Spade Braithwaite

Herbert Brewer's Dirty Little Secret

By Spade Braithwaite
(Banned in China!)

Part of the Amsarnie series of novels
Learn more at www.amsarnie.com

Herbert Brewer's Dirty Little Secret

Published by Spade Braithwaite

Copyright Spade Braithwaite
First edition proof copy
published July, 2016

Spade Braithwaite

Chapter 1

Somewhere, beyond the farthest-away place that you can think of, lies the modern island nation of Amsarnie.

In 1836, driven by the need to hide assets and undisclosed liabilities from a swathe of interested parties, three of Amsarnie's biggest mining companies incorporated their interests and applied for Municipal Status. Far out in the western desert, the Township-Borough of Clausthowler-Snaugler-and-Bogler was born.

Our story tells of how, at the beginning of the twenty first century a bizarre series of events occur that force Clausthowlersnauglerbogler to the very brink of civil war.

The only way to tell the story is through the experiences of the five main protagonists and some of the millions of other people that get caught up. **Do not** attempt to remember names, the narrative will gently remind you of anything you need to know.

Just try to appreciate how, in the modern world, a very remote town and region with its very own, very intense, "fuck-your-own-wheelbarrow!", attitude might exist.

Herbert Brewer's Dirty Little Secret

Our story starts on a Friday morning in the middle of April, relaxed, with a tentative optimism almost tangible in the air. Winter had gone and summer was close enough to believe in.

In his office, Police Chief Gary Crozier read the monthly overtime reports, signed a couple, threw the rest away and drank his coffee. It hadn't been a bad winter. Soon, the bums would start drifting out of town for their walkabout season and the kids would start hanging-out after dark. One menace replacing the other.

Gary picked up *The Independent* and drifted around the globe. There was a lot going on in the world, all of it very far away.

In Paris (Gary's favourite city since he'd travelled there to interview an Australian back-packer about a pair of murders) a disgruntled policeman had slain four chemistry students for being young and hopeful. In Seoul (Gary's least favourite city since, during his brief period of National Service he'd been invalided to a camp there with three frost-bitten toes) the new, conservative government had approved a coalition reunification with North Korea.

In the United Nations, British Prime Minister John Wivell called for a military initiative against the Marxist Guerrillas terrorising peasants and British mining workers in north Bundawa, citing reports of atrocities but not mentioning who was committing them.

Spade Braithwaite

Gary read the stories and smiled to himself because they fell into a category that he filed under S.E.P., which was to say, "Somebody Else's Problem", and fuck their horrible luck, whoever they were.

Gary was just looking for the crossword when his door burst open and Detective Ian Metcalfe sauntered in with his lunch, a, "**Moo-Rama beef sandwich and root beer, lunch on the run – special meal in a bag**".

Half the billboards in town currently claimed that it came with a choice of, "**eight exotic mustards!**", and Detective Metcalfe's face gave evidence that he might have been trying at least five of them.

Gary kept his calm, as ever.

"Metcalfe, next time you walk in here without knocking there's a fuckin' good chance that I'll shoot you. I have a theory that it might only take a couple of well publicised fatalities, and you fuckin' bastards might learn to knock, and wait to be invited in!"

"I'd completely understand, boss. How's it goin'?"

Gary was not finished with the issue.

"I could o' been playin' with m'self, or anything! Is that what you want? You wanna catch me playin' with m'self?"

"You always play with yourself first thing in the morning, when you first get in. Everybody knows that."

"Not always! Wha' do you want, Metcalfe?"

"Nothing much. You fancy lunch?"

"Bo-Bae's picking me up in a few minutes. We're going to

see Jim's tutors."

"He's in trouble again?"

"No, dog-brains. He's never been in trouble. It's a regular thing they do, in schools, parents meeting the teachers. You'd know if you'd ever been to one."

"How often do they expect you do that, then?"

"Well..., we've never done it before, but we could have if we'd wanted to."

Metcalfe paused to savour a particularly intense burst of horseradish.

"Hmm..., say hello to Bo-Bae for me."

"She'll be up in a few minutes. Say it y'self."

Gary put the paper down and stared out of the window. Across the street Constable Fitzroy frog-marched Adam Doughty back into the newsagents to apologise and pay for whatever he'd done. An attractive, blond woman in neo-flares and crop-top paused theatrically to light a cheroot. Bo-Bae Crozier drove past in her shiny, yellow Ford Monitor and pulled into the Brewer Building car park.

Gary smiled to himself and the sun shone down.

In the centre of town, just behind the Galipoli Street financial section, in a district known as Oxpens, Jenny Won Baker also enjoyed the warmth. At eighty-three years of age, spring no longer surprised Jenny. Not so much an event in itself as a ripple on a far greater swell.

Spade Braithwaite

On the roof of her apartment she opened a chair and parked to enjoy the ripple.

The first day of spring, just as welcome as the heat waves, the lightning, the gales and the snow, but infinitely more pleasant. Jenny rolled her skirts up past her knees and allowed a bit of nature onto her rheumatoid joints.

Before settling she poured herself a big jigger of cloudy rum and lit her pipe from an ancient, gasoline lighter. Twenty per cent opium the boy had told her. Three per cent, if lead were heavy and twenty per cent if grass was pink. But she didn't blame the boy. He'd charged her nineteen fifty-seven prices and probably all the neighbourhood had bullied him. What did they think? That an eighty three-year-old lady was going to die young? God bless them.

For the most part, Oxpens was a village unto itself, which was good, or the Borough might have discovered that Jenny owned most of it without ever having a deed in her name. Most of the capitol that had opened the Shoop-Shoop Saloon, over which she lived, had been her savings in nineteen forty-three. And most of the local investment since then had come from "Mama Jen Unincorporated."

Ten per cent or two per cent on the dollar, or send your kids to college, Jenny Won was happy with life. Oxpens never let her miss a meal or pay for a taxi.

On the roof, the sun shone, the rum made her happy and the tobacco did nothing except burn.

Herbert Brewer's Dirty Little Secret

Across the courtyard one of the girls came out onto her roof and waved at Jenny Won.

"Lookin' good, Mama Jen! Get some sun on those knees!"

Jenny smiled and raised her glass. The girl stripped off to bikini briefs and settled in a sun lounger.

The world had changed a lot since Jenny had started in the business seventy-four years ago. In those days girls weren't allowed out of the house without a Madame and every inch of flesh had to be protected from the sun. Men rode into town to consort with beautiful little dolls and then rode home to perform sanctioned relations with their weather-beaten, farm-fraus.

Jenny admired the girl's muscular, tanned body. Nowadays, the men wore rubber-jonnies. The girls insisted on it. No rubber-jonny, no jig-a-jig. Shoop-Shoop had been the first house in Amsarnie to supply rubber-jonnies, the first to employ bouncers, the first house to beat-up a punter for slapping a girl and the first house to employ a lawyer when the punter demanded to see the girl horse-whipped.

That was then. Nowadays, the girls had it and the girls sold it. Supply and demand. More power to them! The world had changed beyond recognition and Jenny Won was slightly proud of her part in the never-told story.

The rum was beginning to make her light-headed. One perk of being an eighty three-year-old legend was that people made room for your strange behaviour.

Jenny sat up in her chair and lifted herself onto her feet.

Spade Braithwaite

"Miss! I say, Miss!"

The girl on the lounger opened her eyes and sat up.

"Is everything all right, Mama Jen?"

"Do you have a drink?"

"No."

"Well get one."

The girl bounced into her apartment and re-emerged with a half-full bottle of champagne.

"Miss.."

"Kate."

"Miss Kate, the world is yours! Clever men think they're clever and rich men think they're rich, but it's pretty girls that really run the world, nowadays. Pretty girls! Cheers!"

"You and me, Mama Jen! Cheers! Good health!"

(Authors note: In real life Joshua Matenach is a big, burly redneck attending Penn State University in Pennsylvania. The author worked with him on a construction gang one summer and asked him if he minded having his name used in a novel. Josh said that he didn't, as long as his character didn't get, "butt-fucked by fat guys." ...Sorry Josh.)

At the bottom of Gothburton Street, behind the old railway terminal complex by the river, Joshua Matenach swung his BSA motorcycle into the alley behind his building, pulled the clutch in and rolled the last thirty yards to his garage. As the bike came to a stop he killed the engine, kicked the side stand down and hopped off in a single, familiar movement.

The garage door was unlocked because nobody except him could open it anyway. He wedged his toes under the left-hand side and slammed the door with both hands as he kicked it upwards.

It was a beautiful morning. The air was thick with spring and the gourney bushes were brilliant yellow, punctuated red and brown with old machinery and rabbit warrens.

Inside the garage, Josh peered under the blanket covering his "project" Triumph Daytona motorcycle and rubbed the tank tenderly.

"August, I promise. Maybe we'll even get to the coast, this year."

He pulled the BSA in next to it and wandered up the path to his back door.

"Maybe, Baby, I'll have you. Maybe baby, you'll be true! Maybe baby, I'll have you-oo someday."

The back door was open. Not what Josh needed after ten hours on the line. He pushed the door and walked into his kitchen.

"Yo! Who and why?!"

The kettle was cold. He filled it with water and put it on the hob.

Movement upstairs.

"Who the fuck is that? Get down here!"

Josh unlaced his boots, propped the back door open and lit a

Spade Braithwaite

cigarette.

Feet clumped down the stairs and a pimply youth appeared through the kitchen door.

"Yo, Geezer!"

"Bishop. What the fuck d' you want?"

"We was wanderin' if you could score us some gear, nah-wah-a-mean?"

"You little fuck. You come in my house again I'll tell your dad. You hear me?"

"An' I'll tell him you got drugs in here an' he'll kick you out."

A second teenager squeezed, sheepishly past the first and made his excuses.

"Casual, Boy!"

"Yeah, catchya mench!"

"Bishop, get your spotty arse out o' my house before I kick it up the street."

"Seriously man! DezzFest's comin' up soon and the whole street's gone dead with it. Nothin' anywhere! We was wanderin' if you knew someone?"

"Just do me a favour an' fuck off!"

"Don't get tense, man. I was only thinkin'."

Josh jerked a thumb towards the open door.

Rupert Bishop shrugged.

"If 'it be, mench. See ya royally!"

"Fuck off Bishop!"

"Later!"

Herbert Brewer's Dirty Little Secret

Rupert Bishop strutted down the path as though he'd made the big deal and then iced the bad guys just for sport.

Josh poured the hot water into a pot of tea leaves and sat on the back step to smoke another cigarette while it brewed. It certainly was a beautiful morning.

Across the river the old blanket mill was beginning to look more green than grey. The ferns, clumped together in every broken window, just happy to be there. The big, old Juilimar tree growing out of the engine pit, up through the gap in the roof, rightly proud of a brilliant display of new leaves.

When he'd finished his tea Josh pulled his boots off and padded upstairs to clean himself up.

In the bedroom he performed a very personal ballet routine, flicking his socks, then his shirt into the corner, emptying his pockets and becoming a dying swan to pull his trousers down. He shifted tempo to disco out of his under-pants and noticed that his jewellery box was sitting on the shelf with the scuffed side facing outwards.

"Shit! You little bastard!"

He popped the lid up and counted the foils. Eleven out of sixteen left.

"You little bastard, Bishop!"

Josh counted them again, trying to keep in mind how the Lord Buddha might have dealt with the same situation.

"You little fuck! I'm gunna kick your bollocks."

Spade Braithwaite

At Clausthowlersnauglerbogler International Airport, flight BU113 from Paris, via Johannesburg and Gunswale, landed fifteen minutes late and a bus carried the passengers to International Arrivals.

Charles LeFevre claimed his luggage and strolled through the officialdom just like all the honest men, looking forward to conducting honest business.

Damn, but this was some kind of town! Two international flights a week and they acted as though they were rushed off their feet. If he'd realised how alert they were then he would have brought his Captain Krumble Passport, with the birthdate, 2012 and the place of birth, Planet Hedrush. In Charles' occupation every passport-stamp was a liability. You lived and you learned. "Clausthowlerlersnauglerbogler: Piss-easy!", was what he'd learned today.

He was to learn very different, before too much longer.

"Name?" the man repeated, more loudly.

"Ughh, sorry, miles away. Charles LeFevre."

"Reason for visit?"

(To fleece you cretins royally and retire to Saint Tropez.)

"Business? My company, Cambridge GeoSpeck, specialises in evaluating geo-real-estate and acting as agents, thereof. We're..."

The man nodded his head to the cadence and smiled.

(Yeah, yeah, yeah... D' you want to hear what my company does? Just fuck off! It's a long shift and I'm really not interested!)

"Thank you! Have a nice stay in Amsarnie!"

The man stamped Charles' passport and shifted the glare of his enthusiasm towards the Colombian talcum representative that was next in line.

Charles pocketed his passport, picked up his case and ambled out through the glass terminal to the taxi rank.

The doors opened automatically and Charles sucked his first, real lung-full of Amsarnie air. It tasted surprisingly good. The town looked fucking-awful, but then every town looks fucking-awful from the airport. Bite-the-pillow and think of baccarat season on the Côte D'Azur.

"Taxi!"

A yellow taxi swung into the gap.

"Mate?"

"A good Hotel. Not the famous, overpriced one, but a good one."

"Shoop-Shoop?"

"No."

"The Blandford?"

"Restaurant?"

"Betcha! Spiro Agnew ate there once. Remember him?"

"Yeah, of course. Pool?"

"I think so."

"Okay, the Blandford."

The driver popped the trunk for Charles to put his case in and

Spade Braithwaite

then drove them both back to town.

Clausthowlersnauglerbogler was a lot dirtier than Charles had imagined a desert town.

Driving in along the southern bypass, he watched the vast acres of black-stained, redbrick terraced buildings on either side. Company housing projects. Little, old pubs and little, old shops. A little, oily looking river. Ancient factories given face-lifts and divided into business units. Wide areas of forgotten industry, abandoned to nature, unable to compete with the virgin outskirts for new construction.

After a few miles the taxi turned off the bypass and towards the town centre on Morecombe Boulevard. The architecture quickly changed. Bigger, grander houses with ornamental gardens. Recognisable chain stores. Cinemas and restaurants. Wine bars, banks and parades of boutiques.

"So what do you get for taking a fresh tourist to the Blandford?"

"A bottle of brandy at christmas, if I'm lucky. If you end up at the Shoop-Shoop, do me favour and mention me. They give air-miles and a discount on drinks."

"I certainly will, my friend. Nothing wrong with incentives, the grease in the machinery."

In the centre of town the car pulled into the entrance of a clean, modern hotel with a landscaped forecourt and a doorman.

Charles paid the driver, retrieved his case and stood for a moment to look at the surrounding buildings before checking in.

Herbert Brewer's Dirty Little Secret

A four-storey office complex, a big, new pub-restaurant, a department store, a multi-storey car park and a pedestrian shopping precinct.

"Town, be good to me!"

It was a beautiful day. The sky was blue, the air was warm and the pigeons shat everywhere.

The doorman opened the door and invited Charles inside. Charles had a good feeling about Clausthowlersnauglerbogler.

A very long way away, late at night, in a different time zone, British Prime Minister John Wivell sipped a bloody great big brandy and rubbed his temples.

"Gentlemen, and ladies. You all know what's going on. Bundawa's going all to shit and we've got to pull the fat out of the fire. Ughhm..., did you get me those figures?"

(Fuck figures, and fuck advisors.)

"Yes sir. Let me see..."

In the sub-private conference room, on the first floor of number ten, Downing Street, John let a nasal young man explain the situation.

"If we, da, da, da..."

The man danced his pen down the page, looking for the statistics. John gulped down a lungful of the fiery liquid.

"If we..., no, can't do that. We can't lose the mining revenue from Bundawa. It'd mean an austerity budget that'd pretty-well break us, electionally speaking."

Spade Braithwaite

("Electionally speaking"?! God preserve us from the London School of Economics!)

"I know what we bloody can't do! What can we do!"

"Ughhm..., consider our diplomatic options, perhaps. Or send in the army."

Around the room John's council of "wise men" considered the suggestions and then mentally equated what it had just cost the taxpayer in "consultancy expenditure."

John Wivell pushed his eyebrows towards each other and pretended not to be very pissed off.

"Thank you, ughmm...," (What the hell was your name? I want to remember it so that I can have you convicted of treason, and public indecency!) "...David. So, people, what have we done, and what can we do?"

Foreign Secretary, Duncan Shorting sat up.

"I've been putting the moves on a few chappies in the UN, and I reckon we could dry-up the flow of rifles to these rebel-chappies if we put a bit of pressure on Russia to stop supplying them. You know, embargoes and what-not. Italy seemed jolly keen."

Sue Lunden, John's most trusted advisor intervened to prevent the discussion from degenerating any further.

"Mr Shorting, the rebels recently shot down an ionaspheric, satellite guided, recognisance missile, using Korean-made, isotope-seeking launches. I think you might want to focus on more contemporary alliances, and events in general."

Herbert Brewer's Dirty Little Secret

Linda Dalglish, the Director of MI5 stroked her moustache and made a suggestion.

"Zaire! Next-door neighbour! Political nightmare! Parachute half a dozen of my boys into the interior, set up ground-control, Budawa, minus five klicks! Instigate domestic conflagration. Sweep north and south! Bundawa commies storm up to take advantage, Zairian, anti-insurrectionist factions sweep down to mop them up. G&T's in Luanda! Sweet as a nut!"

Alexander Murdoch, the unofficial Director of MI6 smiled enigmatically. He had a collection of colour photographs of Linda being taken "doggie-fashion" by a muscular dominatrix with strap on apparel, so everything she said made him smile. He also had genuine film of Silus Mantè, the President of Bundawa, bayoneting a screaming school-girl, and a photograph of Abraham Unduwe, the rebel leader, and a couple of his guerrillas wearing dresses in Paris. But they were his little treasures, not for general consumption.

"Perhaps we could waft the stink a bit. I happen to know a couple of Head-Men in that region and I'm damn sure that we could stoke 'em up with a bit of gossip about Marx, Lenin, Mao, Castro and that lot. Buggers and thieves, to a man! Give me two years, I'll have them voting for inclusion in the Commonwealth."

John Wivell had heard damn-near enough.

"How do you come to know any of the Head-Men in Bundawa?"

Spade Braithwaite

"One makes contacts!"

(Alex had met them at Eton, where everybody met everybody else. He'd shared a dorm' with a couple of them and lost his virginity to one of their drivers.)

"Two years?"

"Four, tops."

"Any other bright ideas?'

Everyone had spoken except Home Secretary Gordon Piffe.

"No? Okay. Re-convene Monday, four p.m. Good night, ladies and gentlemen. Gordon, hold on a mo', will you? I'd like a word."

The crowd shuffled out, well pleased with themselves. Sue shook another shovel-full of coal onto the fire and turned it with the poker.

Prime Minister John Wivell watched his council's exit and then deflated.

"Am I the only fucking grown-up in Parliament?! What the bloody hell were they talking about? Parachutes and embargoes! What's to be done, Piffe?"

"I think you know, sir."

"That bad, eh?"

"Not really that bad, sir. We have the moral high ground, so a few of our friends might support us. President Sharpton's up for re-election in two years an' he could use some glory. And, Amsarnie owes us, big-time, so we can practically name our terms there."

Herbert Brewer's Dirty Little Secret

"You know, I don't want to sound like a, "wet", but the idea of sending men off to war really gives me the willies."

"Not "War", sir. We call it, "Strategic, tactical, ground deployment." "War" is something you talk about in hindsight, just before an election, if you won."

"Okay, do the biz', Piffe. At least the army 'll be pleased. New boots and an excuse to paint their faces. And, God forgive me for what I do."

"In a month's time it'll all have blown over, sir. You know how it works."

"You're very young, Piffe. But I sincerely hope you're right."

The Brewer Building car park had a section reserved for police vehicles. Bo-Bae Crozier pulled into the space next to her husband's car and parked.

The dirt in the cracks was beginning to dry out and there was a soiled condom next to the bin. Spring had surely arrived.

She crossed the lot to the entrance, weaving to avoid lunchtime traffic and smiling at the people who said hello. Inside the big doors it took a moment for her eyes to adjust to the gloom before she could find the buzzer to call the receptionist.

In the back office, Old-Eddie peered out from his newspaper and grinned. He pressed the lift-call and pottered into the front office for a friendly chat.

"Oh my lord, if it isn't yourself. Nice, to see you. Damn, but you look as fresh as a sweet-pea. It does my old heart good."

Spade Braithwaite

Bo-Bae was ready for him.

"You flirt with me, you dirty old man, an' my husband "fit-you-up" with cattle-rustling charges. You go to prison!"

"It wouldn't stick. I couldn't recognise a cow in a line-up. An' I can account f' my whereabouts."

"Well, you flirt with me anyway, an' I promise not to tell him."

"I think y' should leave the useless bum! I always thought that you could do a lot better. You know, I just happen to be available."

"Maybe I will. He good husband and father, an' all, but what every girl really yearn for is exceptionally dirty old man. Other night I dream that me and my girlfriend kidnap you and tie you up and rub tiger-balm into your ligaments, and then..., but you don't want to hear about my dream!"

"No, I honestly do! I think I had the same dream!"

"Later, Eddie."

"Think about it, seriously!"

"You are a dirty, old beast. Maybe that what make you so damned attractive."

The elevator arrived and she let it take her to the fourth floor, "Police Department, - detection, administration and complaints (Payment of fines on seventh floor, Taxes and Municipal.)"

Gary intercepted her at the front desk and guided her back to the elevator.

As they walked out Old-Eddie winked at Bo-Bae. Gary shrugged and tried not to say anything.

Herbert Brewer's Dirty Little Secret

"Eddie, if I catch you messin' with my wife, I'll kill you dead. Do you understand?"

"That's a big "If", sonny-boy! See ya' both later."

Bo-Bae winked at Old-Eddie over her shoulder.

Neither of them said much on the drive to the high school, with the windows down and the radio tuned to an oldies station. It was just too lovely, being out together on a week day in the sunshine. The first day of spring.

At Snaugler High, Bo-Bae parked in the very farthest parking space and they walked, with five minutes to spare. It was ten past twelve. The appointment card said 12:15, Language Lab' 312, which, according the ground plan in the foyer, was in the old Newton Building, back behind where they'd parked.

Three minutes to spare, two hundred yards. Newton building side entrance, second floor, language department, room 312, Mr Epstein - Form teacher.

Mr Epstein ushered them into his room enthusiastically.

"Mr & Mrs Crozier! Lovely to meet you! James is one of our very special products, we're all very excited about him, as I'm sure you understand."

Neither Gary nor Bo-Bae understood at all.

"He's expected to do okay in his exams? Isn't he?"

Mr Epstein smiled like a gargoyle.

"James is one of those rare creatures that, quite honestly, it doesn't matter. We're confident that James will find a suitably challenging career in one of the local semi-conductor industries.

Spade Braithwaite

But if he doesn't, then a representative of Infocorp in Seattle, America has expressed an interest. And several others. But they would all involve him emigrating."

Gary tried to match Mr Epstein's smile for enigma, but without the ugliness.

"James Isaac Crozier, right? Our son? Good natured lad with a bit of a slouch? Needs to get involved in sport more?"

Mr Epstein chuckled and his face screwed up like a goat's udder.

"Your modesty does you credit. I've always believed that my choice of teaching, as a career, might be vindicated by the discovery of one such as James. And I was right."

Bo-Bae contained herself no longer.

"What this, "local semi-conductor industry" that Jim has to work in?"

Gary scratched his chin, authoritatively.

"Transistors, or something. You know, like radios."

"Oh, much more than that, Mr Crozier. James wrote a speculation on the cultivation of micro-biological intelligence, for his Physics G.C.E., that made us all weep with impotence."

"James Isaac Crozier? Big, skinny lad?"

"Ha ha! I'm sure young James is a bit of a wag! You can't help but admire him. I've gotten the impression that he's more interested in going into industry than pursuing an academic career. That's the way of the world, nowadays. I know that Braithwaite and Randolph have both offered him scholarships, but he doesn't seem interested. And a few of the international universities have written to us, King's-Oxford, Harvard, Heidelberg, Sou-Cal. It seems a shame to spurn such great honour, but that's young people!"

Bo-Bae was almost sure that she was pleased with the way this meeting was going.

"What he say, "great honour"?"

Gary retreated to regroup.

"When does he leave school?"

"Oh, five weeks, as soon as he's sat his last exam. But if something urgent came up before then we'd be quite willing to graduate him with high honours immediately. It reflects positively back on the school, you know. His "non-mobilised conscription papers" will be mailed in June, so he'll have to be in Clausthowlersnauglerbogler to report to the Auxiliary Defence Officer, but that's just a formality."

"You really think our James is something special?"

"I have no doubt that "our James" is going to change the world."

"What he say, "great honour"?"

"Darling. Darling, it seems that our James is a bit of a dark horse. I think we should have a talk with him this evening. It seems that there might be a lot more about him than we realised. Harvard, Heidelberg, Sou-Cal, and, what was the other one?"

"Oxford, in England."

"Any good?"

Spade Braithwaite

"American President William Clinton went there."

"But the others, they're alright?"

"The very best!"

"Well I'm fucked. Our Jim!"

"What he say, Harban-Hidlebun-Sowcow?"

"I'll tell you in the restaurant. I think this calls for a celebration. Is there any history of genius on your side of the family."

"Uncle Choo invented implement for disabled person to look inside their own ears."

"That's not it."

"So what Jim do?"

"Thank you very much, Mr Epstein. If you have any parking violations, and I don't normally do this, but drop them by and I'll sort them out. Good Day! Have a nice life!"

"So what Jim get up to?"

"He's a clever little bastard. Who'd have thought. D' you think he looks a bit like his ol' dad?"

"He look a bit like a pipe-cleaner. But I never doubt his genius."

"Would you believe little Jim?!"

"He get it from his mother. Exactly what I expected. You should have, too."

"Oh yeah! Look, I'm goin' to phone back to the office. I think I want an expensive lunch."

"Good idea. What-all he say about Jim?"

Herbert Brewer's Dirty Little Secret

"I'll tell you in the restaurant."
"Okay."

Chapter 2

After a short sleep, international swindler Charles LeFevre snapped back to crisp awareness.

Naked on top of the blankets, warm, blissful and semi-erect, the dream he'd been enjoying was a recurrent one. He was walking down the street of some town, he never knew where, just wandering in and out of all the shops and businesses, handing out money and fondling the girls where they stood. Waitresses, receptionists, customers, police women.

It was all comfortingly familiar. Often, but not this time, Charles passed a lot of other buildings, looking for a bank. There was something particularly horny about walking in to a bank, walking behind the tellers windows, giving the prettiest girl a bag of money and then ripping her blouse open.

Nice, crisp, cotton blouse, with just the outline of a lacy bra underneath. He gripped the front and tore it open, buttons flying everywhere. The girl didn't mind, she was being well paid. Then he groped the girl's breasts through the underwear while she

Spade Braithwaite squirmed.

Charles made a mental note to look in at the Shoop-Shoop Saloon after dinner that evening. He was in character now, and that was what businessmen did when they were away on business.

It was going to be a pleasure investing four hundred thousand dollars in Clausthowlersnauglerbogler.

The scam was embarrassingly simple, but the rewards grew geometrically every time. Move into a town and spend a bit of money settling down. Discreetly investigate the mineral rights to a lot of worthless desert. Appear to pay a lot more than face value for the rights to a few controversial sights. Allow the town's leading citizens to invest in the project in return for them using their influence to remove political obstacles. Spirit their money out of the country and leave them owning a very expensive company with rights to a lot of worthless land. It would be extremely difficult to prove that anything criminal had ever occurred.

This was to be the last time. The big one. Four hundred thousand dollars of Bolivian sucker-money to play with, this one was going to pay for all.

Charles rolled off the bed and turned on the shower to let it run hot.

On the desk was the newspaper that Charles had picked up at reception, the "Claust Howler."
He read a few pages, trying to get an impression.

Herbert Brewer's Dirty Little Secret

During the past week vandals had tied a dog to a weather balloon but the owner had shot it down and a number of high-school students were being questioned in connection. Somebody had stolen a case full of bathroom-dispenser tampons and dumped them in the canal. Police suspected that the perpetrator had been trying to steal cigarettes, which were delivered in similar boxes. Retired Ernest Bishop was to be honoured by the Knights of Queen Fatima for his donation of land for the new lodge. Philip DeBiere had filed suit against his ex-employers, Contemporary Extrusions, claiming that he'd been sacked for pointing out safety violations in their procedures. Contemporary Extrusions claimed that he'd been sacked for tardiness, alcoholism, urinating in a truck container and telling a female co-worker that too much brandy gave him a "nine-inch stiffy that could see day-break in anybody's knickers."

What a bloody dreadful town!

Charles read it all with morbid delight.

Steam started to appear around the bathroom door. Charles put the paper down and got ready to have a look at the town.

The sun went down and a lot of people came out to enjoy the start of the weekend. Too cold yet for any but a few school kids to contemplate outdoor sex. Too early for tables and chairs on the sidewalk but warm enough to get a taxi into town and then walk from the restaurant to the theatre, to the pub. Jackets and wraps for later on, shirt sleeves for now.

Spade Braithwaite

Upstairs at the Shoop-Shoop, retired Ernest Bishop enjoyed his party as much as anyone and more than most. A free bar and all the girls on duty, even a couple of new ones. Ernie reckoned that the guest of honour ought to have first crack at the new girls because Ernie was the guest of honour.

Bridgette refilled a few glasses and then called for quiet.

"Gentlemen! And the rest! You've asked for it, so we're proud to give it to you, "Of Inhuman Bondage!" Big hand for the girls please!"

Whistles and a few cat-calls.

The curtains over the little stage parted and room lights faded to spots. Joanne and Kate dragged Tina on from stage-right, manacled her to imaginary shackles in the backdrop and then stepped back.

Fast, frenetic, funky music started playing as Tina writhed.

Suddenly, Tina broke her moorings and expressed her individuality through the medium of erotic dance. Joanne and Kate re-appeared to express their own individuality.

Whistles and cheers.

"Hoo!" , "Hoo!" , "Hoo!" , "Hoo!"

Ernie Bishop stopped rubbing himself and ordered another brown ale.

"Y' know, Stav', it's an honour!"

Stavros Nicolaus slapped Ernie's back and really didn't care what the old fart was talking about.

"Like-wise!"

Herbert Brewer's Dirty Little Secret

"No, man. It really is an honour, to be a bachelor in good company."

"I'm divorced, twice, you're widowed, and everyone else here is married."

"Haa! Ya fuck! Y'know wha' I mean. Y' mates! Y' can't beat the company o' blokes."

"I think you're up first, f' the new girls. Go on, boy, get it all out o' y' system! There's a good lad."

"Cheers!"

Ernie marched past the front of the queue and down the corridor to the Wide Room with a soul full of un-told, karmic debt and a scrotum full of dirty water. And, by God, he shed one of them in the Wide Room, with Ffion and Charmaine dressed as policewomen.

Downstairs in the Lounge bar, Charles Lefevre bought himself a large brandy and stepped back from the bar to give other people a chance.

Shoop-Shoop was a lot of fun, for a hick-town, whore-house. A lot of people got in there on a Friday night. The hostesses were all gorgeous, but not the obvious, thin, whorish gorgeous that you normally got. They were real girls, with real smiles and real tits. A couple of them were real boys.

Charles tried to absorb as much as he could. Most of the men seemed more interested in having a beer than going upstairs. Quite a few had brought their wives. Little social groups spilled into each other with everybody seeming to know everybody else.

The room itself was wide with a low ceiling. Four thick pillars supported the upper floors and divided the room into several, separately lit areas.

The bar ran the length of the back wall with three middle aged ladies and a young man serving drinks, quietly and efficiently. No sign of a bouncer anywhere.

Charles leaned against a pillar and tried to listen in on a few conversations.

"She's only gone with 'im 'cause he's got a Porsche. I know f'r a fact that she won't go down on him.", "He always wears that cardigan!", "Exactly!", "Did she go down on you?", "Had t' padlock m' pyjamas to keep her out!"

"So, 'ow much d' y' reckon it's going to cost if they stop subsidisin' it?", "They can't. There'd be riots in the streets, and old Cartright likes a bi' of it.", "I reckon I'm gonna stock up, just to be sure!"

"It was wider than it was long! Like a can o' cat-food!", "Makes yer eyes water, thinkin' about it.", "Lucky bastard!"

Charles felt someone poke him in the side.

"You got here, then?"

"Ughhm, yeah." Obviously.

"Taxi from the airport!"

"Oh yeah! I'm sorry, it's been a long day. Can I get you a drink, ughhm?"

Herbert Brewer's Dirty Little Secret

"Barry Ntongi."

"Charles LeFevre. Pleased see you again. Drink?"

"Go on then, pint. What do 'y think of the town?"

"Very lively, for a desert town. A lot more fun than most of the places I get sent. What else is there in town?"

"Allsorts. You got here at just the right time. It gets a bit dull in winter but we make up for it in the summer. Most of the blokes I bring to town are more interested in the young skirt than anything else. You like that?"

"Young ones, old ones, I don't care."

"All the kids go to the Owahu Lounge. You'll get high-school girls there that'll go home with you just to have a look inside the Blandford. But, d'y' want my advice?"

"You've done me proud so far."

"Every Summer they have a few dances at the Exeter Hall, just down the road from the Blandford. First one's a week tomorrow. Black tie, an' all the old-town class comes out to pretend it's the good old days. Lots of neglected wives! A good-looking foreigner, like yourself, could get enough phone number to last you quite a while. And it's a fun night. Old Claust's got a lo' of class, f'r a shitty, mining town. I usually work the shift when it's on."

"Barry, my friend, damn your air-miles. I'm going to buy you a ticket to Jamaica for a fortnight."

"I've always wanted to go to New Orleans."

"New Orleans it is! Are you working tomorrow?"

Spade Braithwaite

"From noon."

"Could you get me at noon? I really need to lease a car and I'd be glad of someone who knows the locals."

"No problem. By the way, that bloke over there, the fat bugger with the white jacket, he's the local BMW dealer, Duncan Adamson. He's talking to Gary an' Bo-Bae, the Police Chief an' his little Asian wife. I'll introduce you, if you like."

"Barry, drinks are on me, tonight."

Same time zone, East Coast, the political capitol of Amsarnie, Gunswale. A hundred yards from the Parliament Assembly Building across the Hermitage Lawns, at Duncarin, the official residence of the Prime Minister, a special, late-night meeting was just coming to order.

Prime Minister Dereck Cartright wasn't his normal, sparkling self.

"Sammy, Bernie, just fuckin' sit down, I'm not in the mood! Sorry to get you all here, blah blah blah. We've got a fuck-up and I want it sorted. Chas?"

"Sir, Mr Cartright, ladies and gentlemen, the situation is this,"

"Get to the fuckin' punch-line!"

"Sir! We received a communication from the British Government tonight, to the effect that they intend to embark on a policy of hostility towards the Bundawanese anti-government factions...,"

"To the effect that they want us to support some fuck-up in

the UN, and then send a boat-load of soldiers off to fight in some fuckin' jungle somewhere. Where was it?"

"Northern Bundawa, sir, in the Congo Basin."

"The Fuckin' arse-end of nowhere!"

Dereck's cabinet tried to look interested.

"Sir, what did we tell them?"

"We told them, "Yeah!" We had to. They pretty-much bought us in the last election. So what's t' be done?"

"Sir, how many soldiers do you think they're expecting?"

"What could we get away with?"

"We only have five thousand soldiers!"

"What about the air force, and the navy?"

"Five thousand! That's it!"

"Reserves?"

"Five thousand servicemen, including reserves. And disabled veterans and pensioners."

Dereck paused to imitate a slab of very unhappy granite.

"You've got to be shittin' me! Five fuckin' thousand?! So how many actual, mobilised servicemen is that?"

"Slightly less than two thousand."

"Holy mother of God! Do you think the enemy know about this?"

"We would assume, but we're of no strategic importance to anyone, therefor...,"

"Shut up! Two thousand servicemen! Probably five hundred combatant riflemen?!"

Spade Braithwaite

"Mostly currently employed in civic duties, under the Municipal Mandate of 1994, article 347."

"Do we have an army, at all?"

"Not as such, sir. Not a defensive one."

"Oh my good God Almighty, Jesus Christ! D'you reckon we could we cobble one together?"

"Technically, sir. It's in the statutes whereby all the young men have to report for National Service before they start work. But it'd kill us, politically, if we tried to exercise it."

"It won't do us a lot of good if we don't! I want a map of everywhere that didn't vote for us, and I want a lot of good, political excuses to conscript from there first."

"Sir...!"

"I know exactly what your shitty, ethical, middle-class minds are thinking! And I don't care! Get on it, tomorrow!"

"Sir! It'd take half a year to supply them and train them!"

"As long as we can send a few plane-loads of lads over there, in green outfits, that's all we need. It'll probably all have blown over before any fighting starts."

"Sir...,"

"One fuckin' word out o' you, an' you'll be on the first plane!"

"Yes sir."

Back in Clausthowlersnauglerbogler, in Sherwin Park, behind the bushes screening the old pumping station, Rupert Bishop laid his leather jacket on the ground for Jane Walton to sit on.

"I really dig you, woman! You're well-'ard!"

Jane smiled and patted the ground for Rupert to sit next to her.

"I've seen you lookin' at me in lunch. I knew you fancied me."

Rupert sat, and nervously shuffled closer until one of his legs was underneath her knees and the other was behind her bottom. Close enough to smell her. He reached out with one hand to stroke her neck, waiting for the nervous shrug that told him to stop.

No shrug. Closer to another human than Rupert had been since his mother died. His heart knocking like a worn, big-end bearing.

Jane pulled his chin towards her and clumsily kissed him on the lips.

Rupert nearly burst out through his ears. It was now or never.

"D'you want to.., I mean...,"

"Allright then. Have you done it before?"

"Lots of times."

"Have you got any thingies?"

"Always."

He casually undid the first, then the second, then all the buttons on her shirt.

Jane arched her head back to look at the sky. A clear night, with lots of stars. A great, big moon, hidden behind the Luker building, betrayed by its aura. A few, wispy clouds, platinum against the dark, moving just enough to make the trees whisper.

Spade Braithwaite

Really beautiful.

    He'd decided beforehand that he was going to try to touch her tits first so that, whatever happened later, he'd have touched one.

    He slid his hand inside the material and gently cupped her little breast through the bra. Her little nipple hard as a bean. With his other hand he stroked her back, looking for the clasp.

    Jane suddenly shivered and stood up.

    Rupert was ready for it.

    "I'm sorry, I won't...,"

    "That's alright. Sit back against the wall. There, that's more comfortable."

    "Ughhm, do you...,"

    "Be quiet. Don't tell anyone, will you?"

    Rupert had already told Geoff that he had, but it was okay because he didn't think Geoff believed him.

    "I promise!"

    Jane pulled her blouse out of her skirt and hitched her bra up, letting him see her proud little chest, in the dim, yellow security light.

    Rupert nearly died.

    "You..., you're really beautiful!"

    "Sure I am. So are you."

    She sat in his lap and guided his hands inside her shirt.

    Under her skirts, Rupert felt his zipper being pulled down and his penis being pulled into the clear.

Herbert Brewer's Dirty Little Secret

He winced as it bent to clear his belt. It hadn't wanted to bend for three days, since Jane had agreed to meet him in the park on Friday. He'd beaten it with everything but a stick, and there it still stood, a monument to young love.

"Thingy?"

Rupert scrambled in his seat pocket for the little package.

"Here. D'you want me to...,"

"Relax."

Jane tore the package open and held the thingy up to the light, looking for the entrance.

It disappeared under her skirt and Rupert felt her fingers roll it down his length. God, but it felt delicious to have someone else touch him!

A little shuffle and he was in!

Jane smiled and looked at the sky. The moon was slightly visible now. Full, but for a shaving off the top. Slowly, she gently rocked up and down, savouring the intimacy.

It took Rupert a few minutes to overcome his surprise at the situation. He'd done it! Should he die tomorrow, he'd been there!

As the shock wore off a fresh urgency reared its head. A three day, veteran boner with as much feeling as a lump of mahogany.

He shuffled away from the wall and rolled Jane onto her back, enthusiasm taking over.

"Careful!"

Spade Braithwaite

"Sorry!"

Rupert took a breath and galloped away for all he was worth, occasionally getting close only to find it elude him in the short strokes.

"Yeaaghh!"

Jane saw stars for the third time after twenty minutes, the third time in her life.

It was getting close. Rupert felt a little glow and focused on it with all his attention. It had to be soon.

Closer. Closer. Closer. There!

"Uuuughmmm...,"

Boof!

"Urghh! Fuckin' hell!"

Rupert felt himself turning inside-out through the end of his penis. Wrenching spasms of relief, gripping him in shock-waves.

"Ooh, bloody hell!"

Half a minute that seemed a lot longer, holding Jane as though fate might snatch her away.

Relaxation. Warm, glowing, good feeling.

Rupert shuddered and opened his eyes.

"Are you okay?"

Jane had to blink a few times to regain focus.

"Wow!"

"Are you okay?"

"Just give me a minute. Phew! I didn't really believe that you'd done it before."

Herbert Brewer's Dirty Little Secret

"I try to be discreet. D' you want to do some stuff?"

"Drugs?"

"Yeah. It's the perfect night for it."

"What kind of drugs?"

"Gear. Pure Colombian hoss."

"Heroin?"

"No. Speed."

"Have you done it before?"

"Lots of times. See, it comes in foil wraps, one per dose."

"I'll do half a line. Have you go' a mirror?"

"You look great, don't sweat it."

"Here. Pour it onto the sleeve of your jacket, then I'll chop it into a couple of lines with my library card. Have you got a dollar?"

"Two halves."

"No bills?"

"Only a ten."

"That'll do. Give it here."

Jane rolled the note into a straw, closed one nostril and sniffed most of a line up her nose.

"Hyaagh! Phew! That's gear! Here y' go."

She gave him the bill and sat back to see stars.

Rupert did exactly the same.

"Hmmmn, hoo! Bloody hell!"

"You're a cool guy, Rupe'!"

"You're a cool chick. Can you hear your heart roarin' in y'r

Spade Braithwaite

ears?"

"I can hear ice melting in Argentina."

"Wow! I can hear my lungs crystallising. Does your arm ache?"

"I think I just melted into the desert and reincarnated on the surface of the sun."

"I don't feel so good."

"That was some kind o' sex we just had! D'y' think we might be soul-mates?"

"I really don't feel so good."

"Wow! I need to piss. Don't follow me."

"Could you get me home?"

"I'll see you tomorrow. Don't quote me, but I think I love you."

"Could you phone someone? Tell them where I am. Ask them to come and get me."

"Take i' easy, Bish'. You d' man! See ya tomorrow."

"Yeah! See ya!"

Upstairs at Suzie's, Ernie Bishop had nearly had enough.

"The party's over! It's time to call it a day!"

"Your singin' isn't a lot better than your dancing."

"You know Kate, you're a lovely girl. You really are. I'm a bit worried about my son. He's healthy enough but, since my Janey died, I worry that he misses a woman's influence. Could I bring him in?"

"How old is he?"

"Fifteen. But he's a good lad. I don't understand a word he says, mind. Come to think of it, he might be bloody 'orrible! I wouldn't know. Can I bring 'im in?"

"Fourteen's the legal age, f' boys. Bring 'im in. We'll see if we can't make a man out of 'im."

"I'd be touchingly grateful! I worry about 'im, with no mother an' all."

"Bring him in. I'll do 'im m'self!"

"Good lass!"

Mayor Humner Spielding scraped a handful of bubbles off the top and tested the temperature with his elbow.

"Perfect. D' you want candles?"

"Yeah."

"Josticks?"

"Yeah. The works. It's been a long week."

Stephanie Spielding lowered herself into the bath.

"My mind tells me to milk this for a few days, and then deal with whatever it is. But my heart has to know. What's going on, Humner? Have they caught you doing something?"

"No! Nothing like that. Am I that obvious?"

"No. You're a stone-wall. What is it?"

"I've been thinking. I've been Mayor f'r nearly twelve years, since old Herbie Brewer karked. That's a long time, I reckon I've done my bit."

"Go on."

Spade Braithwaite

"How about, I raise the salary of the Borough Co-ordinator a few thou', and then allow myself to be shuffled sideways at the next election. It'd mean a lot more vacation time!"

"The Borough Co-ordinator already earns more than you, with kick-backs. Do it. We could semi-retire. You know, I've always wanted to see the Cote D'Azure."

"I know. So you think it's a good idea?"

"What's bad about it?"

"It's not exactly honest."

"More hot water. You're a good man, Humner, but you do have some bloody stupid notions. Just retire, and do us all a favour."

Chapter 3

Ian Metcalfe got the call at shortly after eight the following morning. Constable Bomar at the scene of a youth, found by lady with a dog, dead in the park.

"You sure he's dead?"

"Cold. Been dead all night."

"Anyone we know?"

"Can't see the face properly, but it looks a bit like Ernie Bishop's boy."

Herbert Brewer's Dirty Little Secret

"Shit! Any wounds?"

"Nothing visible. No obvious sign of a struggle. Used condom next to 'im though."

"Any idea what the procedure is?"

"I'd phone the hospital first. See if there's a coroner, or something. Then phone the boss."

"Okay Bomar. Where a' you now?"

"At the scene. We've got the area taped off an' it's takin' both of us just to keep people away."

"Okay. I'll get every available man over there. Keep 'old of the woman with the dog, will ya. I'll be there in 'alf an hour."

Ian hung up the radio handset and phoned Gary Crozier at home.

"Hello?"

"Hello Bo-Bae, is he up yet?"

"Ian? Yeah, he's up but I send him out for groceries later. You come round then."

"Seriously, I need to talk to him."

"Problem?"

"Yeah. A body in the park."

"Shit! Here he is."

"Metcalfe? What's up?"

"We've got a body in the park. Might be Ernie Bishop's kid."

"Oh shit! What's the state o' things?"

"A woman with a dog found him and reported it. Andy Bomar's on the scene. He's got the area taped off and he's

Spade Braithwaite

keeping the woman with the dog until we get there."

"You don't need me. Call the hospital. I think Dr Payne's the Official Medical Examiner. Get her to have a look at the body before it's moved, then get it sent to the hospital for an autopsy. The Procedure File's on the shelf, next t' the atlas. Handle the scene like a bank robbery, rubber gloves an' tweazers. Get someone from Estate Management to photograph everything before anything's touched and keep them on the scene in case you find anything, get it photographed before it's picked up. Find out who he was and where he went to school. Find out from his form teacher who his mates were. Find out from the mates what he was into. Perhaps if you mention possible manslaughter proceedings then they'll grass each other up. If it's drugs find out where he got 'em. Oh, and better tell the parents."

"If it's Ernie's kid, d' you want to tell 'im?"

"No I fuckin' don't. You're in his little, "Queens of the Night" gang. You tell 'im."

"Knights of Queen Fatima." It's a lodge."

"You tell 'im. An', come to think of it, I remember signing a firearms certificate a few months ago for a couple of big pistols that he keeps at home. When y' tell him, better stay with him for a while. All night if needs be. Cook 'im dinner and make sure he isn't goin' t' do anything psycho."

"Cheers boss. And you have a happy weekend aswell!"

"Any problems, I'll come out. But only real problems. See ya Monday."

Herbert Brewer's Dirty Little Secret

"Cunt!"
"And you."

At the bottom of Gothburton Street, just over the road from the Flying Sandboy, Joshua Matenach opened his front door with the key, took his groceries inside and closed the door behind him.

Pretty much the only time he used the front door was Saturday morning when he walked up the hill to the store. All part of the weekend ritual.

Frozen food first. A big bag of sweet-peas, two pork chops, a pack of turkey fingers, a sachet of chopped spinach and a box of assorted power-pops, all in the small, empty, freezer compartment. Dry goods in the cupboard. Bacon, milk, lettuce, tomato, cheese and Aroogah-Burgers in the fridge. Toilet rolls and toothpaste on the stairs to go up. Carton of cigarettes in the cupboard under the stairs.

It was going to be another lovely day.

Josh lit the grill and got a couple of bacon croquets out for breakfast.

One of these days, if he wanted to get to the coast this year, he'd write a note advertising for a lodger, and put it on the board in the post office. But a couple more weeks of living on his own wouldn't do any harm.

Twenty one years old. The first time he'd lived on his own and didn't it beat all. No room-mates freaking-out at four in the morning, no parents hammering on the floor, no mates "staying for a few days" and stealing his sleeping bag.

If Josh's house had been detached he could have stood on one side and thrown a truck- battery clear over the top. The furniture was 1940's, loan company, reposession-auction reject, with piss stains. But the lease said, "Joshua Matenach, sole."

When he locked the door, no one could come in and shout at him. No one could tell him to get up or go to bed. No one could freak him out while he was tripping.

Soon it would be time to get a lodger. But not today.

He ate the croquets off a dirty plate, with a dirty knife and a mug of rum and coke, watching a Chanel Eighty Nine, Laurel and Hardy marathon, with the grill pan left filthy for next time.

For a month or two, it was worth the overtime to be able to afford it.

Maybe if he got a female lodger it wouldn't be so bad.

Or maybe he should go to the coast next year. It might be good just to have a bit of space to get his head together. Maybe he could just hang out and play the local games while the weather was nice. Perhaps he could get some girly-action going with one of the women from the laundrette.

Perhaps he should go back to bed for a few hours and then wander over to the Sandboy for a couple of pints with the old-boys while the racing was on.

"When I nod my head, you hit it!"

Josh smiled at Oliver Hardy's buffoonery.

Herbert Brewer's Dirty Little Secret

Things were all right, for the time being. Soon, but not too soon he would take the situation in hand and get a lodger. Definately not today.

Across the country, exactly the same, wonderful sun shone on the nation's capitol, Gunswale. Rising at five forty seven. Positively warm by nine o-clock.

At nine o-clock, give or take a few excuses, a super-secret, extra-governmental meeting of the Cabinet convened in Inland Attorney Samuel Guarthje's family room, safely out of sight of Parliament, to discuss the Prime Minister's recent behaviour.

"So! We were all there yesterday, we all heard him. Comments please!"

Foriegn Advocate, tired, fifty eighty year old Bernard Kent asked the question on everybody's lips.

"Has he lost the plot, or what? How's he been acting lately?"

"He's been spot-on! That's the puzzle. If he'd been dictating to Elvis or writing poetry then we might have expected something, but he wasn't. D' y' think he knows something we don't?"

"How? All he knows is what we tell him."

"Maybe he's got a source. An Advisor!"

"Fuck, has he! He's been there too long and he thinks he knows everything. Thatcher-Syndrome, that's what it is!"

"So what do we do?"

Charles Mintion, Cabinet Secretary, "I'm the oldest man here.

Spade Braithwaite

I suggest that we let the silly bugger screw it up badly and then force him to resign. We lose an election, do four years in opposition, and then we come back, with one of us in charge. Every man f' himself, I say!"

"Chas, if ever you get into power then I'm shipping my sons out of the country until they're old an' ugly!"

"Cheeky!"

"So, let him get an army together and send it off to some war. How d' we keep our own hands clean?"

"If we let him create a War Ministry, promote some duff bugger from the back row up to Minister of War, we could coach it all from the sidelines with never a mention."

"What if we sent each others departments strongly worded memos, criticising the whole bloody affair? No one need see them until after the event and then we could produce piles of official documents making our positions more than clear."

"So, who should be the stooge?"

"Who don't we like?"

"Chalfont?"

"No good. There's always the outside chance that he might pull it off, in which case, whoever it is is going to be up there, looking down on us! I couldn't stand Chalfont sitting further up the table than me."

"Snapper?"

"Perfect! A first-rate, private school half-wit. And a nice bloke, by all accounts."

Herbert Brewer's Dirty Little Secret

"What exactly are the legalities of all this?"

"All perfectly constitutional. It's in the Original Charter, whereby all young men have to register for national service when they leave school. They're kept on the register for five years, during which time, if a threat to national security, or the security of an allied nation, arises then it's at the discretion of the government to call them in."

"I don't remember registering."

"Your parents probably sent a servant. Mine did."

"Five years! I had a wife and a daughter three years after I left school!"

"School's out in a few weeks. Two hundred thousand male students over the whole country just about to leave school. We only want about four thousand, of which, probably only a few hundred will ever get sent abroad."

"What about university, or college?"

"Automatic college deferment. All entitlements deferred until the end of National Service."

"It'd be nice if we could catch the arts and humanities scholars, and give 'em a bit of combat experience in lieu of university education!"

"Homosexuality, automatic disqualification."

"That might be a good one for someone to repeal! Apparently liberal, and yet common-sensical at the same time. "The Army, an Equal Opportunities Employer!" I think I'll introduce that one."

"Job done!"

Spade Braithwaite

" I wouldn't want to be stuck in a combat situation with anyone I'd shagged. My secereatry's bad enough, telling the bloody career-men what their business is!"

"Lose her. Put her on the board of some fact-finding mission to the Caribbean or somewhere. They forget everything!"

"So where are we going to put this Ministry?"

"Throw the fuckin' press out and stick 'em in there!"

"Contracts?"

"There's five of us here, I say we just divide them evenly. I'd like first call on the clothing contract. There's a little Pakistani fellow in my constituency who always contributes way beyond his means, and I'd like to give something back to his community."

"First call catering!"

"I call medical and transport!"

"So, we're all agreed?"

"If he wants a damn war, let him bloody-well have one!"

"Any opposing? No? Gentlemen, war it is! God bless us!"

Saturday morning in Clausthowlersnauglerbogler. Everywhere was open by nine o-clock, even the bars. By ten o-clock the all-nighters were drinking-up and heading home for lectures and sleep. In St. Peter's Plaza the skateboarders were already slapping high fives and sweating under woolly, ski hats and baggy sweaters.

"Yoh, Bwye! Givin' i' all tha' 'n' then some! Dead casual!"

"Oh my goodness! Fearsome!"

Herbert Brewer's Dirty Little Secret

The City of Quebec had their benches and umbrellas out front but table-service was still very chancey.

Jenny Won Baker parked herself on the end of a bench and flagged down a furtive, tip-toeing, security-guard to fetch her a Pimms.

"Sure thing, Mamma Jen, I'll find somebody. Just give me a minute to see where that woman's going."

The woman got into a brown, 1984 Austin Taglia, driven by a man twice her age. The guard wrote the registration in his book and then went into the pub to order a pitcher of Pimms for Mamma Jen outside.

"Take care, Mamma Jen."

"And you, young man. Could I encourage you to join me for a snifter?"

"I'd be honoured! I just have to report back, I'll only be a mo'."

Mamma Jen nodded serenely and surveyed the square.

A young woman coached her heavily-laden husband out of Up-Country Camping and Outdoors, and towards the pharmacy.

"We've got to do something. The malaria tablets 'll interfere with my Pill, so you'll just have to wear 'em if you want some!"

"We're only going for two weeks. Can't we just do oral?"

"You can!"

The pigeons strutted under Mamma Jen's table, tormenting a discarded burger bun. The security guard returned, poured Mamma Jen a tall Pimms and snapped the cap off a beer for himself.

Spade Braithwaite

Two young boys, a fat, stupid one and a thinner, only slightly less stupid one rode into the square and lounged around on their pushbikes, looking tough in that very special way that only spotty, seventy pound, thirteen year olds can.

Kev, the skinnier of the two farted and remembered a joke that had made everybody laugh on Hey, Hey, It's Saturday.

"'Ere, what comes in pints?"

"Ughhm, milk."

"No."

"Fuckin' does!"

"I know, but that's not the answer."

"What kind of a fuckin' question is that then?"

"The answer's elephants. Elephants come in pints! You know, "cum" in pints!"

"I don't get it"

"Me either, but my dad reckoned it was really funny."

Josephine and Hailey hung out on the retaining wall around the landscaped mini-palm trees and did everything they could to attract attention without attracting attention. Smouldering, mean, moody, magnificent postures and stretches. Everything but eye contact.

Josephine yawned and arched her back, advertising her brand-new bosoms inside her Frisco Teen-Top.

"J' reckon they're poofs, or somethin'?"

"They're too stupid!"

"Don't say much for us!"

"Ahh, Kev's alright."

Hailey hawked a lung-full of tripe into the pit.

"Gi' us a gasper."

"Go on then. Last two."

They broke the filters off their extra-mild Kemptowns and lit them backwards from a book of matches.

"Ughh, hoorgh agchh, h'h' hoorugh!"

"Hach, hach urch, brrr, huugh!"

"Urghh! Can't beat the first puff!"

"Say that again. Where are they?"

"They've gone!"

"Wankers!"

"Yeah."

Stephen Bintuey opened the door of Saltzman Bros. for his wife and held it open while three women and their husbands and children filed in.

"I'm not going to get anything here!"

Stephen's wife, Pamela, followed the throng.

"You could at least look! It wouldn't do you any harm to try a few things on! Colours aren't deadly, y' know! It's not like getting acid on your skin, wearing a plaid sweater! Humner wore a tartan wind-breaker at Alms-Giving, and he's the Mayor!"

"It just isn't me! And it isn't as though I used to wear poncey clothes and then I changed after we got married! I've never worn red! I like blue!"

"It isn't red. It's blue with a whassaname. A hue!"

Spade Braithwaite

"It's bloody tartan!"

"It bloody-well isn't!"

"God give me strength! It's not what I want!"

"Just try it. That's all I ask."

It was a small honour sitting with Mamma Jen in public. It made the security guard feel gallant, as though he was escorting the Queen Mother to a function.

"What's your name, young man?"

"Ughhm, Darren, miss. Darren Kelvin."

"I thought so. Related to Beany Kelvin, I'd guess."

"My dad. He died a few years ago."

"Yes, I was sorry to hear about that. A very gentle man, very handsome. You're quite like him."

Darren glowed and blushed.

"You're a fine lookin' lady, y'self, Mamma Jen."

Mamma Jen smiled and sipped her drink.

Andy Bomar knocked on the door and took a step back. The house wasn't that big but it looked very comfortable. Ernie had enough money for it to be anything he wanted, and all he wanted now was comfort. Mowed lawn, black-topped driveway, windproof porch, repainted woodwork and clear gutters. Andy knew that the inside would be just as organised.

He closed the porch door behind himself and knocked again. God let him get a call on his radio about a robbery in progress around the corner. Shit! He'd left his radio in the car. God let him get abducted by aliens, or something.

The door opened.

"Andy-boy! The last person I expected to see. Good do last night, eh? Fuck-me, I had a good time. I did, didn't I?"

"Ughhm, yeah. Look Ernie, can I come in?"

"Sure, lad. Come into the kitchen. Breakfast? I was just doing some gammon in the mike'. Drink? Come on boy, have a belter."

Ernie took a second glass from the cupboard and filled it with ancient malt before Andy could answer.

"Yeah, chears! Look, Ernie, I'm here on business. Rupert's dead."

Andy Bomar poured half the glass into his mouth to get rid of what he'd just said.

"Rupert? He's in bed. Never see him before noon at the weekends. If at all. Here y' go, top-up. No, Rupe's kushti in 'is pit. I'll get 'im if you want. He isn't in trouble, is he?"

Ernie trudged to the back of his house and hammered on a bedroom door.

"Rupert! It's the fuzz! Wha' 'ave you been up to?"

Andy heard the door open and close and Ernie trudge back.

"Little bastard hasn't come home. Good job 'is mum isn't here, she'd go spare! Bloody kids!"

"Ernie, Rupert's dead. We found him in the park."

Ernie Bishop put his glass down without looking up.

"If you tell me, right now, that this is a joke, then it's funny. If you try to carry this on any longer, then I'll be really angry."

"I'm really sorry, mate."

"What, what are you saying?"

"We found Rupert in the park this morning. Coroner thinks it was probably a reaction to kettamine or amal or amphetamines. We'll know more later."

"Drugs?"

"Yeah."

Ernie pulled a chair out from the kitchen table and sat down heavily without looking up.

"That little bastard could 'ave dropped out of school or shaved his head or knocked up the fuckin' cleaning woman. I would 'ave shouted, but I wouldn't 'ave cared! It's not much to ask, for ya fuckin' wife an' kid to outlive you, is it? Maybe not y' wife. But y' kid? That's only fair! I want the bastard that did this done for murder! I can pay..."

"Ernie! You know we're going to do everything!"

"I want the bastard's head on a stick, an' I want 'is cock in my deep-freeze!"

"Ernie, I'm goin' t' use your phone t' call in sick. Then I'm going to cook us both breakfast and drink the rest of that scotch. I suggest that you get a couple more bottles out f'r the duration."

"What do I have to do?"

"You have to drink lots of scotch. I identified him, and Fishy's organising a funeral f'r next week."

The word "funeral" caught Ernie's perception like a punch in the eye. His family was all gone. He slumped forward and howled like an engine.

Andy stepped closer and patted his head, uncomfortably.

"I want the bastard who did this!"

"Don't worry mate, we'll get 'im! Scotch?"

"Cheers!"

Chapter 4

It was nearly five a.m. in Bundawa. Steamy hot, but comfortable for a few more hours. Upcountry, along the Manuli River a thousand species of brightly coloured birds were waking up, three types of bat were going to sleep and Abraham Unduwe could have gone either way.

Beneath the embarkation pontoon at Porta-Bintutu, Abraham and eight lion-hearted, lion-witted soldiers of the Bantu Nation Redeemist Guerrilla Force dozed and waited for dawn. Abraham might have caught forty winks himself if his wet trousers hadn't kept creeping up his arse and chaffing his mosquito bite every time he shifted.

Being a jungle guerrilla warlord wasn't easy but every once in a while it was fun.

Before sunset, the previous day they'd trekked through the

Spade Braithwaite

forest to a bend in the river half a mile upstream. There, they'd bivouacked down and played bridge till three in the morning when the sherry ran out. Then, they'd solemnly painted their faces and swum silently down stream to the village.

To be perfectly honest, in their desert camouflage, combat boots and dirt-brown faces painted bright green, Abraham felt as inconspicuous as a normal person in a California porn' flick. But in guerrilla warfare, mystique was all.

If it had been more politically provocative they could have caught a bus into town, blown up the town hall, attended a wedding and played volleyball at the YMCA until the bus came back, but Abraham had an eye for world politics and this was how it had to be done. No hint of anarchy. No award-winning video footage of "darky" villagers looting the liquor store and dancing around their neighbour's head on a stick.

David Ben-Gurion, right down the line. Nelson Mandela, without all the years in jail. Intellectual, realistic, political alternative. Terrorism that the west could embrace and shake hands with on their own national television stations.

There were eighteen Europeans in town, including the "Patron", Gerard Barone. Abraham had had a long lunch with him in Tel Aviv a month ago and Gerard had promised to, "recall for inventory" all the militia's rifles for a week, while things were, "working out". Neither of them wanted the town shot-up. Casualties, on either side, were bad for the cause.

Exactly *not* the publicity that would win them friends in the

Herbert Brewer's Dirty Little Secret

UN. Not nice friends, anyway.

It was starting to get light. An exodus of blow-carpies dug themselves out of the mud and limped back to the river on their fins. Adolescent rainbow monkeys crawled out of their fragrant bowers and screamed frustration from the upper canopy. Leopards, sloths and mature rainbow monkeys shooed the mosquitoes out of their ears and rolled over. Everything that was green felt the gentle, sensual sunlight stroking their cells. Everything else buzzed, bit, snored, hid, grazed, preyed, played or laid eggs.

An old man that they hadn't noticed, already asleep under the pontoon, woke up and coughed bile all down himself.

"Ooh my Lor' Lor'! Y'nam bissn't bwye gahn be rootin'-tootin' aaal-ower de town! Me can' believe it! Me say, me caan' believe it!"

"Have you quite finished?"

"Naah'm! B'n ifn't dis d' livin' end!"

"Look! Just piss off!"

The old man lighted off into a field of cassava like a tired, asthmatic with a throbbing head and a bladder close to bursting.

"Stupid old bastard!"

"Focus, people! Eyes on the prize! Weapons, check?"

Eight Kashmirnikov, nine millimetre, short burst elephant-stoppers and a close-quarters, armour-piercing grenade launcher. Not that there was any armour in Porta-Bintutu.

"Check."

Spade Braithwaite

"Check."

"Facepaint, check?"

"Really, Bernard, you need a bit more black over you' cheekbones. You look like a water melon!"

"Facepaint, check?!"

"Check."

"Check."

"Explosives?"

Eighteen American, ariel-drop, submarine locating, limpet charges. Five thousand US dollars each. A present from Bernard's Uncle Muschè.

"Check."

"Duct tape?"

"Check!"

"Okay guys, time to do it!"

Porta-Bintutu served seven copper mines, all within a hundred miles. The ore was driven by truck to the West Africa Mining Company smelting plant at Jamaa. From there, the black, pig-ingots were carried forty-five miles to Porta-Bintutu by rail-shunt. From Porta-Bintutu they were shipped downstream to Kinaida and the world.

Seventeen percent of the country's copper passed through Porta-Bintutu. Point seven percent of the world's total output. Abraham had done his homework; he had the figures and he had the connections.

If he could de-stabilise the flow of copper enough to attract

Herbert Brewer's Dirty Little Secret

British attention then maybe he could convince the right people to ship their copper upstream to Lake Komganerka in Zambia. And from there, by rail to Port Mtwara, on the coast of Tanzania.

It was a plan that didn't involve any construction and only the minimum of diplomacy. The river and the rail links were all there. Tanzania and Zambia would enjoy a few years of unexpected bonus and strong alliances could be forged.

The Bundawa government had no real power up-country. After six months without copper revenue they would flee to France for retirement in abject luxury. Abraham could march into Kinaida, with his eight commandos and cut the padlock off the Presidential Palace without a shot being fired.

Then copper could come through Kinaida again and some of the revenue might actually stay within the country.

The first explosion sank a barge laden with copper, eight feet to the riverbed. The second explosion tore up the railroad track into a huge crater that would need at least five hours work to repair. The third explosion destroyed the McDougal's restaurant. Abraham didn't rate their burgers anywhere near adequate. A poor imitation of a western classic, although their Veggie McDoug was spicy, tasty and a real alternative to meat.

The fourth explosion woke John Shutu, and John Shutu didn't like being woken.

"Dis better be a big one!"

John Shutu marched into his living room to see what was going on. Across the street Bernard Bwarre taped a bomb to the

Spade Braithwaite

wall of Radio "FA-Africa" and ran back to shelter behind John's own porch wall.

John Shutu fetched his revolver from the nightstand.

The bomb exploded, tearing a big hole in the side of the radio station. John Shutu opened his screen door and shot Bernard's brains all over his patio.

Young children, excited by the fireworks and the shouting, ran indoors to hide from angry John Shutu. John Shutu felt the energy roar up his spine and gather behind his eyes.

"Little acquereur bastard!"

If there was one thing, and there were many things that made John Shutu's blood boil, it was little acquereur bastards. The friends, relatives and courtesans of Silus Mantè that had "acquired" control when Bundawa nationalised foreign holdings. Parasitic, pseudo-intellectual, bourgeois brats with foreign educations and enough time on their hands to play games.

It wasn't Philosophy or Sociology that kept things rolling. It was John Shutu and his deputies. Labour didn't gravitate towards the townships because conditions were good. They came because if they stayed in the villages their wives and children would be raped, their animals stolen and their homes burned down. And they worked till their little hearts gave out!

There were a few things that John had wanted to do for a long time, and now was a chance, if ever he was going to get one. Still in his perjamma, he rolled his jeep out of the garage and drove up the hill to the compound.

Herbert Brewer's Dirty Little Secret

The jungle began even before the edge of town. The last few buildings were overgrown and tumbled into nature. A brothel full of refugees, repatriated from South Africa when they tested HIV positive, a red cross shelter with a Catholic priest and a bottle of iodine, a dormitory for foreign mine workers, long abandoned, and a "Come As You Are, Painless, Pay-Less Dentist!" Semi-abandoned.

Half a mile out of town the growth had been cleared for seven mock-Spanish villas facing into a quadrangle, with a big fence all around and a big, wrought iron gate at the front. The Compound. Home to Gerard Barone, his wife and three sons, four Belgian engineers and their families, an African tutor, his wife and eight other blacks.

One of the engineers had a fifteen-year-old daughter. As John Shutu drove up, the gates opened without him having to slow down. Just inside, he stalled his car and bounced out to tell the guards what was going on.

"What a' bin gwann'n?"

"Ahh'l shit hittin' de fan. Me reckon it ahh'l gan pear-shape! Do wha' ya can, an' fuck it ahl!"

"Oh! Me Lor'!"

"Seriously! Gan a' fuck whar y' can, bwye! 'M' be away wit' yal! Me be sayin' g'bye now! Y'hear?!"

"Oh my Lor' Lor'!"

The two guards ran into their dormitory to get their swords. John Shutu kicked open the door of the fourth house, shot four people and raped the shit out of the little, fat, fifth person.

Then he tied her to a banister and chopped her father open to eat his liver.

For all their soap, white people's insides smelled like nothing on earth! His liver, or it might have been part of his bowel, flopped like a fish in John's hands! John Shutu ate some of it and barfed it up all over the polished wood floor. He could eat a McDougal burger after this, in fact, he positively relished the prospect!

Next life, half as black, half white, half the devil, twice the power. All it needed for the spell to work was for himself to die a vainglorious death before the child was born. And God knew that it was coming.

In London, at a club called Radnors, on Victoria Embankment, Alexander Murdoch, the unofficial Director of MI6, sat down to breakfast with the Bundawan Trade Consul, Muschè Bwarre.

"So, Alex, are you sure that this is kosher, meeting here like this?"

Radnors was a large, imperious gentlemen's club that almost nobody outside of politics knew existed. It had two oak-panelled ballrooms, eight snooker rooms, three conference rooms, a reading room, overnight accommodation for twelve and their secretaries, a beautiful restaurant overlooking the Thames and a back entrance into the Ministry of Fisheries and Agriculture in

Herbert Brewer's Dirty Little Secret

Whitehall. The land value alone was more than most African presidents siphoned off in their entire lives.

Bundawa had two secret agents in London. Between them, they couldn't infiltrate the Book of the Month Club without getting caught. Alexander Murdoch felt fairly comfortable in Radnors.

"Muschè, I've seen your agency's files, and they're less informed than our Parliament! Elizabeth Taylor could get a sex change and Bundawa wouldn't hear about it until the television movie had shown on channel five. Relax! What's the scoop?!"

"My Bernard, you remember Bernard?"

"Of course, great wicket-keeper."

"Bernard's got an idea that if we shipped copper upstream, through Tanzania, for a few months, then Mantè might do a runner and Bundawa might be up for the taking. Bloody keen mind, our Bernard! No diplomacy involved at all. Just flaunt a bit of revenue in front of Zambia and Tanzania for six months an' they'll be tame enough to stroke. Bernard has the connections, you know. And then it'll all be kushti-pie in Kinaida again. Bernard and his boys dishing out the favours, instead of madman-Mantè. More copper than you can shake your dick at."

"I could shake my dick at quite a bit of copper!"

"I know. But seriously?!"

"If he can do it without scaring the international community, then we're in clover."

"You think?"

"I could get the copper shipped via the moon, as long as

Bernard doesn't piss anyone off."

"Is it a plan?"

"Tell Bernie, Uncle Alex 'll sort it all out. Just keep it clean, for the sake of the UN. As long as no one gets massacred, we can start on Monday. I just need things to be kept clean. No nastiness, you know what I mean?"

"Yessum, Bwannah. No nastiness. No problem!"

Muschè Bwarre tugged his forelock.

"Muschè, don't be a cunt! I'm Bernard's God-father, remember?"

"I'm sorry, Alex. Are we sorted?"

"Consider yourself "sorted". And young Bernard. He's quite the kiddie! Isn't he?"

"Lor'! I could tell you some stories!"

"I don't want to know. And nor does anyone else! Okay!"

"Okay!"

Breakfast arrived as it always does in fiction, exactly at the moment the conversation reaches it's natural conclusion. (Can you imagine a technical hitch in a novel? The toast getting stuck in the toaster, or the waiter taking it to the wrong table. And then the principle characters having to sit around, making small talk with nothing actually happening. "We are sorry, but due to a technical hitch, narrative has been temporarily suspended. We hope to return to normal story telling as soon as possible!" How weird would that be?!)

"So, ughmm. How's life at the embassy?"

Herbert Brewer's Dirty Little Secret

"Oh, you know. Same old "same old". How's things in international espionage?"

"Good days, bad days. You know."

"Yeah."

"Yeah. Ughhm?"

"Yeah?"

"Oh, nothing. How's old whassisname?"

"The same."

Breakfast arrived, thank God! ("Where the hell were you?! We were dying out there!")

Abraham Unduwe and his commandos regrouped under the freight hoist at the engineering dock at seven hundred hours minus ten, exactly. One last explosion to say goodbye. Buffy Chumba climbed the gantry and taped a mine to the cross-member at the bottom of the boom.

The rest of the Bantu Nation hid behind the wall of the dry-dock and counted down. Buffy turned the screw, energised the ignitor, dropped ten feet and hit the ground running. The timer counted to one second and erupted, destroying the ancient crane and dropping four thousand pounds of twisted angle-iron onto Buffy's shoulders. Buffy hit the ground like a dollop of jam flicked off a ruler. His face caught in anticipation of horror but his brain gloriously oblivious before the pain even got there. Two tons of twisted steel on his back.

Behind the wall the Bantu Nation Redeemist Guerrillas pissed

Spade Braithwaite

their trousers without anyone looking away.

After a minute of silence, Abraham first, then the rest, they tiptoed up to the wreckage and shuffled their feet uncomfortably.

"How the hell are we going to get him out from under that?!"

"Soldiers lay where they fall."

"You tell his dad! I'm not telling him!"

"I'd rather go to England and work for a bank than tell his dad!"

"I'll tell him. Where's Bernard?"

"Last I saw of him, he was looting apple pies from McDoug's."

"It's Bernard's man that's picking us up at Twomey. I think he'll bloody notice if Bernard isn't there! Did he get to the bank?"

"I heard the radio station go up."

"Did anyone hear the bank go up."

Six jungle guerrillas and a jungle warlord replayed every moment of the raid in their heads, searching for evidence that Bernard might be on his way to join them. Possible, but not likely.

"Muschè's going to be pissed!"

"Oh my God!"

"Oh, f' Christ's sake! We're guerrillas, and this is a revolution! For what we've achieved today, two casualties are a fair price to the nation. We'll build a bloody statue to them, if it makes you any happier!"

"Muschè's going to be pissed!"

"Fuck Muschè! Fuck you! I'm going home."

The surviving guerrillas bickered, half-heartedly for a half a minute then shrugged their shoulders, waded into the river and swam half a mile downstream to Twomey for their lift home.

The sun rose a little higher. Not painful yet but enough to hatch swarms of devil flies and boil some shower water in the few solar panels.

The two guards at the Compound killed everyone that they could find and then chopped Gerard Barone's head off, mutilated his body and stole his pistol.

Then they borrowed the East Africa Company's Jeepey and drove home to their village to carry on the fun.

Chapter 5

Joshua Matenach ate his meal in stony silence. Gary Crozier watched him through the observation window and wondered what to do with him. It had been over forty-eight hours so it was time to formally charge him or let him go.

They'd arrested him at six o-clock on Sunday morning, at home, at the bottom of Gothburton Street, and found enough speed in his bedroom to last him through six weekends or two weeks of very intense work.

Since then he hadn't said a word, except asking for cigarettes and the bathroom. Gary was quickly developing a harsh respect for Joshua.

Drugs had never been a problem in Clausthowlersnauglerbogler. No gangs, no junkies, no organised crime, no problem.

A lot of people indulged but everyone turned up at work everyday and nobody cared. It was a tough, industrial, desert town. What did people expect?

Gary could see a lot of difficulties in contriving an acceptable solution to this particular situation.

Ernie Bishop was understandably distraught and wanted a culprit.

The Senior State Magistrate, Judge Tethers would probably want to try the case himself. He would probably try to find an excuse to let Joshua off. If Josh got off then Ernie would shoot him dead in the street and every punk-kid in town would see it as a green light to sell drugs to school kids.

It was a high-profile case and everyone had an opinion. It'd take a whole lot of arse-kicking and overtime to return the town to normal.

Gary had a few ideas. Judge Tethers was a reasonable man. If he sentenced Josh to twenty years, hard labour then Josh would be sent to Randolph Maximum Security for the duration, and that was a long way away. Cars broke down and paperwork got lost. Josh could disappear and no one would ever look for him. Ernie would never know.

Josh didn't even look up when Gary opened the cell door and sat down. He just ate and tried not to get into any more trouble.

"Joshua. Do you hear me? I have to formally charge you. For supplying category "A" drugs to a minor and for being party to unlawful acts that led to that minor's death. Do you hear me? You have the right to remain silent, but that silence might be construed as guilt, in a court of law. You have the right to consult an attorney, if you can afford one, or you can ask for a State Counsellor to be present at your interrogation. You don't have to tell me your side of the story but if another version of events is entered into evidence first then it will be given greater credibility. Do you understand? Do you have anything to say?"

Josh didn't even shake his head.

"Joshua. I don't think you did anything wrong, but the shit's hit the fan, in a bad way. And you stand to spend a lot of years in jail. Can you work with me a little bit? I promise I'll do my best."

A man's head poked round the door.

"Gary, it's Stav' Nicolaus on your personal line. Says he wants a word when it's convenient. Oh, and your wife called half an hour ago and said it's important."

"Okay, thank you. Josh. I knew your dad. I went to school with him and I arrested him twice for punching your mother. I went to Elizabeth's funeral. I arranged for Shirley Brown to be

Spade Braithwaite

your caseworker. You remember old Shirley? The best I could do. You sniff a bit of Billy-Whiz and you work hard. You give a wrap to a mate, and he dies! Not the end of the world. Just talk to me!"

Josh finished his mince and beans and passed the empty plate over for approval.

"Josh! Rupert Bishop was a little bastard! Do y'self a favour! Tell me about it!"

Josh looked up at Gary and remembered long days of being beaten half to death by his father. In his mind there was still a little place that he could retreat to. A little valley of Middle Earth, with hobbits, necromancers, goblins, wizards, heroes and beautiful, elven queens. Dwarves and burglars against all the forces of darkness.

"Josh! This is for real! I'm not kidding!"

Gary stared into Josh's eyes for a full two minutes and then gave up

"Fuck you, boy! You're up shit-creek, without a paddle. Talk to me when you want a break."

Gary locked the cell door behind him and walked back to his office. There were good parts of being a cop but there were bad parts as well. Picking bodies off the railroad track. Telling people that their children had died in car crashes. Telling guys with nine children and mortgage arrears that they couldn't drive to work because their cars weren't road worthy. Taking people with minor, emotional problems out of society and putting them in prison with shag-nasty, hardened criminals.

    Gary rubbed his face indulgently and then called his wife.

    Bo-Bae picked up on the third ring.

    "Hallo?"

    "Babe, it's me. Yo' lover man."

    "Frank?"

    "Very funny!"

    "Honey! Have you seen the news today?"

    "Something about an unusual desert bloom, and..."

    "The draught?"

    "Unusual winds..."

    "No! Fuck head! The draught! Some young men of age being called up for soldiers!"

    "Do what?! If anyone wanted to invade us they'd have done it years ago. Christ! Bangladesh could over-run us in half a week, if they wanted to!"

    "I know, but, let me find it..., the "UN has committed itself to keeping the peace in Bundawa", and we've "committed" ourselves to "providing a peace keeping force"."

    "We can't even keep the peace at Council meetings!"

    "I know! God only knows! "

    "Bundawa?! Where the hell is that?"

    "I think it must be just off the South coast. If Bundawa falls then we all in trouble!"

    "No, I'm sure it's in Asia, or Africa, or somewhere."

    "Then why we care?"

Spade Braithwaite

"I don't know. Why *do* we care?"

"Jim have to report to conscription office, any day now."

"Holy shit, yeah! Give me a while to think. Don't worry. I'll sort it out. What are you wearing?"

"A crisp, white shirt. But all the buttons have come undone! My little nipples are nearly bursting in the fresh air, and my panties..."

"Big, white, cotton panties?"

"Saturated! Good thing Mother Superior not here!"

"I'll be home in an hour."

"I know."

"See you soon!"

"I know. Bye."

Gary Crozier leaned back in his chair and thought about sucking aspic-jelly through a straw, wellington-boots full of mushy-peas, Prime Minister Cartright on the toilet and every other un-sexy image that he could conjure.

"Janet, get me Stav' Nicolaus on the phone."

"Okay."

The phone rang three times.

"Hello! Randolph First National Bank?"

"Stavros Nicolaus, Gary Crozier returning his call."

"One moment!"

Three moments. Then four more moments.

"Gazza, my boy!"

"Stav', What's the problem?"

Herbert Brewer's Dirty Little Secret

"I've had a bloke in here today. He sounds like the real thing, but not quite. Calls himself "Charles LeFevre", from Paris. But he chuckles at my joke about Greek women and then makes a crack about the cycles of the moon! He's a Greek, or I'm the long, lost Kennedy brother!"

"What does he want?"

"He doesn't want anything. He just wants to transfer money here and start a business."

"No loans or anything?"

"Not right now."

"What do you want me to do?"

"Find out if he's kosher. Who he is and what he's after."

"Can you get his fingerprints?"

"Got 'em on a brandy tumbler. I'll have someone drop it off. I'd appreciate the tumbler back. It's one of four that match."

"Sure thing, Stav. If he hasn't got a record then his dabs won't be in the system, but we'll have a look and see what's there. Charles LeFevre, you say? Can I have a look at his details?"

"I'll send a copy with the glass. Do me a favour and burn it afterwards. You know how people are."

"Okay, Stav. I'll be in touch."

Janet came into the office to pick up the day-work sheets and leave a few notes for his signature.

"Janet, how old are you?"

"Forty seven. Forty eight in June.".

Spade Braithwaite

"Do we have any naked photographs of you in the files?"

"Not that I'm aware of. Do we need any?"

"I think it'd be a good idea. A few topless shots in a passport photo booth, to start with. And then a full layout, taken outdoors in a cornfield. I'd take them myself if you wanted."

"I'd love to, except that the "sexual harassment in the workplace" handbook specifically advises against it. You can have some of my old underwear to masturbate over, if you want."

"Good enough. A healthy compromise. When can I have it?"

"You're a sick puppy!"

"Don't you love me for it?"

"Take an early lunch. I think you and Bo-Bae were made for each other."

"Are you saying that my wife's a pervert?"

"Just go."

"Okay. But I'm serious about the underwear. Don't bother washing it. I'll do all that."

"Just go."

Janet couldn't help smiling as she left the office.

At the library Jenny Won Baker read the newspaper, contemplated, and read it again to let her perception creep into all the gaps. Conscription in Amsarnie!

The story read:

Herbert Brewer's Dirty Little Secret

Military Call-Up for School Leavers

For the first time in Amsarnie's history the government has voted to exercise a clause in the Original Charter and summon a limited number of young men into active, military service.

The move, likely to be applauded in several countries, follows weeks of intense dialogue in the United Nations about the sending of an international peacekeeping force to quell internal frictions in Bundawa. UN Resolution 90813, championed by the United Kingdom, against opposition from Russia and China, declared the UN to be committed to protecting ethnic Luban villagers in the interior from intimidation and violence by the minority Mangebutan nomads. The tribes, both nominally Catholic Christian, have a history of hostility since 1912, when a Vatican Council ruled that onanism was still a sin, even when your wife looked more like a man than a woman.

Recently created Minister for Allied Stability, George Snapper said today, "Amsarnie has enjoyed, "head in the sand" politics for too many years. We're now a burgeoning economic and political super-power. It's time we got involved in international affairs and made a difference."

Opposition spokesman, Chip Wellesley said that, "Everybody knows that Snapper's a [vernacular expression for a self-obsessed gelding or a person of little credibility]."

Already, the Mayors of several cities, including Randolph, Precaria and Braithwaite have communicated support for the plan.

Political analysts anticipate that the scheme will probably be implemented in a limited manner at first, in specific geographical areas to assess the sociological

Spade Braithwaite

implications.

Mamma Jen had arrived in the county just after the First World War when she was still a child. Years and experience had dulled her reflexes, but her memory was nearly perfect.

Straight from the wagon she'd started working for Big Kelly's Hotel, clearing tables, running to the betting shop and learning about men.

Half the families in town had sons who'd sailed away to enlist in one army or another. All their fathers drinking together, showing photographs and telling stories about how brave their sons were. The winning and losing were just like a football match. One crowd patted each other's shoulders with grim pride. The other group hugged each other with grim remorse. Everybody still drank together and none of the sons ever came home. Nothing seemed to get any better.

Twenty years later all the young men had gone away again but that time it had been slightly different. They were all on the same side, protecting Amsarnie from a real threat of invasion by Japan. And a lot of them had come home again when it was over, shot full of syphilis, psychosis and holes.

The country had never, ever forced young men to join the army. It wasn't right and it mustn't be allowed to happen!

Mamma Jen read the article a third time and then scoured the other sections looking for a deeper explanation.

It was lunchtime. He parked his car in the cul-de-sac

Herbert Brewer's Dirty Little Secret

adjacent to Bloxham Road and cut through the trees to a footpath that ran along the bottom of the gardens. Three houses down, he pulled an old wheelbarrow against the fence and carefully perched to see over.

There she was, in the kitchen ironing clothes. Short, dark and trim in a grey skirt and white blouse. He shuddered as she held up a pair of panties and folded them onto the pile.

With more effort than was good for him he vaulted the fence and landed on a cane that had once held a vine. The sharp end of the stick caught his taint and snapped as his weight came down on it.

"Yow! You fucking...! Ow! Ow."

He landed like a pig and hopped around, clutching his rear. Then, after a full minute of cursing, he snapped the two pieces into two more pieces, cursed some more, and crept up the garden like a cat.

The french windows were open. He slipped quietly inside and closed the doors behind him.

She was still in the kitchen, singing along to the radio. He tiptoed towards the door.

Suddenly the door opened and she came through, carrying a pile of ironed clothes. He stepped forward. She screamed and ran.

At the bottom of the stairs he caught her, panties and pillowslips flying every way. She struggled but he was too strong. He dragged her onto the hall carpet and pinned her down with all his weight. She grimaced and tried to turn her head away from his kiss.

Slowly, with great satisfaction, he plucked open the buttons on her shirt and ran a rough hand over her belly.

"Ow! Hold it! Something sharp up my arse!"

"I'm sorry."

She wriggled and adjusted herself more comfortably.

"There, okay. You dirty bastard! You dirty bastard! Let me go! I beg you! Please don't violate me! I beg you!"

He let the beast out of the bag.

"Oh no! It's so big! Please don't hurt me!"

He hitched her skirt up, pulled her panties to one side and penetrated her with the biggest erection he'd had all week.

Three minutes later.

"So what about our Jim?"

"What? I don't know. I'll make a few phone calls, see what's going on. What's for lunch?"

"You had your lunch, you eat now. We have pizza, minestrone and crusty rolls, or I make cheese and ham toasty? Then, maybe you have a few minutes left for more lunch?"

"I'm the chief. Who's going to fire me?"

Charles Lefevre picked the real estate agent up at his office and drove back to Gallipoli Street to have a look at an apartment tucked in between the Luker Building and the Town Life Tower. Above the offices of the Domestic Revenue Department. With

Herbert Brewer's Dirty Little Secret

parking space in the Luker Garden and an exclusive entrance and elevator. The bachelor-pad that every married man in Clausthowlersnauglerbogler dreamed about.

Six stories up, with a view over the Geological Chartered Bank into Oxpens and the sunrise. One split level. Two and a half thousand square feet of fanny-magnet. Ultra-modern kitchen, fake log-burning fire, shag pile carpets, enormous bed. Available for nine months while the late Kevin Bogler's estate was carved up in an American court.

"When could I move in?"

"Two thousand down, refundable, and two thousand a month, in advance. Tomorrow, or as soon as the credit clears."

"I think I'm good for it. My funds should be here by now. I'll take it."

"Would you be wanting a domestic service to keep the place? There would be a charge for cleaning if you left the place any less salubrious than you found it."

"I think I can organise my own domestic arrangements, thank you. I'll be in here tomorrow, if that's okay."

"Okay. The keys'll be downstairs, at reception."

"Cool."

"Yeah, cool."

Gary Crozier phoned his old friend in Paris.

"Allo. Interpol, Paris."

"Can I speak to Jon Burofsky. Tell him it's Gary Crozier,

Spade Braithwaite

Amsarnie."

"Could you spell that please?

"C-l-a-u-s-t-h-o-w-l-e-r-s-n-a-u-g-l-e-r-b-o-g-l-e-r."

"No such place!"

"Just tell Jon that Luncheon-Truncheon-Gary Crozier is on the phone."

A French, male voice interrupted

"Gary! Forgive Janice. We get a lot of crank calls here. You must understand. How are tricks? When are you coming back to Paris?"

"Jonny-boy! Soon. I'll bring the wifey this time."

"I hear she's hot!"

"More than you could handle. I need a favour. I need to find out about some guy called Charles LeFevre. Claims to be French, might be Greek. I've sent you some fingerprints over the wire."

"What's he been up to?"

"Nothing yet. But you know us hick-cops. We like to know who's in town, and what they're up to."

"Maybe he just likes sand in his lungs and road-killed camel for lunch?"

"You dip-shit Frog! I'd kick your arse, if I cared enough!"

"You'll owe me. When are you coming over? You third-world cops earn more from road-blocks than we do from blackmail!"

"I've been talking about it for long enough. I think I could commit myself to a trip in Autumn, when the fares are cheap.

Herbert Brewer's Dirty Little Secret

And I'll be bringing the wife. So, best behaviour!"

"The best is none too good. But we'll try."

"Speak to you later. I'll owe you one."

Gary hung up the phone and smiled. It was nice to have a plan. The next number he hadn't dialled for four years so he had to look it up in his rolladex.

Eight one three one seven nine seven eight two. Area code four four four. Gunswale, Parliament.

"Office of the Secretary of the Interior! How May I help you?"

"Harry, please."

A short pause.

"Harry Melchet, very tired, what is it?"

"Harry? Gary Crozier. What's this shit I'm hearing about conscription? Is it gen'?'

"Gary. I was going to phone you. How old's that boy of yours?"

"Sixteen. Leaving school in a couple of weeks."

"Then you've got to come up with a plan, fast. Do you know what voter turn-out in Claust' was at the last election?"

"Piss-poor?"

"Piss-poor. Less than two percent. The winning candidate lost his deposit! You know that they're going to conscript from just a couple of towns first, to see how it goes. Guess where?"

"You're shittin' me?!"

"Straight up! Get your boy a serious medical exemption, or some devious shit, or he's a soldier."

Spade Braithwaite

"He's built like a girl! An' he couldn't hit a stuffed moose with a bayonet!"

"I'm telling you like they're tellin' me. Thalidomide babies, no exemption, cerebral palsy, no exemption. They want a plane full of any-bugger in Bundawa, dressed in green, making up the numbers. They don't care. It's political, and you know how that works!"

"Thanks, Harry. I really appreciate the information. See you christmas."

"Take care, Gary. This is all really bad shit! Even by our standards!"

"Cheers Harry. I owe you one."

Gary hung up the handset, down-booted his computer and signed out for the evening.

At three in the morning a message trickled into the computer network at Clausthowlersnauglerbogler Police Headquarters. Destined for Gary's eyes only.

It read:

"Charles Andropolous. AKA: Charlie Boy, Champaigne Charlie, Charles LeFevre, Captain Crumble. Born: Greece, nineteen sixty-two. Achieved French Nationality: Nineteen ninety-one. Name flagged with registered query from Bolivian embassy (Ignored!) Wanted for questioning in relation with terrorist crime. (More likely, big steal from Bolivian power men.)

Linked to confidence heists in several countries.

Herbert Brewer's Dirty Little Secret

Not considered dangerous, but very, very clever! Beware! Details to follow."

End message.

Chapter 6

At seven o-clock that morning Skinny Andy Bomar got a call to a domestic at the Bourke house. Three houses knocked into one. Twenty seven Bourkes at last count. Any call from the Bourke house automatically brought armed back-up and notified the hospital to wake a few interns up.

Andy struggled to awareness, wiped his eyes and cranked the radio back up to full.

"What was that, Rhonda?"

"Liam's gone off on one."

"Big Liam?"

"Young Liam."

"Fuck!"

"Came home shortly after six and took his sister-in-law hostage. No further details. It's only just seven, I'll break into morning roll-call and get a couple of cars over there straight away."

"Thanks. I'll go and have a look."

Spade Braithwaite

Juno Street wound right across the Burmont estate. At the corner of Partridge and Juno, opposite the Lymington Tavern, the Bourke house. A terrace of tied-houses that used to belong to the Seventh Municipal Fire District before it was incorporated. Now inhabited by the Bourke family.

Every building in town newer than eighty years old had foundations dug, shuttered and poured by a Bourke. Big, burley bastards they all were.

Andy parked outside the house and scoped the situation. No sign of whoever called the emergency, no shouting or fighting, no obvious activity at all. Andy swore a revolting curse on the god of policemen and big, fat, ugly ground-workers. Big, fucking problems at the Bourke house.

The front garden was a loose barricade of abandoned cement mixers, rusted truck parts and rotting wood, discarded and arranged to discourage a direct, ground assault. Andy put the night-stick into his belt and walked up the path to have a look.

"Hello! Anyone call the police?!"

No answer. A really bad sign.

"Open up! It's the Bogies!"

Andy knocked on the middle door and prepared to run.

"Oh, officer! Thank the lord! It's our Liam! He's takin' me brother's wife into the basement and says he'll cut her throat!"

"Okay, madame. Does he have a weapon?"

"Fuckin' great pair o' tar shears. He's been gone three days. Came home this mornin' in an awful moyther!"

Herbert Brewer's Dirty Little Secret

"What're tar shears?"

"It's like scissors, but bigger and blunt."

"Where are they?"

"In the basement, with all the home-brew! We're desperate, so we are! Please sort him out!"

"Show me where."

Andy Bomar entered the house cautiously, stepping over plastic tricycles, grandparents and power-trowels.

"Door on your left. I moved the targets. There, just down the stairs, now."

Andy Bomar tiptoed down the stairs looking for a light.

Young Liam's voice came out of the darkness.

"Is it a pig? It smells like a pig. Come on, pig! Come and get some!"

Andy found the light. Big, fat, Young Liam was in the corner of the basement, holding a huge pair of scissors around the neck of a simpering young woman.

Andy found the floor and evaluated the situation.

"You stupid, big, fat fuck! I really don't have time fo' this bullshit!"

"I'm really gonna cut her up!"

"One less fuckin' Bourke! An' then I'll put you in jail forever! Two less mud-grubbin', fuckin' sheep-shaggers!"

"You little shit!"

Young Liam took a run at Andy. Andy calculated his run, took a step backwards and swung a boot.

Spade Braithwaite

Liam ran violently on to an ungodly kick in the gonads, folded like a sheet and fell in a tidy pile.

Andy reviewed the situation and stamped on young Liam's scissors-hand with all the energy that the day had left. Three or four times. And then his left hand twice.

"You-fat-fucker! I don't fuckin'-need-you!"

"Agghhhh! I'm unarmed! Don't hurt me!"

"Don't-hurt-this! Y' fat bastard!"

Reinforcements arrived in time to arrest young Liam, counsel the sister-in-law and calm Skinny-Andy down before serious mischief was done.

A constable cautioned Young Liam before he was taken into custody.

"You stupid wanker, sir! You're gunna fuckin' get it! Negligible damage to the hands, and minor bruising, probably incurred while resisting arrest. Shit happens. You know what? Your face looks alright, and that could all change during questioning! Just lie back and think of Amsarnie! That's what I tell my wife!"

Liam Bourke was arrested and held for questioning in connection with abduction, false imprisonment, attempted murder, attack on a police officer with intent to take his/her life, and for being a big, fat bastard that everybody was scared of. Maximum sentence, forty-eight years in a federal jail. The very minimum, a damn-good kicking.

Herbert Brewer's Dirty Little Secret

Seven forty eight, a Detective and a Constable identified themselves to the morning porter at the Blandford Hotel, who knew exactly who they were, and asked which room M. Charles LeFevre was occupying, even though they already knew.

The Detective explained that although the hotel wasn't obliged to co-operate the police could be back with a search warrant and a health-inspector within the hour, if it came to that.

The porter shrugged his shoulders, rolled his eyes and begged would they, please, just get on with it and then piss off. Life was too short, and bullshit too plentiful.

The Detective and the Constable rode the elevator to the fourth floor, wound left and turned right at the fire directions, and found room four eighteen exactly where it was supposed to be.

The Constable knocked and then stepped backwards so that the Detective was positioned to deal with the response.

No response. The Detective knocked louder.

"Yeah! Hold on. What's the bloody time?! I didn't want a call. Hold on."

The door opened a slit to expose an unshaven Charles LeFevre, eyes like fat girls' belly-buttons.

"Yeah?"

"Sir. I'm Detective Brodie and this is Constable Fitzroy. We'd be pleased to interview you at the Station about a serious crime that we believe you might have been a witness to."

"What time is it?"

"Nearly eight."

Spade Braithwaite

"What have I done?"

"Three murders and a bank robbery, if you're not careful. Put y' trousers on, Andropolous, it's a bust!"

Charles' blood ran cold.

"Shit..."

Shifting automatically from "game-on" mode to "fight or flight", Charles absorbed a lot of information quickly. Every word, every nuance of body language. Every possible option.

Eyes suddenly wide open, he let the policemen play their games and waited for a contingency plan to present itself.

"We both know I haven't done anything! I've been here a week! You want money? I got money!"

"Very kind, sir, but I think that the Chief wants to piss on you himself. So unless you got retirement kind o' money..."

"Yeah, right."

"...You're in it! Bad luck, sir. Put some trousers on, and a shirt. There's a good lad. We can take you in whole, half, damaged, dead or alive. We don't care."

"Give me five."

"Two."

"Okay. You know, I've been thrown out of better countries than this!"

"If only that were all of it, sir. You're up shit's-crick, without a paddle. I'm damn glad that I'm the public servant arresting you, and not you! You know what we do with bad-guys in Claust'?"

"Just..., save it. I'm not in the mood! Give me minute, and

then bust me, but don't give me the fuckin' the lecture!"

"Very good sir. However you want to do it."

Constable Fitzroy made mental notes and tried not to smirk.

Mamma Jen hailed a taxi to the Brewer building and tipped the driver most of what the taxi would have cost anyway.

"Mamma Jen! We have a company policy concerning you. I'd get sacked for taking money from you!"

"It's not money, it's a gratuity. And it's not for you, it's for your lovely wife. Take me to the Brewer Building and take your time. I need to be there about mid-morning. People are at their best mid-morning, and then again after lunch. Is Humner still the Mayor?"

"I believe he is."

"Good. I knew his uncle and I watched him grow up. He's done a fine job, don't you think?"

"Yeah, I suppose."

"Who's on the Council now?"

"I don't know. I think there's five of them. Or twelve. I think I voted for a black guy."

"Eighteen, or the constitution's changed. They haven't held an election for fifteen years."

"I think it was "Something-Boingo."

"Randolph Maboygnia, that was eighteen years ago. Lost by twelve votes."

"Unlucky!"

Spade Braithwaite

"There was a total of thirty eight votes. He requested a re-count, and it took less than a minute. But I'm glad that you voted. It's important."

"Yeah. I decided then that voting for a politician is like voting for whether you want to be de-frauded, or just robbed outright. I choose not to vote. I don't want to give any o' them bastards my support."

"I'd like to take issue but I can't fault your reasoning. The Brewer Building, if you don't mind."

The taxi dropped Jenny Won Baker at the front entrance of the Brewer building and arranged to pick her up from the Pied Bull Tavern across the road in an hour.

Jenny Won Baker tottered into the reception and summoned Old-Eddie with a buzz.

"Edward! I need to speak to Humner. Are the council in?"

"I doubt it. Maybe a couple of them. The ones that ever turn up. How are you, Mamma Jen?"

"Shit-hot! How are you?"

"Almost as good."

"I want to discuss this conscription nonsense. We mustn't let it happen."

"Humner's on the seventh floor. I'll tell him your'e coming."

"Good man. Give my regards to Rachel."

Jenny Won Baker had attended Rachel's funeral, fourteen years ago. The elevator arrived and Old-Eddie pressed the number seven button for her.

Herbert Brewer's Dirty Little Secret

The policemen ushered Charles Andropolous into the lift and took him to the fourth floor.

No handcuffs or strong-arm tactics. People in Clausthowlersnauglerbogler knew when they were nicked and came quietly. Charles stood in the corner, with his hands behind his back, standing just out of the auras of the arresting officers.

Second floor, third floor, Fourth floor.

No fingerprints, no mug shots. Straight into cell eight, and the Chief would be along sometime.

Clang. Door closed.

The peephole looked out across the typing pool. Three women, picking their noses, reading their horoscopes and chattering as they keyed information into the data base.

"Is it likely?"

"The way Doris was talking, it's definite. Rich or poor."

"What about college kids?"

"They're getting 'em and giving 'em a docket for college when they leave the army."

"Our Ranjit, you know, our Frank's eldest girl's feller, 'e's been a father since he was fourteen. They can't take 'im?!"

"Every fucker! That's what I heard."

"Just Claust'?"

"Limited geographical areas, to start with. And Claust's been chosen."

"Doesn't seem fair!"

Spade Braithwaite

"What about Gary's kid? James, is it? Big daft sod, might be the makin' of 'im."

"Every fucker, man and beast. That's what I heard. As long as they can stand up and see. Every bugger."

"So what does Gary think?"

"Not best pleased I should imagine. He had some deal sorted out so that Jim could coast his exams and the teachers'd all get their parking tickets sorted. Something like that, I heard."

"What about the factories? They're going to need all the new kids when the pensions come around?"

"Fuck Claust'! I think that's what they've decided."

"Where is this war?"

"Bundawa."

"Where's that?"

"I think it's just off the south coast."

"Too close for comfort."

"It doesn't seem right though, just Claust' being involved."

"And a couple of other towns, chosen for their "geographical isolation." So that they can "assess the sociological ramifications." That's what I heard."

"I bet you a doughnut that Gary's kid doesn't go!"

"It's a bet! They're getting everyone. They don't care."

"Seems a bit rough!"

"It happens every forty years, that's what I heard."

"I don't remember it!"

"Me either."

Herbert Brewer's Dirty Little Secret

Gary Crozier wandered down to cell eight to have a look at Charles Andropolous and recognised him straight away. He was only other person Gary had met who'd been to Paris. Last Friday night at Shoop-Shoop. Lots of funny stories about life in Europe.

Gary opened the cell and sat on the bed.

"Good morning Chief! I hope your family is well. I'm ready to take my medicine like a man! What's in store for me?"

"I don't know. I could put you on a flight to Bolivia and earn a few favours for doing it. What were you up to?"

"I'm a representative for a company that..."

"Tell me now, or sit here and tell me in a month. What were you up to?"

"I was going to drum-up a bit of interest in the bog-lands. Then I was going to get lots of money out of a few local idiots and fuck off back to France. Are you happy now?"

"Good enough. Why shouldn't I send you back to Bolivia?"

"I'm a professional, and you need professional help."

"You have my attention."

"Your boy James. Not army material, by all accounts, but destined to do his bit, all the same."

"What do you know about James?"

"He's your son. And he's going off to fight in some smelly jungle unless you get a plan together quickly."

"And your contribution would be?"

Spade Braithwaite

"You know about the law. I know about bending the law. International, domestic, I come, I go."

"I caught you!"

"A fluke! I know the system as well as anyone. I can get your boy out of the army or I'll do time for all the murders you never solved."

"I solved all our murders. We've only ever had two."

"Well everything else then."

"So what's your ideas?"

"We can avoid, evade, or just fake it."

"Go on."

"Avoidance, study the parameters of call-up eligibility, look for a gap. Easiest and most likely. Problems, I get the impression that it'd need a doctors note from the Brothers Grimm, and that might come back to haunt."

"Evasion?"

"Fake death, false identity. New life in a different town. I know some people in Europe."

"Faking it?"

"Send someone else. I'm sure you could think of someone."

"You're a very interesting man... Do you prefer Andropolous or LeFevre?"

"Whatever."

"...Mr Andropolous. I'll have a good think about it. In the mean time, I've spoken to your bank this morning. They received four hundred thousand US dollars, that's about seven hundred and twelve thousand Amsarnie, into your new account yesterday and I've asked them to freeze it. They'll pay your hotel bill and give you six hundred dollars a week cash. I have to make a few enquiries and I'll be in touch. Don't try to leave town. And stay out of mischief!"

"Actually, I just took over an apartment. Could I stay there?"

"By all means! Leave the details with Janet at the front desk on your way out. I'll probably see you about town somewhere. Take care."

"And you."

Humner was a little bit intimidated by Jenny Won Baker. There weren't many people in town, of any consequence, who cared anything beyond planning approvals and zoning laws, but Mamma Jen was one. Humer suspected that she had a lot of important connections that he didn't know about, so he never quite knew what angle she was coming from.

Humner's secretary buzzed into his office.

"A Mrs Baker, to see you. Have you got a minute?"

"Sue, please show Miss Won Baker into the Empire Lounge and furnish her with every refreshment. I'll be there immediately."

That was office code for "Suck-up and look busy!" Sue took her cue.

"Miss Won Baker! The Mayor is currently in a meeting with Heads of Agency. I've told him that you're here and he's eager

Spade Braithwaite

to speak to you as soon as he can get away. I've been asked to entertain you in the lounge. Please, follow me."

Sue led Jenny Won to the good room and seated her in a big swivel chair that looked out over Sherwin Park.

"Coffee, tea, something stronger?"

"It's a bit early. Brown ale, if you have it."

"I'm sure, anything else?"

"No, thank you very much."

"Okay. I'll be just across the hall, typing up requests for emergency social security for the elderly. Just call if you need me."

"Thank you very much. Miss?"

"Sue."

"Thank you Sue. I'm good."

Humner checked his nose for grolleys and his teeth for spinach and then greeted Jenny Won Baker in the Lounge.

"Jenny Won! Nice to see you! What can I do for you?"

"Humner! It's this conscription. It mustn't be allowed!"

"I'm sure! The factories need every able bodied man!"

"Bugger the factories! It's our men! It's enslavement! We must stop it!"

"Of course. Shoop-Shoop needs young men."

"Clausthowlersnauglerbogler needs men! They're our young men! Humner! I'm nominating you the chairperson of a town meeting to discuss opposition to the draught."

"Which particular draught?"

Herbert Brewer's Dirty Little Secret

"Conscription!"

"Ah, yes. What?"

"All our young men being called up to fight some silly war in Africa!"

"Of course! Which war in Africa?"

"Humner! I want you to read the newspapers and find out any gossip that you can from your sources in Gunswale. Call in a few favours, get some inside information."

"Actually, I've been thinking seriously about passing the mantle. Retiring, you know... And maybe taking a less prestigious position."

"Humner! Next Sunday, I propose to host a full town meeting in Shoop-Shoop's ballroom. About fighting this ridiculous scheme. I'll get the council, and a few people who might have ideas."

"All the council?"

"There's only eighteen of you!"

"I'll be there. Shoop-Shoop, on Sunday. Was there anything serious that you wanted to discuss?"

"I'll give Sue the details, on my way out!"

"Good, good. Always a pleasure, Mamma Jen. I'll see you again on Sunday."

"Take care, Humner."

"And you, Mamma Jen. Good bye."

"Good bye."

Spade Braithwaite

Gary wandered into the typing pool and peered in through the peephole at Joshua Matenach. A young man with a lot of good reasons to want to leave town for a while. Under any name.

Maybe! Maybe Not.

But, Maybe...!

Chapter 7

In his office, on the ground floor, rear, of the Northern Provinces Federal Administration Building, in Precaria, Laurence French studied the envelope and put it in a pile of its own.

It was manila, eight inches by six inches and it said:

```
          L French
          Executive Supervisor for the National Office of
Domestic Security
          (Northern Provinces)
          Federal Administration Building
          Connaught Place
          Precaria

          For attention of addressee, and no other!
          (If undelivered, return to:
          National Office of Domestic Security
          Three Wheel Lane
          Gunswale)
```

Herbert Brewer's Dirty Little Secret

Laurence opened his other mail first and tried to surround himself in an aura of white light to ward off bad karma. Somehow, the white light just wasn't there.

As far as he knew, Laurence French was the Senior Career Officer in the Northern Provinces. He'd taken over fifteen years ago, in a sideways move from Probation and Correction, when Jerry Callow had left the office to take up a seat in Parliament.

His job consisted of administrating a co-ordination between the annual labour requirements of industry and the annual output of labour from the education system.
He also officiated the annual report to the Office of Auxiliary Defence.

As far as he knew, Laurence had never accepted any position with the National Office of Domestic Security. But his name was right there. So he must have. Laurence French, Executive Supervisor for the National Office of Domestic Security. It must be true.

Eventually he opened the manila envelope. Inside was a memorandum. It read:

```
Be advised:
     Specific, objective parameters of Auxiliary Defence
policy under review.  Possibility of necessary, non-
optional recruitment to national service, in specific
circumstances and locations, currently under advisement.
     Proceed towards preparation of annual report with a
view to facilitating non-confrontational adjustment of
report-subjects from civilian to mobilised, military
```

Spade Braithwaite

status.

    Particulars to follow. (Likely to involve federal requisition of all personnel listed available in certain, specific areas of geographical and social isolation.)

    (Regards to all the cats in Health Ed'. Tell them Mellissa says hi! Jerry says do one for him!)

National Office of Domestic Security

Laurence read the note very slowly, trying to work out even roughly what the hell it meant. It appeared to mean that the government, by which Laurence was tenuously employed, intended to call up a lot of young men into the army, or whatever it was they had nowadays.

He read the note again, drawing a syntactic flow chart on a piece of notepaper as he went along. It certainly appeared to mean just that. But could it?! And why would it?!

A thousand questions, possibilities, scenarios and outcomes sprang forward and got bottle-necked at the transfer to conscious thought. Nothing got through.

What was already in Laurence's conscious mind was that his June tour had just taken a direct hit right up the arse. A few days in each of the other three cities of the Northern Province. Good hotels, VIP treatment, short days and long nights. Frannie or Joan in Braithwaite. Frannie that liked to make him watch, or Joan that would be twenty-one this year. Lesley in New Basingstoke. Janet in Claust'. The Shoop-Shoop in Claust'!

Thoughts, very slowly, one at a time.

Herbert Brewer's Dirty Little Secret

"Geographical and social isolation"! They meant Clausthowlersnauglerbogler! They were going to pull some bloody stunt in Claust' and they expected him to do the shitty bit! They could fuck right off! Right now!

Steady stream now, slow but moving.

Executive Supervisor for the office of Domestic Security?! Was that really him? Even if it wasn't, then it was now. Job, pension, marriage, perks, (shit-legs' college fund!) all on the line. Suddenly a very fine line.

Snow job! All things to all people. Emergency phone call to Mellissa, (did I ever shag her? I did a few of them in Health Ed'. Wasn't she the dark haired one with the pointy teeth?!) Gunswale.

"Bernard, get me a line to Mellissa at the National Office of Domestic Security."

"Yes sir. Where's that?"

"Gunswale! Three Wheel Lane! Bone'ead!"

"Of course."

All of five minutes.

Baaaaarp. "Sir? Gunswale."

"Yes, hello? Mellissa?"

"Lozzer? Is that you? You remember me?"

"Of course. Is your hair still...?"

"No. I've done it dark now, with curls and straight bits. Nature's own dental floss! That's what you used to call it! Did you get my note?"

Spade Braithwaite

"Yes! Lovely to hear from you. Nice to know you remember us, out in the boonies. What's the gossip in the big city?"

"All of a commotion! Especially here! You've heard about the war?"

"Yeah! The Great one, or the Second one?"

"Haaahaghh! You're still a kidder! No, this Bundawa thing. It's all going to turn nasty, global, unless we pull our weight. I think it's Communists this time, or something. So we have to get involved! For The Free World, or something!"

"So what exactly is going on?"

"We're sending an army to "quell human-rights atrocities" and "restore internal autonomy". Something like that. We're going to send four thousand soldiers."

"How many do you already have?"

"I don't know, it's classified. But we need to recruit four thousand this year."

"That'd be most of 'em, then."

"But we're doing it in a sociologically sensitive way. Demographically. So that we can monitor the sociological ramifications, an' all that."

"Which means what?"

"We're proposing a limited experiment..."

"What, and where?!"

"Everybody on the registers in Claust', Pershing and Haipnath. Just as an experiment."

"Thank you Merrissa. See you at Christmas."

Herbert Brewer's Dirty Little Secret

"Mellissa! See ya. Bye!"

Laurence dropped the phone into its cradle, fiddled with his pen and stopped the thought flow, consciously.

Move the fans and the piles of shit further away from each other. Contingency measures. Phone Gary.

"Bernard! Get me Gary Crozier, Clausthowlersnauglerbogler, Chief of Police. And don't say a word to any fucker or you're toast. You understand me?"

Laurence played alien space ships with his pen and his biggest paper clip for most of a minute.

Most of a minute later.

"Hello, Laurence?"

"Gary. What have you heard?"

"Well... Mrs Calumny on Weschitt Street likes it when men dress up as firemen and carry her onto the roof. Sammy Berquardt's son might not be his. Janet still asks about you. We've got a party planned at Shoop-Shoop that'll make your hair curl. What've you heard?"

"Big shit, is what it sounds like. Have you heard anything about a war somewhere?"

"Many things about many wars. I was in one once, for a few weeks."

"Some crap that we're getting involved in. You know the Auxiliary Defence Party that we always have? This year, I'm supposed to actually conscript everybody into the army!"

"The whole year?"

Spade Braithwaite

"The whole year, plus everyone on the register! That's four, maybe five other years!"

"Can they do that?"

"Fucked if I know. Except that I've been told to do it!"

"What's the plan?"

"I don't know anything except some bullshit letter I just got. And I phoned Mellissa in Gunswale and she confirmed everything I just told you. I've no idea what they expect me to do, but I'm going to have to do it."

"Could you fax me a copy of the letter?"

"Certainly. But can I ask you not to keep it anywhere public? Depending how things develop, I might not be able to phone you again. If you phone here, be discreet. Walls and secretaries have ears. They'd sack me like a shot, and get some real, hard-nosed bastard to do the hatchet work."

"I appreciate it, Laurence. Janet'll be glad to see you. And we've got some girls at Shoop-Shoop that'll make you think you're dyin'!"

"I'll be there. I'm sorry if I have to come on all heavy! You know I'm on your side."

"You'll do y' best, I'm sure. Take it easy. Thanks for the warning. See you soon."

"Soon. Take care."

Laurence leaned back in his chair and felt a lot better about the day. White light all around Clausthowlersnauglerbogler. From the airport, all the way to the tyre depository out west in the desert. And fuck their horrible luck.

At the Blandford Hotel, Reuben Schmettz answered his door. The woman was at least seven inches taller than him. Six foot tall, ash blond hair pinned up. Gorgeous.

"Come in."

"Hi. I'm Joane."

Joane wore a grey business suit. Double fronted jacket and knee length skirt. Black stockings and black shoes. Briefcase.

"Do you mind?"

Joane marched straight in and made herself comfortable in an armchair.

"Please, be my guest. I don't know if the agency said, but...,"

"I'll do it my way! If you have problem with that?!"

"No problem."

Joane took her jacket off and threw it on the floor. Then she unbuttoned her blouse and pulled it out from the skirt. Lacey black bra with very large, sunburned tits bulging over the top.

"Three hundred dollars. Or six hundred for the whole day."

Reuben counted out twelve fifties and handed them over. They disappeared into a very manly wallet in the jacket.

"I..., I want to play at job interviews. I'm interviewing you, and you'll do anything to get the job."

"I want the job. What would I be doing?"

"You'd be, uhhm, let me see. You'd be the Travel Co-ordinator for our whole international division."

Spade Braithwaite

"I want that job!"

"So do lots of other women. What can you offer?"

Joane leaned back, making her bosoms rise with a shudder.

"I can type! And, I can take care of things. It's awful hot. Do you mind if I take my skirt off?"

"By all means!"

Joane stood up, unzipped her skirt and let it fall to the floor. Black lacey panties, black stockings and suspenders. Black shoes. White bits where the sun don't shine.

"I'd do anything to get the job. Are you married?"

"Actually, no. I know all men say that, but I really aren't married. I had a fiancée, once."

"I'd do all those things that your fiancée never would!"

"She'd do most things. For most men."

"Did she do this?"

Joane rubbed herself through the lace of the material.

"Ughhmm! That feels good! Could you help me out, please? I'm so hot."

"Undo your bra!"

Joane reached behind and unclasped her bra. Two very plump bosoms bounced into view. Pearly white, with great, big, pink aureoles and big, pink nipples. Black bra discarded in the corner.

"My nipples! They really need attention!"

"What can I do?!"

"Rub them, and jiggle them up and down in your hands!

Herbert Brewer's Dirty Little Secret

There! That's better. I bet you're big!"

Reuben was as big as he was ever going to get.

Joane pulled her panties down past her knees and off. Big, furry, scary womanhood.

Reuben let his cat out of the bag.

"It's so big! I don't think I can! Don't hurt me!"

"Travel Co-ordinator, or typing pool?!"

"Don't make me beg!"

Reuben nuzzled his penis against the entrance, and in!

"Ohhh! Ohh! Oh? Are you done? Well, you've got me for the day. Do you want to play bath time for naughty girls?"

"I think I'd like that a lot!"

"Did I get the job?"

"Not yet. But you're on the shortlist!"

Stavros Nicolaus got a phone call from Sue at the Mayors office.

"Mister Nicolaus? Sue, Mayors office. We're having an extra-special crisis meeting this weekend to discuss town policy towards the impending call-up. Humner asked me to call round a few of the leading citizens and get them involved. It's at the Shoop-Shoop Saloon Ballroom on Sunday at twleve noon."

"Sue, you remember that hundred dollars I gave you?"

"Yeah?"

"How would you like to earn two hundred dollars, and a hundred for a friend?"

Spade Braithwaite

"How about three hundred, and two hundred for my sister?"

"Real sister?"

"Near enough."

"Photographs?"

"Video cameras and a script if you like!"

"Five hundred dollars, all in for the entire night?"

"Seven till two. After that it's, "We want, you do!" depending on what state you're in."

"Job done. What were you saying?"

"We're having a crisis meeting on Sunday to plan our opposition to the government call-up. Shoop-Shoop at twelve noon. I'd be there if I were you. It sounds like a great big stink!"

"I'll be there. Don't wear any knickers. And tell me that you're not wearing knickers by saying, "Would you like cream or sugar with your coffee?""

"I say that to everyone."

"I know, but say it to me and roll your eyes and I'll know it's true, Fifty bucks if you get a chance to show me!"

"Would you like cream or sugar with your coffee?"

"Good girl!"

"See you Sunday."

"Yeah!"

Gary Crozier was among those invited to the meeting. So were the Senior Executive of the Judiciary, Judge Jacob Tethers, Manager of Social Services, Shirley Brown and half a dozen other renegade outposts of common sense among the town's folk.

Meanwhile, feelings amongst the town's folk were rapidly arriving from every direction at the same sense of outrage. The Government was going too far this time. Clausthowlersnaugler-bogler was one of the few towns that actually generated the revenue that allowed all the other poncey-bullshit towns to have their Universities and civic projects. And the low-income, trainee section of the work-force was a damn-sight more important for what they didn't get paid than for what they did, in addition to their incalculable social contribution to the town. Or, as it was theorised over many a garden fence:

"If our politicians want a fuckin' war so much, why don't they fuck off an' fight it 'emselves?!"

But that's the proletariat for you. What the fuck do they know?

(Author's note to Joshua Matenach: I'm really sorry Josh. I have to do it. You know that. So I'll do it now and then I'll never do it again.)

Andy Bomar took scant pleasure in arresting the Pheobe twins for loitering in a public convenience. Big, fat perverts that they were. One as bad as the other.

Andy had once arrested Huey Pheobe for loitering near a playground which, technically, wasn't a crime but it was near enough because Huey creeped everyone out so much. Andy had kicked some of his teeth out and then arrested him anyway because he just sat on the sidewalk with blood bubbling out of his gums and leered at Andy as though he was mentally undressing him. Andy got to see a lot of unpleasant things but Fat Huey Pheobe, with matted hair and body odour, leering at him vividly and luridly, as though Andy had done him sexual favour was the stuff of nightmares. Not least because Andy suspected that he was being mentally undressed and compared to other, larger men.

So now when Andy arrested either or both of them there were no intimate little kicks in the gonads or manly strong-arm stuff. There were savage little blows to the kidneys that made Huey and Al sit down and suck their breathe until the pain eased off enough for them to cry. That was how Andy arrested the twins and coached them back to the Brewer building, separately handcuffed to the car door on either side.

In the building Eddie had the lift waiting.

"Hey Edward, lookin' good!"

"Hey Huey, Al, Andy. You're some sick puppies, you really are!"

"Hey Edward, that's a cute little arse you got, for an old guy. Did I ever tell you about the old guy that we found asleep in Bishop's Freight Yard? I don't think he liked the kissing much but, you know, I really think he enjoyed the rest of it."

"Lock them bastards up forever. I'll sleep better."

"I'll do what I can, Eddie."

Herbert Brewer's Dirty Little Secret

Upstairs on the fourth floor Janet took one look at the twins and handed Andy a key.

"Cell four? Joshua Matenach's already in there, and he's a good-looking young boy. We've got three other cells sitting empty! Why can't we just put them in separate cells?"

"I don't know! It's something to do with irony. I don't really understand it myself. But they're a pair of big, fat, nasty-lookin' sodomites. It just seems right for the plot that they should spend a night locked up in a small cell with Joshua Matenach, with whom the readers should by now be identifying as a much-misused, stoic, hero character."

"Well, I guess...."

"Go on! You know it makes sense!"

"Uhmm... No I'm sorry Janet. The boss'll go spastic and probably sack both of us. If Joshua Matenach is going to butt-fucked by fat guys then the author will have to come up with a better lead in than this. Put 'em in separate cells."

"OK Andy, I s'pose you'r right."

(Author's note: Damn!)

Gary Crozier was completely unaware of all the plot devices going on in the building. He never heard a thing. He just rested a little bit easier every minute that the Pheobe twins were in jail.

It had been an interesting afternoon. Lots of heated phone calls flying around town. Everyone wanted to be in on the meeting at Shoop-Shoop.

Spade Braithwaite

Everyone in town seemed to have a nephew or son-in-law or catamite who needed saving. And that was a good thing because Clausthowlersnauglerbogler had a lot of good qualities, or a few anyway, but public-spiritidness wasn't usually counted among them. But confront a good citizen with the prospect of their daughter moving home with the grand-children and they suddenly became a vociferous advocate of human rights.

"Gary, you're the god-damn cop! You just stop'em doin' it! If you just arrest all the kids they try takin', and arrest them for tryin' to take 'em, what can they do?"

"Well, they're the Federal Government so they can shoot me for treason, or mutiny or conspiring to bring about the over-throw of the democratically elected government."

"But they can't really do anything, can they?!"

"Well, they can do a few things, after they've shot me. They can install an Emergency Governor, with full authority of the state to keep order however he sees fit."

"But they can't really do anything! Do you see what I'm saying?"

"I know, Bonnie. Apart from my death, and some sporadic slaughter and widespread bloodshed, they really don't have much that they can threaten us with."

"Can I come to the meeting? I know what to tell them bastards!"

"I think that this is more likely to be a brain-storming exercise for the town's executive. We'll throw a few ideas around and then come up with a few schemes that the town can vote on when we have a town meeting to discuss it."

"We're gunna have a town meeting?!"

"I can only imagine that we'll have to."

"Cool! I'll be there! Cheers Gary. And think about it, OK?"

"OK, Bonnie. Speak to you soon."

Gary put the phone down and rubbed his chin. He really did have a very competent consultant on the leash and it would be a shame to waste the man's ability.

He dialled the number and prepared the message that he was going to leave. Charles Andropolous surprised him by answering.

"Hello?"

"Charles. Gary here. Do you remember us discussing my son and the up-coming draught?"

"I've thought of little else."

"Well, we're having a little meeting of local government this Sunday and I'd appreciate your input."

"It would be my pleasure, Mr Policeman. Send a car in case I'm still over the limit from the night before."

"Will do. You know, if you have any productive input I can un-freeze your bank account and get you out of your lease agreement with a moments notice. You can go fuck-over a few of Braithwaite's leading citizens with my complete unofficial blessing."

"I would appreciate that with undignified gratitude."

Spade Braithwaite

"See you Sunday?"
"See you there."

Chapter 8

Sunday, the first of May. In Calcutta the masses were already marching to support their Marxist bretherin in every dying branch of industry. In Oxford they'd staggered into the pubs for breakfast at six o-clock and crawled back to Jericho to sleep the day. In the apartment over the Domestic Revenue Department Charles Andropolous had risen at nine, scalded himself pink in the vast, three-head shower, eaten a restrained breakfast of kippers and toast and at eleven o-clock was just settling in the sun-lounge for a pint of stout and half an hour with the national newspapers before the day began proper.

And the day looked as though it was going to be a bloody lovely one. Low temperature of fifty eight. High of seventy eight. Humidity around forty percent. Winds mild from the south. Apartment the size of a Malaysian tea plantation. Jeans and T-shirt for a business meeting. No need to bullshit anybody. In fact, a rare opportunity to work with people who might appreciate his very real talent. A short holiday between jobs.

Newspapers were always good source of background intelligence. They defined and then reflected the opinions and prejudices of a very large part of the population. The same news telling different stories to every segment of society. Finger-wagging and denunciation for the middle-class paranoids. Statistics and diatribe for the working-class-anti's. Comfort for the old. Pimple cream and heart-ache for the young. Nearly everybody catered for by some publication or other and, the more appalling the rag was, the bigger its circulation seemed to be.

The spread-sheets were full of patriotic rhetoric lauding the government's bold initiative. In the tabloids it was, "Cartright's Cat-fight! New Homo' Soldier Law Shocker!" Stationery Buyers News headlined with a review of the revolutionary new super-paper-clip.

(Authors note: The name has been changed ever so slightly to prevent legal action, but Stationery Buyers News is a real publication! And they really do review new types of paper-clips! The author worked for them once for six months, in the circulation department, and put on a lot of weight.)

What was apparent was that, over-all, the country was excited at the prospect of war. Sabre-rattling and jingoism fromjournalists who'd never done anything braver than denounce terrorism in the vaguest possible terms. Bitching and moaning by columnists who'd never suffered anything worse than an hour wait for a table in a French restaurant.

At eleven twenty eight the bell rang to let Charles know that someone was at the entrance.

Spade Braithwaite

Charles pressed the button and spoke into the box, "Hello?"

"Constable Fitzroy, sir."

For a moment Charles was tempted to let the little bastard wait for ten minutes. The moment passed and the temptation with it.

"I'll be right there."

He slipped some deck shoes on his feet and went down.

Detective Ian Metcalfe wasn't invited to the meeting and he wouldn't have gone anyway. It was the first Sunday that he'd had off in two months and he intended to make the most of it. The previous night he'd gone to bed sober at eleven o-clock just so that he could get up at five o-clock that morning feeling healthy enough to finish his Community Liason Reports and have something left of the day.

By eleven forty five, eight turkey decoys, a fold-up chair, a roll-out, hay-bale hide, three beef sandwiches, a bottle of chianti and a ten-bore magnum side-by-side shotgun were loaded in his car, and he was ready to go.

The decoys and the hay-bale hide had cost a fortune by mail-order through an American magazine. The decoys were about a foot taller than mature, indigenous, northern desert turkeys, and a completely different colour but it didn't really matter because no one had seen a northern desert turkey since eighteen ninety seven when the city of Braithwaite had tested a programme of public canon practice on Sunday mornings.

Herbert Brewer's Dirty Little Secret

Ian had no idea what a hay-bale was but the hide, available in northern-rush or spring-corn came with a standard beer-froster and optional TV arial and it looked like something that a serious turkey hunter might be impressed by. It impressed the hell out of Ian and that was something on a Sunday morning.

One day he'd see a turkey and he'd shoot the fucker dead. In the meantime there were some crows out by the Tyre Depository that were in for a bad day.

Ollie Epstein was enjoying the day so far. He was a fat, middle aged man, shouting at the paper boy from his front garden, wearing the vest and boxer shorts he'd worn to work on Thursday, kept on for Friday and by Sunday, was beginning to feel very comfortable in.

Paper boys, like most things on Sunday mornings, fucked him off. The best part of the weekend was the enormous sulk that he nurtured to its climax on Sunday afternoons with an almighty shouting match and a stormy exit to the club for couple of hours. Two perfect hours, perched at the bar, bitching about cruel fate and sympathising with other fat men who never seemed to receive the respect they deserved.

Little bastard paper boy! Flew past at noon, when you'd already been to the toilet, and sprayed your herbacious borders with a shower of spring-sale flyers. No fucking TV guide and eighteen pages of real-estate!

Spade Braithwaite

"I know you! Adam Doughty! I know your Dad aswell! You wait 'til I tell 'im!"   Smart-arse little sod!

The news section was full of all this crap about the call-up. The objective region of Ollie's intelligence, way down in his subconscious, had been amused by the turn-around in village opinion that had occurred only a month before. Unintelligible, long-haired louts, bleeding their poor fathers dry, with no ambition had suddenly become square shouldered sources of pride. Bursting with burgeoning character. On the verge of making great names for themselves in the world of inter-office mail delivery or refuse collection assistance.

Over the years Ollie's objective thought process had been neglected to a point where it didn't even bother trying nag him distantly anymore. And that was comfortable in a life where misery at the weekends was something to look forward to.

And that little bastard, what's-'is-name, damn sure he was shagging our Melanie, when she was only thirteen and him sixteen. Damn sure they're going to call him up. Then what'll happen?

True love denied. And wha's-his-name such a fine young man and all. Cut his hair and make the effort to understand a word he said. Any man would be proud to have him as the father of their grandchildren. Didn't he have head-hunters from Bishop's Freight chasing him and trying to make him take a position as measurer's-boy, with a view to becoming a measurer himself, in due time?

Herbert Brewer's Dirty Little Secret

If our Melanie's up-the-duff then damned if he's going anywhere. Federal fucking mandate or not.

Ollie scratched his belly and farted.

What was the fucking town council going to do about it? He'd voted for them once and it was people like him that they had to thank for their fucking jobs. They'd better get off their fat, overpaid arses and pull something out of the fucking hat or he'd have something to say about it down at the club. Useless bastards. And another thing,...!

What a fine day!

Constable Fitzroy dropped Charles outside Shoop-Shoop into the care of a charming young man named Reginald who entertained Charles all the way to the ballroom by eleven forty eight. In the ballroom four reception tables had been arranged into a rectangle to create a conference table with settings for about twenty people. All the other places were already occupied by the time Charles sat down. A few of the faces he recognised and smiled to. A few he didn't but he smiled at them and listened hard to catch their first names so he that he could pretend he'd met them. That much was a habit.

As he sat down an attractive young woman with a tray asked him if he would like anything.

"Ughh, cognac please. If you have it. Large one."

"Would you like cream or sugar with your coffee?"

Spade Braithwaite

Charles didn't know what the joke was but the Greek bank manager snorted beer through his nose and the girl smirked like a python to stifle her own giggle.

"Thank you. Just the brandy. No ice."

Gary got things going.

"Ladies, gentelemen. Thank you Mama Jen for inviting us all here. The only person you don't know is my new friend, Charles Andropolous. He's a particularly devious bastard, wanted in half a dozen countries. Charles, Mama Jen, Stav' Nicolaus you know, Judge Jacob Tethers, Shirley Brown, head of Social Services. Fifteen other very important people with strange character traits that I might refer back to randomly, with no real explanantion. Councillors and businessmen mainly."

(Authors note: All the books on writing tell you to keep characters to a minimum by using and re-using. And that's good advice, as far as it goes, but this story just doesn't have enough suitable characters to pad out this meeting with any realism without creating a lot of new ones, and that just puts more pressure on you, the reader. So just take it that there's a whole load of people here, important, but not to us.)

"I'd like to kick things off by reading a copy of the memorandum that was sent to Larry French, we all know Larry, it reads, "**Be advised...**"

Gary read the copy and filled them in on his conversations with Laurence French in Precaria and Harry Melchett in Gunswale. When he'd finished talking he shuffled the tablet of paper that he'd brought and sat back in his seat to encourage comment from anyone. For a full minute everyone at the table stared at their place-settings and digested what they'd just heard.

Mama Jen broke the silence.

"Jacob, what are the exact legalities of this?"

"All perfectly constitutional, I'm afraid. There's always been an annual registration for National Service eligibility, and the government has every right to call anybody on the register into the army or the navy, or whatever they want, anytime they want."

"But just Claust'? Can they do that?"

"They can do it by alphabet, lottery, location, shoe-size if they want. Technically, the only recourse we would have is our democratic right to vote for a different government at the next election, in two years."

Humner put his hand up to catch the pause.

"Can I take advantage of this opportunity to announce that I shall be standing down as Mayor at the next Council meeting and allowing myself to be shuffled sideways into an administrative position."

"Don't we have any town bylaws or local constitutional ordinances that we can fight them with? I remember the town constitution being drawn up in thirty six and I'm sure that the town took over a lot of rights as far as local law-making was concerned. I don't think they've ever been exercised but there's all sorts of local authority in the town constitution."

Spade Braithwaite

"Nothing we can use directly to over-rule a federal law, I'm afraid."

Charles listened and absorbed and found himself strangely interested in the town's problem. Finding the quirks in a situation and then exploiting them was something that he did better than almost anyone. And this was an amusing imbroglio.

"May I make a couple of observations?"

"That's why you're here."

"Thank you. There are three very significant factors that I think you might want to try to work with. One, the federal government are going to be a long way from home when they try to enforce this call up and, two, if they had an army of any real significance then they wouldn't be busting-a-gut to get one together in such a hurry."

"Go on."

"Three, there's been a huge amount of publicity for this call up. Democratically elected Governments stand or fall by public opinion. Very quickly. What if there were two Barney Clarkes in town and the wrong one showed up for roll-call?"

"I had a clerk track down all the specific legalities yesterday. He typed them up and made copies for everyone."

Judge Tethers perched his glasses on his nose and rummaged in his briefcase for the meeting-file. He found a purple wallet and passed a sheaf of papers round the table. When everyone had one he scanned down his own copy to item twelve and paraphrased it for the group.

Herbert Brewer's Dirty Little Secret

"Hughm.. Hughm.. Here we are. Registration is done by National Identification Number. Every citizen is expected to know their own number. The impersonator would be liable for up to forty years in jail for, "Impersonating a federally appointed figure for the purpose of gain." "Gain" is one of those words that they throw in that can be interpreted anyway that's convenient. It can mean any damn thing they like. The person being impersonated would be liable for imprisonment for up to life, for , "Treacherous evasion of federal responsibility." There really wasn't any such thing as liberalism when they made a lot of those laws."

"So, the wrong guy gets arrested. By Gary, I assume."

"Correct."

"And gets bunged in the local nick?"

"Correct."

"Is he eligible for any type of bail?"

"That's up to the local Senior Court Magistrate. Me."

"So the guy gets bail and then doesn't show up for his trial. You issue a warrant but Gary nor his deputies can find the guy. Three thousand cases of impersonation. Six thousand warrants. What would their next step be?"

"Sack all federal employees. That would be me. Then they could impose martial law under the authority of a specially appointed Emergency Governor."

Spade Braithwaite

"We've already decided that they don't have an army to impose martial law with. Okay, so they sack all federal employees. Who else would that be?"

"Me and Gary can both be replaced by federal mandate. I can't think of anyone else. The Abjure Valley submits its own federal tax accounts and occasionally receives federal funding for local projects. I can't imagine that they'd want to interfere with that process at all because the town pays six times what it receives."

"So an Emergency Governor moves into town and sacks you and Gary. His car gets torched, his hotel room gets looted, a big, ugly red-neck threatens to rape him. I think Gary might get re-employed with bonuses in a big hurry. But we'd need a lever to keep you in your job. We'll think of something. Maybe we can have a look in the town constitution to find some other pretext for getting them out of jail so that you can distance yourself from the scheme and pretend to be as outraged as they are."

"You really are a devious sod!"

"I do my best. So then what could they do?"

"Well, all the young men in town would have big federal warrants out for them. And federal warrants don't expire. So the town could never really get back to normal."

"Remember that they're coming in from out of town without knowing anyone. If they never really establish exactly who did what then they'll have a fuck-of-a-time pinning anything concrete on anyone with only you lot for witnesses."

Herbert Brewer's Dirty Little Secret

"Game on!"

Judge Tethers rubbed his eyes and brought things back to order.

"Okay, ladies and Gentlemen. I think we're all going a little bit mad, here, today. It all sounds very exciting but what we're really talking about is an entire town of forty thousand people participating in a bizarre charade that would complicate all our lives beyond my imagination, with the ultimate goal of destroying the constitution and isolating us into practically a separate, siege nation!"

"It'll never get that far. Believe me. The government 'll be expecting a few teething-troubles when they try to get this thing going because it's completely new to them, as well as you. All you need to do is cause enough confusion to kill it dead in its tracks for a couple of months. With all the national publicity it's a safe bet that the government 'll feel the need to invent an alternative. Something that they can stage-manage a bit more credibly. Credibility is a big lever in this business."

"And you really believe that you can orchestrate forty thousand people into this ridiculous farce?"

"Yes. Without a doubt. It's been done on larger scales, with less cause a thousand times. What percentage of the town's folk would you imagine have an immediate family member who would be called up?"

Spade Braithwaite

"I've calculated that there can only be fifteen hundred odd men on the register. That would give us, let me see, average family of five, about one family in five directly involved."

"One family in five directly involved. In eighteen fifty five, over the whole country only about four hundred wheat farmers were affected by the British Land-Act, which was what started the civil war that got you your independence in the first place. See, I did some research before I came here. You can stage-manage public opinion here so much better than they can. And peer-pressure is a wonderful thing, in the right hands. There never was a cause so just that everybody embraced it, but most people is good enough, in a corner. Meanwhile, it really wouldn't serve any purpose to trash your career, Judge Tethers. Do us a favour, distance yourself and send back any information that you can without compromising yourself. All the rest of you need is some flimsy pretext for Gary to let every offender out of jail for half an hour and you'll have the makin's of the most god-awful, constitutional crises that any government never got re-elected for."

Everybody around the table searched their experience for an anecdote. After a minute Mama Jen spoke.

"Mr Andropolous. I remember that in nineteen sixty three Carney Bishop's eldest, Rupert, went over one afternoon and killed all their neighbours dogs with a starting handle for no reason that anyone ever got to the bottom of. So they locked Rupert up but his brother Ernie came up with a plan whereby he

Herbert Brewer's Dirty Little Secret

petitioned the township to get Rupert let out for half a day for a, "significant domestic occurrence." The occurrence being the burying of the neighbours dogs. So Mayor Brewer approved it after Judge Patel told him that it was quite within his authority. And nobody ever saw Rupert Bishop again. I think the Bishops bashed him over the head and buried him in one of the mines out by the Tyre Depository. But nobody ever looked for him again."

"Bingo! Thank you, Jenny Won. That's probably the one. And if it isn't the one then I'm sure you'll find something."

"Mr Andropolous. Could I be allowed to nominate you for the position of Mayor of Claust'?"

It wasn't very often that developments hit Charles completely unexpectedly but this one came in from way out in left field. Charles wasn't exactly sure that it was a joke but felt that everyone would be more comfortable if he treated it light-heartedly.

"Thank you very much, Mama Jen. I've kind'f had my eye on Gary's job, but I suppose the Mayorship would do to get me started."

"Mr Andropolous, I'm deadly serious. I'm sure that our Mayor doesn't earn the sums you're used to but an enterprising fellow like yourself would be well positioned to earn a bit on the side without fleecing our own trusting populace. And it needn't be a life sentence. Just guide us through this particular crisis and we'll cut you loose with all the good will in the world."

Spade Braithwaite

"That would be the highest honour I could imagine. You do understand what I do, don't you?"

"You're a swindler who takes foolish people's money away from them."

"Yeah! I s'pose. And I really don't think I'd make a good Mayor."

"Mr Andropolous. Humner's been our Mayor for twelve years and done a fine job, with a personality that couldn't get ten cents out of a school boy with the promise of an ice cream. And we've been very proud of him. But the time has come for us to get dirty, and you strike me as a dirty fighter. If you'll allow Gary and Stavros to scrutinise all of your dealings I'm sure there are enough bylaws buried in the constitution to make you a wealthy man without taking one cent out of our own town."

"Your serious?"

"Mr Andropolous. I don't say things for the fun of saying them. Would anyone have any objection to Mr Andropolous succeeding Humner as Mayor?"

"I'm confident that Stav and me can keep an eye on him. I'll second."

"Any objection?"

Humner fiddled with his top button.

"You know, I didn't really want to stand down for another month or two, until the full council had had time to discuss my successor. And I haven't really had time to plan my sideways move into administration."

Herbert Brewer's Dirty Little Secret

"Humner, you're a good lad, but kind words butter no carrots. We'll make you Health Care Supervisor. That's something the town really needs. And the kick-backs should be plenty good enough for you. Charles Andropolous, Mayor, Humer Speilding, Health Care Supervisor. Any objections? No? Congratulations Mr Mayor. Congratulations Mr Health Care Supervisor. Game on."

Chapter 9

The situation in Kinaida was becoming distinctly tense. Silus Mantè wasn't comfortable with the way things were developing and when Silus wasn't happy people disappeared.

All of Abraham Unduwe's cousins had been rounded up. And his grand parents. And the relatives of the few other fat, little bastards who's gone to school at Eton in England and were probably sunk to the testicles in whatever treachery he was hatching.

Little acquereur bastards! A lot of rag-arsed, cannibals until Silus had put them in charge. Back when they couldn't even spell their own names with the whole alphabet to work with.

Silus Mantè enjoyed the last laugh. It was his greatest pleasure in life. Abraham Unduwe's paternal grandfather begging to be allowed to hang himself had been particularly amusing.

Ungrateful little shit. Words didn't go where Silus' feelings about treachery extended. Not words that could be translated into English, anyway.

Actually, life in Kinaida carried on the same as it ever did. Outside of the Presidential Palace and the National Assembly, most people expected to endure the day without dying in horrible torment or ironic humiliation.

Old ladies still came into town to trade. With fist-fulls of squawking chickens, swinging upside down by their feet and kit-bags half full of meally, elbowing and scrambling out of sinking plimsoll boats onto the quayside of the Manuli River market. As confident that they wouldn't have their throats cut this day as they were every other day.

Young wives with boxes half full of potatoes, bananas, yams or an occasional undersize cauliflower struggled in to sell their bounty. Bouncing and jarring on the middle seats of death-trap buses or perched atop hard-wood trunks, stacked high on brakeless trucks.

Fishmongers bid, half-heartedly for individual eels. Slightly more excitedly for crates of muddy river mussels and blow-carpies.

Fat publicans patrolled rows of trestle tables littered with breakfast, resting playboys and animated conversations. Splashing centime shots of black rum into dirty glasses and picking up the francs. Keeping a hand close enough to their pinnies to grab the short stick and remind the tomfools of their manners behind their ears if they weren't quick enough.

Bootblacks, weight-estimators and prophet-women squatted in the shitty corners out of the sun. Manifesting intense disinterest and perpetuating their professional mystique.

Small boys chased scrawny cats and chickens and tormented them with unbelievably accurate, brutal, little stones. Older boys chased younger boys and cracked open their skulls with great, big sticks.

Refugees from up-country lived, procreated and died by the side of the road. Settled in shanties near the Beneficent State Refuse Tips or just camped out in the centre of town next to the Beneficent State Drinking Fountains.

In the half dozen shiny, high-rise buildings that were the down-town-district the international business community was on high alert. Pretending that nothing was wrong. Trading just enough to maintain the appearance of normality and keep up with the rumours that were spiralling out of control. Shuffling their less obvious assets towards liquidity. Digging out their spare passports.

Silus Mantè could feel them all. He could smell them and taste them. Their hard-work and their cruelty.

Silus Mantè was their mother and their father. Their God. And they'd better damn-well love him because he could change the rest of their lives into a brief experience of hell with just the wave of his finger.

In spite of his insanity, Silus Mantè was frighteningly in touch with the realities of his country. He breathed and sweated Bundawa. From the mountains all the way through the jungles to Kinaida. The spiders, the snakes and the heat. The bigotry and the heartbreak. Old men in their anxiety at new company regulations. Boom-land developers quietly mocking international logging quotas. Bourgeois, pseudo-sophisticates flirting with revolution.

There had been challenges to Silus' leadership before but they had always come from men that envied Silus' power. Quiet, aggressive characters with personalities that were just a little too large for their positions. Silus could see them a decade before they came. He felt them coveting his style and rearranging the furniture in their heads. Silus saw them coming and he courted them because it amused him to raise them up to the point where they thought that it could be theirs. He let them believe that he was out of touch, losing his grip. That it was time for a change. He let them believe so that he could surprise them so badly when they realised that he knew what was in their hearts. And then it amused him to torture them to death.

The only external threats to Silus' lifestyle had been the Congolese civil war of eighty-seven and the United Nations trade embargo of the same year. He'd dealt with both of them by courting the right people. Compromising representatives inside his own country and giving breath-taking amounts of money to political expedients with the right influence outside of his country.

There had never been any real trouble at home. Silus had created the infra-structure himself. He'd chosen the leaders. Not always popular choices but ruthless enough themselves to convert local scepticism into abiding, unquestioning loyalty. Silus had invented a society that was exactly what he wanted it to be. And the country had behaved itself for a long time but then he'd allowed a few of his favourites to send their children abroad for an education and now there was chaos.

He knew all about Abraham Unduwe. Little Bugger-Boy from the pleasant suburbs that Silus had built for his hand-picked middle class. Never even had his hands dirty in his life.

Silus read the reports and saw traces of Abraham Unduwe everywhere.

Reports telling him that terrorists had kidnapped a Regional Director of the Police, lectured him for an hour on the benefits of a socialist, free-market economy, released him. Then returned hours later to butcher him and his family, loot his house and finally, somehow convince his deputies that they'd been given a week of vacation on full pay.

It didn't matter to Silus that Abraham obviously had nothing to do with any of the nasty parts of the episode. If Abraham didn't posses the subtlety to keep his little displays from getting out of control then he was directly responsible for all the mischief that he unleashed. And it made for good situation-management that

Spade Braithwaite

Silus' ambassador could report to the United Nations what little Bugger-Boy and his friends had been up to.

Silus had friends in London that were about due for a phone call. They'd promised him a damn great army of crack troops. Ten thousand jungle-savants with a hundred and thirty percent supplies and full European wages to splash around. And so far, he reckoned, he'd seen dick.

He'd made the last two repayments out of the National Reserve so they'd damn-well better be on the case or there would be a whole new company called Bundawa National Mining bidding out managerial positions by the weekend.

Meanwhile, back in the jungle.

Abraham Unduwe's latest camp was three external walls of an old, colonial river station, converted to suit. The fourth wall and the roof were cunningly crafted of local bamboo and hardwood panels to evade aerial recognisance and conform to British civil engineering regulation BS189634, concerning acceptable noise insulation. The interior had been partitioned into seven, separate rooms, during a spontaneous demonstration of support by local artisans and family servants to create an acceptable freshman-minimum for Abraham's Jungle Lions and their two new recruits who were on their way.

Even now, Abraham mused, the new boys were probably infiltrating the Zairian border and disappearing into the jungle like falling leaves. On their way to join Abraham and their elder brothers in the Bantu Nation Redeemist Movement.

Younger brothers Dominic and Elijah were indeed just re-entering Bundawa after a five-year absence. From Paris to Kinshasa by regular jet, coach-class. From Kinshasa to Lambashi by charter helicopter and from Lambashi to Kapishi, on the border, by Rain Forest Experience Tours range-rover. Then, secretly across the border for two hundred dollars, seventeen Marlboro Lights and a Pamela Anderson fanzine.

On the Bundawa side of the border Chè Rubello, iron-hard jungle partisan and former chauffeur had waited half the day to rendezvous and spirit them back to camp in an out-rigged canoe.

"Lovely to see you again, sirs."

"Hey Ruby! Nice one! I think the fat guy's got our bags. Don't take your eye off him, thieving swine. What the fuck's that smell?"

"Begging your pardon, sir, I took the liberty of disguising our trip up-country by transporting a number of rustics to a village soirée."

"What did they do, crap in the boat? Fuck me! I'd forgotten what this country smells like. How far to base-camp?"

"Three hours, at most. I could probably employ a boy to help row, which might cut the time down a bit."

"Take on the whole family. I've got three T-shirts and a bottle of aspirin you can pay them with, but don't offer them all three, straight out! I'm fucking knackered and I need a bed. Sort it out. And count our bags on board! Eight, including my water-skis and the box that Muschè had us pick up in Kinshasa."

"Very good sir."

"And get a fuckin' lick-on! I'm ready for bed."

"Very good sir."

John Shutu was making good time out of the mischief. He still booked office hours and submitted his staff reports on time but with all the rebel activity going on he hadn't had time to do any policing lately. Although a lot of chores were getting taken care of.

At two forty in the afternoon he woke up in the master bedroom of the residence of the Overseer of Logistics for the West Africa Company's plant at Jamaa. Despite the bottle of port wine that he'd drunk earlier he knew exactly where he was.

After a minute he picked himself up and went to review the extent of the damage.

"Hulloo? Anybady?"

His deputies had all left over an hour ago when the action was finished. They'd better have had the good sense to leave him a bottle of port wine or he'd be visiting some of their houses tonight.

Rupisha, widow of the very recently deceased Overseer of Logistics was herself dead at the bottom of the stairs. It looked as though she'd been broken at the waist. Dirty bastards! She'd been alive when John had gone upstairs to lie down. Good sex and port wine always made John sleepy.

Five thousand US dollars were piled on the table in the kitchen.

"Good boys!"

His boys knew better than to try to steal from him. He scooped the money into a bread bag and stuffed it inside his shirt.

The dining room was a mess. It always amazed John that people facing absolutely certain, horrible death tried as hard as they did to avoid telling John where things were hidden. As though they might need anything ever again. John explained to them very patiently but something in their heads prevented them from believing that they would soon be dead.

Carmine the Overseer had been filching from the company for as long as he'd been with them. Everyone knew what a good number it was. Million dollar budgets passing across his desk. John felt that he should have had a lot more than ten thousand dollars salted away by now, but then he'd married that little minx three years ago and everybody knew that young wives were the bane of a man's good sense.

John shook his head at the remains.

"M' sorry, Cyar-mine. Y'only should 'a' belief m' sooner."

The door of the liquor cabinet was on the floor and the cabinet was bare except for a bottle of port wine and a presentation bottle of Glen Butanaya whisky.

Spade Braithwaite

"Good boys!"

John left the whisky and took the port.

The end was rushing towards John like an out-of-control diesel shunt. John could feel it barrelling down on him. Vainglorious annihilation. Blessed violent death. With unaccountable wealth hidden away and a couple of bastard seed buried in the woodpile.

Good ol' John Shutu! Hell of a man.

It had better come soon because the pressure was on him to go up-country to that river station where they were camped and kill all those acquereur playboys that were causing all the mischief. But he could let it last a few more months. And that would probably be more than enough.

In London, at number ten, Downing Street, Prime Minister John Wivell had bran-flakes and a pot of decaffeinated tea for breakfast. It was a strict rule of government that nothing should disturb the P.M during his breakfast or his B.M. If they had to wake him up for an emergency then that was fair enough. But if he slept until seven then anything that happened after that could bloody-well wait until seven thirty, when he'd eaten and been to the toilet.

At seven thirty two, after a piss-poor breakfast but a pleasantly invigorating trip to the bathroom John dressed himself in grey and strode into his sub-private office to catch up on the world.

Herbert Brewer's Dirty Little Secret

"Sir! The markets in Sydney are in free-fall. They want to know what you're going to do about their mutton blockade."

"Fuck 'em! Anything interesting going on?"

Sue Lunden, John's most trusted advisor had a snippet.

"Dereck Cartright's office phoned from Amsarnie. They want to know what sort of an army they should send. I get the impression that they don't have a whole lot of military experience. They wanted to know how many soldiers we needed, what kind of rations they'd need and what camouflage to wear."

"What did you tell them?"

"I said we'd have someone phone them back. I don't think their army's going to be much good for anything except making up the numbers. Which leads me to.., we had a phone call from Silus himself. Frothing at the mouth, he was. He says that if we don't get some soldiers in there damn quick then we can kiss the West Africa Company goodbye."

"What did you tell him?"

"I blagged him! I said we're on our way."

"Good girl. You know, I think, after all the publicity, we could send a few troops. The S.A.S. are always looking for something to do. Send them over but don't give them any guns or explosives. Tell them it's a training mission to experiment with the use of bamboo blow guns, or something, in a jungle format. Cook up some non-confrontational missions for them and warn them that anybody who actually kills anybody is going to be held liable by the local system. And send a thousand squaddies to Kinaida. Not the Para's. Send 'em via..., what do we have anywhere?"

"We're still welcome in Ghana, if we're spending."

"Send 'em via Ghana. Give 'em a couple of weeks to get used to the smell. The Tabloids 'll love it. "Our brave lads abroad but where is the rest of the world?" Tell Amsarnie that we expect a thousand of their finest on the same day. And try to make sure that none of our crew ever sets foot outside Kinaida. The last thing we need is a fucking Vietnam round our necks."

"Sir, just a thought. You know Andy Johnson, Earl of Brinclyde, who keeps on shooting down our black-top bill in the Lords?"

"That fat idiot! Just because there's no fucking roads in Brinclyde he thinks we can all get to work by mule-train, or whatever it is they do in Scotland."

"Well, he's an old-boy of the Highland Blues and Fusiliers Regiment. Always wittering on about the tragedy if they have to merge with the Strathclyde Light Foragers. If we sent the Blues and Fusiliers it'll give them a five year reprieve and Lord Johnson might be ready to negotiate his position on a lot of issues."

"Good girl! Get on it. And make it clear that I hold him personally responsible for their behaviour. Blood-thirsty fuckin' Scots! What exactly do the Blues and Fusiliers do?"

"I think they do fire-work displays. I don't think they've ever actually been in a battle."

Herbert Brewer's Dirty Little Secret

"Perfect! Get 'em out there! Tell Psycho-Silus that we're on our way! And make sure that Amsarnie sends an army out there at the same time. Just in case there's any fighting."

Abraham Unduwe sat cross-legged by the river for over an hour to be perfectly positioned when the two new recruits arrived.

Chè Rubello and the employed boy guided the canoe to the bank.

"Hoo! Got two sleepy boys f' ya', boss."

"Hey! Jungle Soldiers to alert!"

"Oh, Man! Are we there! Fuck, I'm as stiff as Lucifer's cock."

"Jesus', angel tears! Hey Abe! Good to see you, man. Where are we sleepin'? Show me the way."

Elijah put a foot into the river as they clambered ashore.

"Fuck! That's my Corvani boots done for! A hundred and twenty nicker from that shop in Shepherds Bush. Fuck! Give me a fuckin' hand, will you!"

Abraham closed his eyes and sighed. Dominic and Elijah looked more like fat publicans than terrorists. Still, a few hard weeks in the jungle would make them thin, tough, and self-reliant.

"Did you get the box from Muschè?"

"Yeah, and it was bloody heavy. We had to get a taxi just to take us across the airport. What is it, anyway?"

Spade Braithwaite

"Something very special. What did Muschè say about Bernhard's death?"

"Didn't seem all that bothered, to be perfectly honest. He seemed more concerned that you'd remember him when things get sorted. So what is it?"

Abraham and Chè Rubello lifted the packing crate gently out of the boat onto the shore. Rough wood and nails, about twenty-four inches square and half again as deep.

"Pass that hammer."

Elijah passed Abraham the claw hammer and chisel that Abraham had brought to wait for their arrival. Very gently Abraham prized the lid up and surveyed the contents.

Beneath a thin layer of packing was a lap-top computer with a download attachment duct-taped onto the side, a reel of wire and about forty, audio-cassette sized mechanical inserts with ten inch aerial wires. Underneath them, separated by another thin layer of packing were about forty small, steel boxes, painted mat grey, with slots for the mechanical inserts.

"What are they?"

"Instability! And chaos. Our deliverance."

"Go on!"

"Should be about forty bombs. Completely harmless until they're primed and detonated. With the explosive power of about three hundred pounds of dynamite, each. We can spend the next month hiding them in Kinaida and then blow them up, one by one, in any pattern that we want, whenever we want, from here! And if, by any chance they find one and try to have a look at it then they'll take whatever they learn about it, during the milli-second that they have, straight to hell with them. Leaving the other thirty nine ready to go."

"Bloody hell! We carried that thing half way across Africa! If you want me to carry bombs again you can bloody-well ask me! We could have been blown to bits!"

"They're completely safe until they're primed."

"You fuckin' tell me when I'm carryin' bombs! We've been kicking that thing about and striking matches on it! Fuckin' hell, man!"

"Go to bed!"

"I don't mind guns and things but bombs you have to fuckin' warn me about. It's a miracle that we weren't in a car crash or something! Fuck me, they'd have seen the explosion in Moscow!"

Abraham closed his eyes and sighed.

"Just…, go to bed."

"I not scared of doin' it, I'd just appreciate a bit of warning, is all."

"Bed! No reading. Fatigue parade at oh-seven-thirty. Sweet dreams."

"Good night, man. Jesus! Did you see those fuckin' things! Must ha' been enough there to blow Kinaida out to sea! I've gotta read something to calm my nerves. I can't sleep if I don't read."

"I've almost finished my Dick Francis."

"I'll swop for a Grisham. Have we got lights or should I dig out my torch?"

Abraham sighed again and lit a cigar.

"Goo' night, guys."

"Night Abe. See you tomorrow."

"Night, man."

Chapter 10

Stella Davenport rolled the stocking up her thigh and clipped it on her garter belt. Always silk, never nylon. With no one to appreciate the difference except herself.

She checked herself in the wardrobe mirror.

Damn tidy for forty-five years old. Trim little tummy and a tight little bottom in French knickers. Boobs not quite what they were when she was eighteen, but good enough in a bra.

Stella wondered again if it was normal for a healthy, heterosexual woman to find her own body so attractive.

But she didn't wonder too much.

Covering it all, a serious, dark blue set. Skirt and blouse.

Herbert Brewer's Dirty Little Secret

Skirt to the knee. Never shorter. Rarely longer. Blouse tailored just enough to show off her twenty six inch waist.

Stella knew that quite a few of the young men in her classes fantasised about her. She knew because she knew what men were like. And she'd intercepted a few notes and drawings travelling from desk to desk. Crude sketches and smutty speculations. She'd punished the offenders and kept the sketches.

Today, though, wasn't a school day. Today was Saturday, the Seventh of May. The day of the Town Meeting. An event unprecedented in the town annals. Announced only the previous week, it was to be a public forum to discuss the town's opposition to the imminent military call-up. Scheduled for eleven o clock at Sherwin Park, around the bandstand. Everybody welcome.

Stella would be there. Miss Davenport. Spinster of the Parish. Dedicated mentor of the young since her own college experience, twenty-four years earlier. Vociferous champion of the immature.

"Sarnie"-Sinebaun, the Principal would be there aswell. Poor old Sarnie who just wanted a shag. It was embarrassing to talk to him. He emanated desperation like an aura. Stella often toyed with the idea of going into his office, demanding to talk about exercise books and then just slowly unbuttoning her blouse while she talked, keeping her eyes on his, waiting for him to break down and worship her.

Spade Braithwaite

The old fart would probably have a heart-attack. Either that or he'd leave his wife and want to marry her. Life was too short.

Stella felt that it was appropriate for her to attend today's Meeting to make sure that everything was conducted with decorum.

Stella was nothing if not professional.

Ollie Epstein was going to the Meeting. The council had finally got off their high-arses and decided to ask the proletariat what they thought should be done. He fully intended to give them his opinion. His opinion was that the federal government should be told to go fuck itself.

The government didn't have to put up with his Melanie rolling in, pissed as a wheelbarrow, at midnight every night, with her knickers in her pocket. Just about the time when Ollie normally had his quiet beer. Her boyfriend dropping her off at the gate and aiming her at the front door. Not even pretending to care a toss because they were sending him off into the army, or whatever it was they had nowadays, whether he got Melanie in the family-way or not.

Ollie would allow himself to be fucked-over by black men before he let that spotty, little wha's-'is-name leave his Melanie up-the-duff with never even a backward glance!

The crowds were already thick when Ollie pulled into the carpark of the Office of Domestic Revenue. Every single space, including the chevroned areas and "disabled" section was occupied. The fire lane and the lawn, right back to the Standard Life Building, packed solid with cars and motorbikes. The fervid hoards already thronging towards the park.

"Fuckers! Yeah, you!"

Ollie followed a new Chrysler through every aisle and back out onto the street.

The entrance to the multi-storey was backed up a hundred yards down the street. The taxi rank was full of cars, leaving taxis to disgorge in the road and move on. Finally, six hundred yards away, down two side roads, behind Papajorge's Fish & Chips and the Reject Card Shop, a "ten minute" loading bay with no cars in it. How many deliveries did a chippy or a card shop get in a week? Not enough to make Ollie search any further.

Ollie locked the car and walked back, cursing loading-bay slopes, old people, people with dogs, people that looked as though they probably thought they were special because they hyphenated their names, and itchy underpants.

There were a hell of a lot of people making their way into Sherwin Park. Claust' was only supposed to be forty thousand people but it looked to Ollie as though twice that many were already there.

The largest crowd that Ollie had ever seen in his life had been the twelve hundred people who'd turned out to see Monsignor Woomera bless the airport fifteen years ago.

The crowd that was fighting its way to the park must have been at least three times that size. Maybe more, including children and hawkers. Fuckin' hawkers. Three dollars for a fuckin' hot dog!

Balloons! Ollie liked balloons. But not buskers. Scroungin' bastards.

Shirley Brown got a taxi to the meeting. The queue of cars crept the last half mile along Gallipoli Street at walking pace. Shirley paid the fare and slithered out opposite the pedestrian entrance to Sherwin Park without stopping traffic.

"Two o-clock, Shaky Man Pub. The public bar."

"Gotcha Shirl'!"

"Behind the restaurant."

"I know where the public bar is! Close the door before I hit something!"

"Two o-clock!"

"See ya' at two."

Shirley slammed the door and wove through the crawling vehicles to join the droves herding towards the event.

It looked as though there might be five thousand people, including the people still streaming in. An incredible showing for a town where two and a half percent of the electorate had bothered to vote in the last election.

Four Donner Kebab vans contested the cut-through into the park. A bald man and his girlfriend played Moody Blues on a recorder and an acoustic guitar. Shirley listened for half a minute and dropped half a dollar into their bedpan.

Herbert Brewer's Dirty Little Secret

It was like the Street Fair weekend that marked the end of summer. Only better, because everybody was here on the same day and the atmosphere was better.

Families with every size of child. Mothers pushing strollers and dads with ketchup-faced toddlers on their shoulders. Teenagers forming peer groups on the periphery. Laughing too loud and lighting cigarettes when they were confidently out of sight.

Traders had been allowed to set up stalls along the jogging circuit, selling balloon sculptures, kiss-me-quick hats, luminous jewellery, walking sticks, pet stones, carved bread-boxes and every other type of crap.

The Shaky Man had organised the beer tent, Fort Shaky-Stake. Two trestle tables equipped with taps and a cash register under a canvas awning. Bottles and plastic cups stacked behind. Lager, bitter, whiskey, brandy or vodka. No ice. A crate of warm coca-cola bottles stashed somewhere in reserve for the unlikely event of an emergency.

At the west end of all the activity was the bandstand. A forty-foot diameter circle of concrete with thirty-two, six-by-six pine braces supporting an eight-plane roof covered with locally mined slate. Water-proofed with locally made pitch-sheet.

Radio station Clausthowlersnauglerbogler, 101.1 FM, The Most Music in the Desert, was conducting an outside broadcast, live from the site. Commuter-Commissar disk-jockey Des' Res bouncing off the airwaves and echoing across the field from the forty mounted speakers that had been hurriedly borrowed from the High School. With More Music in the Morning and That Special Oldie that says, "I Remember When!"

99.9 had been the committee's first choice. Classic Album Tracks and The News Every Hour. A better station in every way but, as Stav' had pointed out, their broadcast could be picked up all the way to Braithwaite, on a clear day.

Not that it mattered. There really was nothing they could do to prevent rumour getting back to Gunswale but Charles hadn't seemed concerned. He didn't think that anything credible would get back to anyone important, quickly enough for them change direction. And he didn't think that it mattered if it did. The plan would work.

Shirley found Mama Jen, wrapped in a blanket, chatting with Stav, the new Mayor and a few of the leading-lights.

"Mama Jen!"

"Shirley! Over here. We're all pleased that you could get here."

"Mama Jen! Have you ever seen the town get this excited about anything before?"

"There's been issues in the past! Don't think the old town doesn't have a soul. What time do you have?"

"Ten fifty five."

"Close enough. Would somebody ask Mr Res to give the public a three minute warning. Ladies, gentlemen shall we arrange ourselves like a meeting. Has anyone seen Humner?"

Herbert Brewer's Dirty Little Secret

"Here Mama Jen!"

Fifteen fold-out chairs were set in a semi circle, facing east towards the main area of the park.

"Humner. I suggest that you open the meeting and introduce Charles to everyone. Shall we sit?"

Three councillors, two company chairmen, two bank managers, a local soccer star who featured in a nation-wide tyre commercial, Humner, Shirley, Charles and Mama Jen. Mama Jen was ushered from the sidelines into centre seat, the place of honour. Everybody recognised Mama Jen.

"Gentlemen, Shirley, I'm sure that this is a new experience for most of us. Mr Des'Res tells me that, when he's ready he'll give us a ten second signal. That'll be him holding up ten fingers and counting down, a finger at a time, and then we're on the radio. Are we ready? Humner?"

"Mama Jen. Ready when the time comes."

"Okay. Eight, ughhm, three, two, one! Humner!"

Gary Crozier listened to the radio in his office. It had taken a few minutes to find the station so he's stuck with it, even though Des' Res was such a wanker that it was painful to listen to.

No reports of any disturbances yet but every policeman on duty, just to be safe.

Gary checked his watch. Gone eleven. Get on with it!

Des' Res cut the end off Bohemian Rhapsody! He always did that.

Spade Braithwaite

"Yes indeed! Queen there, with, ughh, Bohemian Rhapsody!" (Gary winced, "We know what it fuckin' was!"), "And, ughh, time to go over now to the Meeting that's just starting here in Sherwin Park. Ladies and Geezers, give it up for Humner Speilding! The Mayor!"

Adam Doughty had been in the park since nine o clock. He'd sat next to the bandstand since half past ten.

The 101.1 Babes were pretty horny in their cheer-leader outfits but Des' Res was a complete twat. Why did radio stations all hire the worst tossers they could find, and then pay them so much money? It was a mystery.

"And, ughh, time to go over now to the Meeting that's just starting here in Sherwin Park. Ladies and Geezers, give it up for Humner Speilding! The Mayor!"

"'my new appointment as…, I'm sorry. Thank you Des'."

The park went quiet with eight thousand people trying to hear. A carousel organ, celtic music, screaming children and Humner reverberating out of forty loud speakers and innumerable radios.

"Ladies and gentlemen, I'm afraid I have to open this meeting on a sad note. Due to family commitments, I've had to stand down as your Mayor, after twelve glorious years. But don't be sad because we've found a wonderful man to step into my shoes. I'd like to introduce a new face to you. Our new Mayor, Mr Charles Andropolous!"

Herbert Brewer's Dirty Little Secret

A handsome, elegant man in grey pegs and deck shoes hopped up to the microphone, obviously caught by the brevity of Humner's departure.

"Thank you for that gracious introduction, Humner. I'm sure you'd all want to join me in thanking Humner for the twelve years he's spent guiding us through some troubled times. Ladies and gentlemen, Humner Speilding!"

Sincere applause from most of the crowd. The most appreciation Humner had experienced during twenty years of public service.

"And don't worry. Humner isn't leaving the scene. He'll be right there on the council, telling me how it's done. Okay. Without further ado. We're all here today because of a serious threat to Clausthowlersnauglerbogler's future. The call-up. I know that you've heard all about it but I'd like to start by sharing with you all the information that we have."

The new Mayor had thirty five thousand people's unchallenged attention as he read the notes and transcripts. Bringing the town up to date without compromising sources. Leading them towards the plan that Stavros, Mama Jen and himself had cobbled out of the town constitution.

"..."four thousand kids. As long as they're kitted out in green, that'll be good enough!" Those, I'm told, were his exact words. So... Can I invite input from the first few rows?"

Adam put his hand up.

Someone fifty yards back shouted, "Tell 'em to fuck off!"

Spade Braithwaite

Fatty Epstein. Adam knew his shriek from three streets away.

Charles smiled with the crowd and pointed to Adam, "Excuse me, the young man at the front. Here, could somebody pass him the microphone. There, thank you. What do you think?"

Adam stood up, kicking peanuts into the cleavage of the red and white dress that was shouting at her children right by his ear.

"..........,"

"Press the button when you talk."

"Yeah! Ughh, I think I'm going to be called up. I live down Gothburton Street and I used to be a member of the Young Ornithologists Club."

Sniggers from the fringes.

"Yeah! Well, they've got my number and my address and everything, in their computer! I'd rather just go, than go to prison for not going."

"Do you want to go?"

"I don't know. Not really, but if I have to, I don't want to go to jail!"

"Well, it's your choice but we've done some research and we're confident that we can keep anyone out of it, who doesn't want to go."

"Without getting me into trouble?"

"A little bit of trouble. Would one afternoon in jail be too much?"

"I don't want a criminal record."

Herbert Brewer's Dirty Little Secret

"We can see to that. I'm sure you didn't know, but, as your Mayor I can legally change your name to anything I want, without even notifying you? All I have to do is notify Gunswale, officially, in writing and your name's changed. If I changed my name to…, what's your name?"

"Adam Doughty"

"Okay, If I changed my name to Adam Doubty then what's to stop me reporting for induction in your place? And getting rejected because of my terrible physical condition."

"Cor! Would ya?"

"No. Because I'd get out of jail and disappear but they'd issue a federal warrant for your arrest, for evasion. But if we changed everybody's names, then they wouldn't know who had turned up and who hadn't."

"Cool! Can I be called Jimi Hagar?"

Laughter and applause from half the crowd, glad of a break from the information.

"Yeah, well, good one! I'll call you Jimi, even if no one else does! Actually, the computers are already working on a list of name-changes that we're going to send to Gunswale, officially changing all our names. Any questions? You sir, grab the microphone. Yes you, in the olive-drab."

"Me?"

"Yes. You."

"It's beige!"

"Whatever. Do you have a question?"

Spade Braithwaite

"Yes. Ughmm, Scott Sienbaum, Principal of the Catholic Vo-Tech High School for Special Teens. Does my jacket look olive-drab?"

"No, it looks beige. I'm sorry. Lady next to you, in the blue set. Do you have a question?"

"Stella Davenport, Senior Secondary School Teacher. I believe that registration to the Auxiliary Defence Officer is conducted according to National Identification Number, not name. So how can changing everybody's names help? We'd all still be liable according to our numbers?"

"Good point. Registration is calculated according to National Identification Number, but the N.I.N. isn't mentioned in the documentation, and the post office has no record of N.I.N. numbers, so who they deliver the papers to is their own business."

"But they have addresses!"

"I can change street names, aswell. Didn't I mention that? We're in the process of renaming every street in town, eight hundred and thirteen streets suddenly called, "Coronation Road". Just on paper."

"But, it'll be so easy for them to catch people! Like Adam says, they know where we live. And where we work."

"We can afford to let them catch us. I can let people out of jail as fast as they can catch them! Then, they'll have to re-catch them, or at least prove who it was that they caught. We only

Herbert Brewer's Dirty Little Secret

have a limited police force and it's far too busy solving more important crimes to give up any time to helping them."

"But what if they send in the army?"

"If they had an army, they wouldn't be bothering us! You sir, Constable Fitzroy! How are you today?"

The microphone passed hand to hand, three rows backwards and two along to Ken Fitzroy, undercover in the crowd.

"Uhhm, good, sir. I was wonderin', I registered when I left school, four years ago, so I'm on the register for the last year. If I don't turn up, what's to stop them freezin' my assets as though I was evadin' taxes, or something? 'Cause they can do that! They can tap into your dealin's from Gunswale! Without askin' the bank, even! Wha' are you gunna do about tha'?!"

"Good question! Stav'?"

"Ah yes. What to do about the banking system? Interstate transactions, pensions, benefits, credit-cards et cetera! All I can tell you is that we have a cunning plan! I think that you've been given enough information to digest, for one chapter! But, rest-assured, we have it all worked out! It's devious, but it'll work!"

"Next question! Lady with the fan?"

"I don't wanna change my name! I've been a Dixon since I was born, and a Dixon-Cox since I got married! I don't want to be changin' my name, at my time o' life!"

"No one will ever expect you to use any other name. Unless you want to volunteer to turn up for conscription?"

Spade Braithwaite

"Not bloody likely! And what if they ask me to identify 'oo my paper boy is? I've known Adam since he was a sprog. I'm not goin' t' perjur myself just f'r 'im! I'm not goin' to!"

"It'll be a hell of a process for them to force you to identify anybody. They'll have to get both of you together, in a court of law, with a judge and a jury, and, "prove your ability to authoritatively identify" Adam, with evidence, "documenting your relationship and your sure knowledge of his Identification Number", and then ask you to swear as to his identity. Unless they can get that together, then don't worry. They have every right to instruct Constable Fitzroy to arrest any person they suspect of complicity. I have the legal right to instruct Constable Fitzroy to let that person out of jail for up to forty-eight hours. Another question. You, the distinguished gentleman with the balloon sculpture!"

"If you're changin' all our names, what are going to be called?"

"We had a long discussion about that and it was decided.., Mama Jen, would you like to tell the people what was said?"

Mama Jen nodded and rose serenely to the microphone.

"After a lot of thought, it was decided that we might do a lot worse than adopt the name of our greatest statesman. We chose the name, Herbert Brewer!"

The man winced and shook his head, "Seriously?! Me, and my wife, and my children, are all called Herbert?!"

"Yes."

"Fuckin' unreal! When does this all take effect?"

"Thank you Mama Jen. We're preparing the paperwork now. We expect to be able to deliver it to Gunswale next Thursday morning. Exactly the same time that the mobilisation orders will be arriving at our own post office. So that I can personally instruct the post office exactly which Herbert Brewer, in which Coronation Road they can send them to. I'll be proud to answer the summons myself. I believe that Mamma Jen and Shirley also intend to be there. We'd appreciate five hundred volunteers to come along. The worse your physical condition, the better! We've budgeted for door-to-door pick-up and drop-off, two catered meals, bingo and cabaret. The first five hundred totally unsuitable callers get the tickets. Operators 'll be on duty at ten o clock, Monday morning. Good luck, guys!"

Chapter 11

On Tuesday morning a front of warm, ocean air swept the country, bringing unseasonable showers, breath-taking cloud formations and a rainbow to the nation's capitol.

In his splendid office on top of the National Parliament Assembly Building, Inland Attorney Samuel Guarthje was

Spade Braithwaite

enjoying a morning of idle contemplation. Sitting in his very modest leather chair behind his ergonomic desk, flicking through the links to every witchcraft related site that he could find on the internet. And there were hundreds of them.

    Wiccan Recipes for Animal Ailments. (Pass.)

    Apocalypse Shock Cult. Die Now and Rule Your Enemies from Hell. (Bloody hell! Pass.)

    Shropshire Women's Gardnerian Poetry. (Pass.)

    Imagine Lucifer Managing Your Portfolio. (Come back to that one.)

    Wyoming Teen Coven do Nasty Stuff in the Buff. (Worth a look. Click.)

    The Resource Department had only installed the computer four months ago, as part of an initiative to bring the Cabinet into the modern world. He'd regarded the plastic monitor and keyboard as an ugly, intrusive desk sculpture until he discovered the internet. Now he was addicted.

    It was particularly significant that he'd only taken the internet class as an, "In Service" day to avoid having to listen to the Opposition whining about the lack of technology in schools. Some stupid Expenditure Bill they were lashing together to challenge the Government. The Government would oppose the bill while the Opposition would use it to try to win a few local elections. A motion would be passed for the bill to be moved down to the House of State, where it would be shot dead in the water. All part of the game.

Herbert Brewer's Dirty Little Secret

An image of a red bat started to appear on Samuel's screen.

This site contains adult oriented material. Have your credit card ready to confirm your age. You will not be billed.

"Fuck!" Back.

Where was that one he liked.

Real Spells for Sex and Success.

Samuel's new blue phone grunted like a pig.

It could make eight different animal noises. They were supposed to express an ascending order of importance so that he could decide whether to pick up or not. He hadn't been able to remember the order and he couldn't ignore a ringing phone anyway. Or a grunting one.

He picked up.

"Yes?!"

"A Mister Eddie Haffenschaft. Schlagel Holdings. Put a lot of time and money into Cartright's Industrial Reform Bill. Don't mention the wife. His sons are Edward and Andrew."

"Put him on. Eddie! How are you? Andy and Eddie-Junior keeping you on your toes, I bet! When was it...?"

"Christmas! A good time, had by all! Look, Sam, my man's just phoned me from Claust' and I thought you might want to hear the story. It seems that the whole town had a big meeting on Saturday, over the radio and everything, and they're going to change everybody's name so that you can't catch them with this *army* thing that you're doing."

Spade Braithwaite

"The draught?"

"Yeah. My man, and he's been rock-solid forever, he reckons they had a big do in a field and the Mayor spelled it all out. Everybody's got to change their name to Herbert, and then you guys won't be able to get them. It all sounded bloody unlikely but I tell you, he's been paying the bills since before I was born. I'll give you his number if you want to talk to him."

"Yeah, no thanks, Eddie. But I really appreciate the tip. A nod to the wise can tip the scale in this business. You know what I'm saying! Under the hat, man!"

"Yeah! Look man, about that hotel. You know I wouldn't...,"

"Eddie! You're one of the only people I can rely on, anymore. If you ever need me for anything. Otherwise...,"

"Yeah, Chow! See you next Christmas. I appreciate it, man."

"Take it easy!"

"Yeah! Hope it all works out, the *army* thing."

"Chow!"

"Yeah."

Samuel pressed the button and released himself.

What the bloody hell was that all about?! Clausthowlersnauglerbogler having a meeting and changing their names to Herbert so that they could avoid call-up? Bloody perfect! It was exactly the type of Tom-foolery that he'd have expected from those bumpkins. What the hell did they know about politics?!

Herbert Brewer's Dirty Little Secret

Samuel had read their statistics and been amused to notice that the number of people on Claust's register of citizens with learning difficulties was fifty per cent more than the turnout of voters in their last election. And now they were all changing their names to Herbert! That was really funny. Maybe he could tell that story at the next session. With a bit of embellishment it could bring the house down.

Changing their names to Herbert? Surely the silly buggers knew that the register was determined by National Identification Number, not by name. They couldn't be that stupid. Or could they? The town had that freaky Mayor that gave Samuel the creeps. Could he possibly, secretly be very smart, with something up his sleeve, or was he dumber than even Samuel had imagined? Difficult call. Maybe it would be better not to tell the story until he knew for sure.

Who did Samuel know from Claust'? A couple of the girls in Admin', but they didn't have a clue between them. Harry Melchet! Harry practically ran the Interior Office on his own. He'd know.

Samuel lifted the handset on his blue phone and pressed a button at random.

The reciprocal blue phone in the outer office gobbled like a turkey.

"Mr Goa-u-arth-jay?"

Samuel closed his eyes. What the hell was so difficult about, "Guarthje"?

Spade Braithwaite

"Do you think…, do you think you could get me Harry Melchet at the Interior. Please."

Herbert? Samuel had known a Herbert at school. Got caught sniffing the school nurse's bicycle saddle. No one would choose to be called Herbert.

"Mmmooo!"

Samuel closed his eyes and shook his head. The blue phone would have to go.

"Yes?"

"Harry Melchet. Stressed and a little bit hung over. Wha' can I do f' ya'?"

"Harry. Samuel here. You're from Claust', aren't you?"

"Samuel! Yeah, I get back there every christmas. Other than that…,"

"I've just heard a really strange story. What sort of a crew do they have governing your town?"

"'Bout what you'd expect, for the location. Half a dozen village idiots. They're not all that big on government in Claust'."

"What about that Mayor of theirs? What's his name, Humus or something?"

"Humner? He's harmless. His personality wouldn't stand out in a crowd of filing cabinets. But he's okay."

"Does he spout-off?"

"No. He doesn't. I'll give him that. What've you heard?"

"Between you and me?"

"Samuel! You're talkin' to Harry!"

Herbert Brewer's Dirty Little Secret

"I had a reliable source call me this morning and tell me that they've come up with some scam whereby they intend to change everybody's name to Herbert to get out of the call-up."

"Herbert! That's really funny!"

"Why?"

"Old Herby Brewer! The main-man. Silly buggers love him as though he built the town, single handed!"

"So what do you think?"

"Well..., you know, I might be given to speculate that you wouldn't be heart-broken if ol' Cartright took a bloody nose over this one...,"

"God forbid...,"

"Yeah, I'm sure. Okay, I'll tell ya. Claust's a shitty ol' town, but you don't impress people there by talkin' about stuff if you can't deliver. And if two people tell you that the end of the world is at hand then you don't bother buying a long playing record. If y' know wha' I mean."

"Gotcha, Harry. Under the hat, boy. Could y' do me a favour an' phone home. Find out what's really happening."

"I can, and I'll tell you some of it, but it's my mates, and my family...,"

"Understood. Tell me whatever you can an' I'll consider it a favour."

"Cheers, Samuel. Speak t'you later. Take it easy."

"Yeah, and you, boy."

"Chow."

Spade Braithwaite

"Chow."

    By the middle of the morning the frontal system had passed right over Clausthowlersnauglerbogler, leaving a warm, indolent, low-pressure system for the slide towards lunch and beyond.

    At, "Operation Herbert" Headquarters, an empty hardware megastore, loaned to the borough for the duration, Charles was almost ready to seal the document and send it on it's way.

    And it was a piece of work. All of Charles previous career had been based on calculatedly vague circumventions of specific legalities and expeditious retreat with the spoils. "Operation Herbert" was a whole different kind of animal. Confrontation!

    The format of the document had been draughted the previous week, under the advisement of Judge Tethers. A written notification that forty three thousand, eight hundred and two residents of Claust' were legally changing their names to Herbert Brewer. Two computer guys, borrowed from the Randolph First National Bank had printed out the official, Residential Register, including three thousand false identities, generated randomly, interwoven and extrapolated back into history. With a note at the beginning apprising the government that they were all, hereafter, called Herbert Brewer. Eight hundred and thirteen streets renamed Coronation Road.

    Charles read the opening paragraph one last time.

Herbert Brewer's Dirty Little Secret

"Notice to the Clerk of Registrars, please recognise that, as of Wednesday, June eleventh of this year, the aftermentioned persons will be renamed Brewer, Herbert.
Aalbein. Jousef, Mohamed. N.I.N. 025-57-66389-47.
Aalbein. Christina, Nicola Joy. N.I.N. 025-57-74373-53..."

Exactly enough to legally change everybody's name and not one word more. Thirteen hundred pages of computer paper, with the sprocket holes left attached for extra contempt, in three boxes. To be delivered to the Office of the Clerk of the Registrar, Three Wheel Lane, Gunswale, by guaranteed, two-day delivery

Charles was beginning to like Claust'. It certainly seemed to produce more than its share of large characters.

Stavros Nicolaus, manager of the Randolph First National Bank had put in four straight fifteen-hour days to get a system up and running. By lunchtime on Tuesday, he felt that he deserved an afternoon off.

The first problem, the development of a numerical identification system to replace names in the computer system had been fairly easy. Stavros and Charles had worked out a code that was the last four digits of a person's N.I.N. number, doubled to create a five digit number, the person's first and last initial transposed into two, two-digit numbers and three random digits tacked on the end.

Spade Braithwaite

Everybody in town with a bank account had called into their local branch during the past week to pick up a printed notification of their number. If, at anytime, the customer lost their number then the computer could generate a new one.

The number was based on information that was already stored in everybody's files. It had taken three lines of code to make it work.

Every transaction would still require a signature, but the computers didn't record signatures.

It had been slightly more difficult to hide all the financial records so that they couldn't be accessed from outside the system.

Fortunately, Randolph First National had been in the process of opening a new branch on the Burmont estate so Stavros had an entire, chaste computer system to work with. The opening of the new branch had been postponed, with compensation. The new computer had been set up to do nothing except decipher code numbers and accounts, on line to the other branches, via a diversionary link through the main-frame of the Cheap-Thrills, Sex Outlet Stores Head Office in Galipoli Street.

The government could open anybody's personal details as they saw fit, but if they managed to find any financial information then they were better men than Stavros had reckoned.

If there was one thing that Stavros enjoyed it was a bit of scam.

Herbert Brewer's Dirty Little Secret

Actually, Stavros enjoyed nearly everything. Especially big lunches, good red wine, Malaysian cigars, unhurried, dirty sex and an occasional, little sniff of kettamine.

Which was exactly where Stav's afternoon was heading.

Shirley Brown was ready for lunch. She'd parked in the multi-storey and walked through to St. Peter's Plaza because it had lots of cafés and she wanted to look at a few until one took her fancy.

Shirley was sure that there had always been lots of cafés in Pete's Plaza' but, when you were hungry, there were only three. Spankey's Giros and Kebabs, La Dolcè Vita, closed until three, and Sharon's Pantry.

Sharon's Pantry was upstairs with a glass front that faced onto the square.

At the top of the stairs Shirley put her shoulder against the heavy glass door just as it opened automatically.

Two empty tables by the window. She sat at the cleaner of the two tables and moved the dirty cups and the ash tray onto the windowsill.

It was a good day.

Shirley paused for a moment to try to focus all her attention on her own breathing. The slow in, and the even slower out.

She'd pulled a few late nights this week. At "Operation Herbert" headquarters or Charles' apartment in town. Ironing out the small stuff and editing the, "Rules of Engagement" down to a final draught.

It had been a lot of fun. Working on something so different from everything else she did. Working with Charles.

Shirley lifted her bag and folder for a waitress to wipe the little table.

"Ready to order?"

"Thank you. I'll have a cheese and ham toasty, an English-Toffee Mocha, with milk, and a large cognac."

"Decaf' or regular?"

"Regular. Thank you."

It would be good to get an early night, tonight. Nine thirty, straight after, "Return of the Native: Masterpiece Theatre" on channel two.

The waitress came straight back with the coffee and the brandy.

It was a funny thing, brandy. Shirley had never much cared for it but it was Charles' drink, and it seemed appropriate now, as she wound down.

The, "Rules..," were finished and delivered to the Claust Howler newspaper. The editor had been only too eager to put a copy in their Thursday edition. The only charge had been $150, paper and printing. And the print run was being extended to four thousand copies for the day, to cope with projected interest.

Shirley had the rest of the day off. She put her glasses on and took a copy out of her folder.

Herbert Brewer's Dirty Little Secret

White foolscap. Large lettering.

Operation Herbert!

Rules of Engagement.

As you are, no doubt, aware, as of Thursday the Twelfth of June your name will officially be changed to Herbert Brewer, and your address to Coronation Road.

This is only a legal measure!

Do not attempt to use the name in your daily activities!

Only if you are arrested in connection with any crimes concerning the evasion of military service will you be expected to give your name as Herbert Brewer.

If you are arrested, **Do Not** give your N.I.N. Number! You will be released from prison within a few hours and you will not incur a criminal record.

Spade Braithwaite

If you are at risk of arrest then we strongly suggest that you conduct any non-cash financial transactions through the **Randolph First National Bank**, using your code number instead of your account details. Sign all documents with your old name, just as before.

If you do not wish to participate in the scheme then that is your right. No official retribution will ever be dealt. **It is requested though**, that if you choose not to participate, you refrain from involvement in legal testimony that might identify others. **Although, no official retribution will ever be dealt!**

We anticipate a speedy, satisfactory return to normality with the minimum of inconvenience.

Thank you for your Co-operation!
Mayor Andropolous
and
The Town Council

Herbert Brewer's Dirty Little Secret

It was funny to read it again. Charles had asked her to write it but nearly every word of it had been his. Shirley had wanted to explain the whole plan and invite the town's participation but Charles had talked her out of it. He'd told her that people would enjoy a limited amount of complicity but would resent too much involvement.

And he was right.

She sipped the cognac and stifled a grimace. There was something about hard liquor that was unpleasant. For all its emotional attraction, it tasted downright nasty.

She took a sip of the coffee but it burned after the spirit.

Keep it simple. That had been Charles' advice.

"Cheese and ham toasty?"

Should have had a steak sandwich! Far too nice a day for a toasty. Damn!

"Over here! Thank you very much. D' you have brown sauce?"

"Mmm…, I don't think so."

"Okay. You can run up the bloody road an' get some. I'll be waiting. Thank you."

That evening, back in Gunswale the sun set westward in a breathtaking exhibition of impossible colours. Streaks of yellow, through gold to blood red. Dragging a canopy of purple edged, blue-black night time across the sky towards the interior horizon.

Spade Braithwaite

By nine o clock, Dereck Cartright, Prime Minister of Amsarnie, was costumed, wigged and ready to bowl.

One other person in the world knew of Dereck's passion for bowling. John Sumwun, Dereck's chauffeur.

Every other Tuesday, come hell, or Extended Parliamentary Question Time.

"How do I look, John?"

"You're Eric."

Eric Fontaigne, Dereck's secret identity. Unspecified labourer and dedicated member of the Parquet Pirates Bowling Team.

"Hair?"

"Michael Cane."

"Shirt?"

"Jonny Cash."

"Perfect!"

Most countries employ an intricate network of security operatives to guard their senior politicians. Amsarnie chose not to bother.

Dereck had once seen John Sumwun bite a man's nose off during a bar-scuffle over a double-canon into the side pocket. He felt safe enough.

Down the back stairs, through catering and emergency hospitality. Across the lawns, with their heads down, to a brown Ford Malta hatchback, parked outside the Republic Archives Museum.

Herbert Brewer's Dirty Little Secret

John unlocked the passenger door. Dereck climbed in and slid across to lift the knob on the driver door as John walked round.

Out of the carpark, onto Three-Wheel Lane. Straight across six lanes of stragglers. Off the main drag, into town.

Gunswale came to life on summer nights. Even on Tuesdays. The nightclubs were switching their signs on. A thousand Mini-Golf courses, pubs and "Legal-Raves". Every type of fast food.

"I fancy Malaysian! Go on, there it is! Just before the sign for the Book Drive-Thru."

"I hate Malaysian. They sprinkle little fish on everything."

"Did'ja vote for me?"

"No!"

"Then fuck'ya! Pull up to the speaker. Yeah! Two Nasi-Goreng, with extra fish-sprinkles. And a couple o' cokes! No ice."

"You fucker!"

"*I beg your pardon, sir?*"

"Two portions of y' best crap! Wi' cokes! No ice."

"*Would you care to Up-Size that?*"

"Jus' give us the fuckin' food! An' fuck off!"

"*You're a wanker! Sir.*"

"What?! I heard that! What's your name?!"

"*Nothing, sir. Please pull up to window-one to pay for your meal.*"

"I heard you, you fucker! I know your boss!"

"*I said, your mother pays me to fuck her up the arse! An' I hope I get sacked 'cause my boss keeps askin' me to suck him off!*"

Dereck and John collapsed across the seats.

"He knows your mother!"

"Shut-up, dick-head. You little bastard! D'you want a job in the civil service? I'll start ya' tomorrow. Media Liaison. Lots o' prospects!"

"*Thank you sir, but Malaysian food is my life. Please pull up to window-one to pay.*"

Dereck found a twenty-dollar bill in the door-pocket and they collected their food, still chuckling.

The Parquet Pirates trounced the Fat Men at the Bisley Bust-out Bowl-A-Rama. Fifteen lanes and a bar, right in the middle of the Bisley Public Housing estate.

Upstairs, the bar was wide and wooden with gambling machines and a long window that looked out over the action.

It was a modern tradition of the East Coast League that the members of the winning team each bought a round of drinks, after which it was every man for himself. When the Pirates won, John Sumwun was an honorary fifth team member. When they lost he made himself scarce.

Dereck always paid for three times as many beers as anyone else.

Herbert Brewer's Dirty Little Secret

"Lagers? Five lagers, darlin'. And, what can I get you guys? Lager? Lager? Nine lagers! Cheers!"

"Cheers!"

"Cheers!"

"Cheers chaps! Chaps! Can I toast our gracious hosts, the Portly Gentlemen of Bisley! Cheers!"

"Cheers!"

"Fat Bastards! Cheers!"

"Thank you. And can I ask you to raise a jar for our own captain, a veritable Machiavelli of the polished boards. Our own Lecky!"

"Cheers!"

"Veritable what?"

"Cheers! God ol' boy!"

"And...,"

"Fuck! He's on a roll!"

"And, can I suggest that we drink some lager and pause for a moment to think of our brave boys, that, as we speak, are about to answer the call to defend our great country from the threat of international disgrace, on the battlefields of Bundawa. Our brave lads! Cheers!"

"Cheers!

"What the fuck's Bundawa?"

"Cheers!"

"Hey, Eric, you want to hear a funny story?"

"My mother pays you to fuck 'er up the arse!"

Spade Braithwaite

"Well, yeah! But no, another story?"

"Go on, boy!"

"You know Clausthowler-what's-it's-flavour?"

"Yeah, out in the desert."

"They're not sending anyone for the army 'cause they're all changing their name to Herbert Brewer!"

"What the fuck are you on about?"

"They're all changin' their names to Herbert Brewer so that the government can't catch 'em and make 'em go in the army! The whole fuckin' town! It was over the radio!"

"Hold it! What was over what radio?"

"We've got an engineer at our works who's just come back from Claust', an' he reckons they had a big town meetin' an' they're not sendin' anyone for the army 'cause they're all changin' their names to Herbert Brewer!"

"The National Service Register's calculated by National Identification Number! What did he hear over the radio?"

"I told you! They're changin' their names to Herbert Brewer so they won't get called up. I don't know. I'm only tellin' ya what I heard."

"Herbert Brewer was their mayor for twenty seven years. He pretty much pulled Claust' out of the nineteenth century and turned it into an industrial powerhouse. They think they can change their names and avoid the army?!"

"It was just a story I heard. I don't know. Don't get weird on me."

"Lager anyone? Lager? Lager? Ten Lagers, please love."

"Hey Eric, you follow current affairs pretty close, huh? Wha' is it you do?"

"I'm a labourer. It's a Federal crime to evade the draught! Big jail time, an' warrants that don't expire!"

"It was just somethin' I heard from a bloke up at our works! It was only a story!"

"What d' they think they could do?"

"I dunno. It was just a story I heard! I thought it was pretty funny. Lager? Lager? Nine more lagers! Cheers, pet."

"They can't get out of anythin' by just changin' their names! I'll 'ave the bastards if they try it!"

"Eric, what type of labourin' d' you do, exactly?"

"Oh, whatever I can get. Lager, boy?!"

"Cheers, boy! Can't be hard work, from the look of ya!"

"Yeah, good story, mate, but it can't be done. If they're picked they gotta go! Cheers, anyway!"

"Yeah, cheers. Who's shout is it?"

Chapter 12

"..., an' so, with the time coming up to eight o-clock, we go over to Des Res', on tight-blouse patrol in St. Peter's Plaza. Des, what's the morning nipple situation in...,"

Spade Braithwaite

Laurence French, Senior Career Officer (recently appointed to the National Office of Domestic Security) turned the radio off and indicated to exit the expressway.

Four hours of straight driving from his front door in Precaria to the exit for Clausthowlersanuglerbogler. The southern bypass, with Claust' growing on either side like bowel cancer.

Smog-scaped, terraces of red brick. Contour lines of dirty roofs, sown with gas stations and fast-food in the burned-out spaces.

The black, little stream that eventually became a river in Precaria.

Morecombe Boulevard.

Laurence turned onto Morecombe Boulevard and pulled around the back of Elaine's Diner to park.

Hide the briefcase on the back seat, breath-mint, turn the lights off, take a deep breath, door.

Claust' might look like a loose arrangement of all things nasty, but at least you could rely on the weather.

Laurence stretched and let the sun massage his shoulders for a few seconds.

Four hours of road with one truck-stop in the middle. Laurence had meant to ask Gunswale whether having the second job entitled him to double his travel expenses. Next year he would fly here and rent a bloody car.

That was assuming that he still had either job.

Herbert Brewer's Dirty Little Secret

Elaine's Diner always seemed to do a good trade. Breakfast, lunch and dinner.

Laurence sat at the counter and tried not to hear the radio.

"Mr Government Man! We were expectin' you any day now!"

"Hullo…," Laurence squinted at her badge, "Jane! Nice to see you! You're lookin' lovely, as ever."

Jane had been waiting tables every time he'd eaten here in fifteen years. He'd remember her name next year.

"Can you keep a secret?"

"No."

"I've changed m' name."

"I like the name Jane! First girl I ever fell in love with was called Jane. I was eight, she was fourteen. Lovely girl."

"I've changed m' name for political reasons. I'm Herbert now."

"Y' tag still says Jane."

"That's all part of the plot."

"Fair enough, Bert. May I call you Bert? I was going to ask you to run away with me and live in the desert, in a tent, but I don't think I fancy waking up with someone called Herbert."

"I'll change it back! You can pick me up at lunch time. Make sure you 'ave a good breakfast, 'cause I'm insatiable, in a tent!"

"I don't doubt it. What's good?"

"All of it. 'Specially the western omelette. Are they makin' you stay at Shoop-Shoop again, this year?"

Spade Braithwaite

"Omelette, please. Shoop-Shoop? Yeah. I keep tellin' them that I'd carry more authority if they put me up at the Blandford and gave me an expense account. But they just assume that I'd squander all the money wining and dining saucy, young waitresses into bed. I can't imagine why they'd think that!"

"That's terrible! A dignified, sexy man like yourself havin' to stay at Shoop-Shoop. With all those whores probably pesterin' you all the time. And you'll probably be here for a while, what with the call-up an' all."

"What about the call-up? What've you heard?"

"Nuffin'! Only what everyone says. An' Gary reckons they might try to give you a hard time of it, so we've got to look after you as best we can. I reckon I could look after you best, in that tent you were talkin' about."

"What's Claust' got planned?"

"I aint heard nuffin'! 'Cept you might be here for a week or two. Coffee?"

"Thank you. You haven't heard anything, huh?"

"Only what everyone's sayin'. Hey, our Darren's got a tent. I'll bring it in an' you can pick me up anytime you need to get away. Can I get an all-over tan, out in the desert?"

"I'd like to see you try. I mean, not being funny, I really would lIke to see you trying to get an all over tan. Can I get home-fries with that?"

"For you, anything! Home-fries, western and coffee. Onions?"

Herbert Brewer's Dirty Little Secret

"Please. And a glass of water, no ice."

Gary got into his office at quarter past eight. He didn't really need to be there until half past nine but Bo-Bae had woken him at six o clock to have sex and once he was up, he was up.

Also, it looked good for the boss to get in early, sometimes, as though he had important stuff to do.

The records were up to date. The National Liaison and Co-operation Report wouldn't take ten minutes. Criminals from other towns never came to Claust'.

Gary turned the radio on, forgetting that it was still tuned to 101.1, Des' Res.

"...looks like a good one! Here she comes! Miss! Here, miss. What's ya name?"

"Melanie Epstien!"

"Where a' you goin', Melanie?"

"School."

"How old are ya, Melanie?"

"Thirteen."

"Okay Melanie. We like your blouse, an' we were wonderin' if you could touch your elbows together behind your back. Go on, Melanie. There's fifty dollars in it for you, if you can touch your elbows together, behind your back!"

Gary turned the radio off and pressed his intercom button.

"Janet?"

"Gary?! What the hell are you doin' in so early?"

Spade Braithwaite

"Get Bomar on the radio. Tell him to cruise over to Pete's Plaza and have a quiet word with Des' Res. Get him to tell Res that pesterin' thirteen year old girls is against the law. Tell him to give Res a fuckin' great kick in the bollocks, live on air. And then get him to tell Des' Res, unofficialy, that the next time he cuts the end off My Generation, he'll be be looking back, fondly, on the days when he had bollocks to howl about."

"Okay. I think that we've got about eight criminal, civil-rights violations right there. Enough to send you to prison for the rest of your life. I hope you like black guys, 'cause Bubba's probably going to make you his girlfriend."

"I'll admit that I'm not unattractive. Is there any coffee out there?"

"On its way."

"I'd be very grateful."

Gary stared out the window and fought the urge to phone the post office to check on the conscription notices.

Across the street, Adam Doughty and three other teenagers ducked, inconspicuously into the walkway between the newsagents and the Pied Bull Tavern. Gary watched it unfold. One of the kids had money and Adam had the stuff. The two other teenagers kept watch, as inconspicuous as monkeys on a motorcycle.

Gary wondered about the drugs they did, nowadays. Kettamine, whatever that was.

Herbert Brewer's Dirty Little Secret

Every generation of teenagers believed that sex and drugs were something new, that they'd just invented.

Gary remembered his grandfather taking him to one side and warning him about the dangers of opium. His thirteen year old disgust at being warned about some stupid drug they did in historical times.

Acid had been where it was at, in his day, man.

Janet came in with two cups of coffee.

"What happened to people knockin' on doors, before they come wanderin' in? "

"I was hoping to catch you wanking. Metcalf says that you always have a wank first thing."

"Not always! I'm gonna sack that bastard, one of these days."

"What's going on?"

"Nothin'. Just how I like it, touch wood."

"Is everything okay?"

"Everything's bloody perfect. When Bomar's done over on Pete's Plaza, get him to pick Adam Doughty up and give him the "slippery-slope" lecture."

Charles was standing guard over a railway carriage full of Swiss bankers, with a pair of shoes that, he hoped, looked like a weapon. His mother spat on a handkerchief and was trying to get some dirt off his face, while all the bankers laughed and pointed at his shoes. Piss off, woman! Just...'

"Mmmhhh...?"

Spade Braithwaite

"Got to go!"

Stella Davenport kissed his eyebrows.

"Class in thirty minutes. Thanks for the wine. Take care."

Charles opened his eyes. Stella, with clothes on, disappearing through his living room.

Charles closed his eyes again.

"Call me!"

No answer. Being a Mayor was more fun than being a swindler.

Thursday. Call-up day.

The Post Master would have everything under control. By now, approximately five hundred call-up notices should be in the vans, starting to go out. Gary and Charles had certainly made it simple enough.

A couple of postal workers should have gone through the whole sack, rubber stamping every one, advising mail carriers that the name was now Herbert Brewer, and the address, Coronation Road. The names and addresses of five hundred totally unsuitable draughtees, also subsequently re-named Herbert Brewer, had been written out on three pads of removable sticky-memos, one for each envelope.

After that they could just be sorted with the other mail and delivered to exactly the wrong person at the wrong place.

Five hundred Instruction Notifications arriving at Clausthowlersnauglerbogler main post office at…,

What time was it?

Herbert Brewer's Dirty Little Secret

...four hours ago.

Charles should be receiving one himself, any minute now.

By eight thirty, Prime Minister Dereck Cartright had already been at work for three hours.

It irked him that the media spent so much energy bitching about his personality. Let them put some fucking boy-scout in the job. Let them watch their country go down the toilet.

Three hours of working out how he was going to make the economy last another day before he even started on the phone calls that would make it happen.

In high politics, you never actually solved anything. You struck deals to defer disaster until you had the chance to work out other deals.

A lot of Prime Ministers went grey in their first year. Dereck thrived on it.

The intercom burst alive. (JESUS! Mary and Joseph! Don't do that to me when I'm thinking!)

"Mr Cartright! Phone call from the office of the British Prime Minister!"

Fuck them! Why did they always phone at the crack of dawn? Wasn't it the middle of the night in London?!

"Okay. Hello?"

"Mr Cartright, Sir?"

"Hello?"

"Please hold for John Wivell, the Prime Minister."

Spade Braithwaite

Doh, de dee, de do dum dum. Dereck drew a hairy monster on his blotter and tried not to get annoyed.

"...and make sure that they understand that that's' the answer, not a bloody question! Hello Dereck?"

"John."

"Dereck, how are you? How's the job?"

"The hours are great but I don't see much chance of promotion. How's things in London?"

"Dire! How's that army of yours coming along? We're shipping a thousand troops out on Monday. They'll be in Kinaida the following Monday."

"We're getting it together. We've been conscripting a force to augment our regular army. We should have fifteen hundred ready to fly to Kinaida...," Dereck scraped a diamond-hard bogey from the roof of his nostril, "a week next Thursday. That's two weeks. Fifteen hundred more a week after that. Can you wait?"

"Well, I don't want our boys going in and doing anything unsupported. It looks bad. It's supposed to be an International Peace Keeping Force. Silus Mantè's been on the phone all week, bloody moaning. How well trained is this force of yours going to be?"

"After their basic training, we've set up a shock camp to give them a week of jungle instruction before they leave. We're a martial people, us Amsarnians. Never happier than when we're in some smelly hell-hole, blowing-up the locals to pacify them."

John Wivell recognised irony when he heard it. And bullshit.

Herbert Brewer's Dirty Little Secret

From what John had heard, Amsarnie's recruits would be lucky if they had time to look up "jungle" in the dictionary before they were shipped out.

"Good! Good. Solid, professionalism. That's going to be the key to this situation. I'm sure this sedition-thingy will all just dissolve, as soon as they see us coming. Got to put on a good show, though. So, I can promise my Generals fifteen hundred armed chaps, arriving in Kinaida two weeks from today?"

"Roger! Anything else?"

"Nothing our people can't sort out, between themselves. I'm glad to have you with us, on this one. Speak to you soon. Good bye, Dereck."

"Yeah, good bye. John."

English wanker!

Dereck had half a mind to let the USA buy him in the next election. At least America financed its wars properly.

He pressed the button on his intercom.

"Will ya' see if you can track down General Mussbiere for me."

John Wivell pissed Dereck off. They were both Prime Ministers. They should be able to talk honestly with each other, if no one else.

The British government knew bloody well what they were getting. Four thousand kids, with shaved heads. Why did he have to act like that he was expecting Force Ten from Fuckin' Navarone?

Spade Braithwaite

It had been six weeks since Dereck had been asked to produce an army. At that time Amsarnie had possessed two hundred trained riflemen and one General. Two of the soldiers had previous military experience in the Indian Army. To Dereck's best knowledge, the rest hadn't seen a shot fired in indignation between them.

In six weeks Dereck's War Ministry had created a training camp, organised transportation, found a caterer and outfitted four thousand expected recruits with boots, clothes, kit-bags and rifles.

Actually, the secret training camp was a Good-News Revival Missionary summer camp. It's loan to the government had been negotiated while the Domestic Revenue Department reviewed the Mission's non-profit status.

The four thousand kit-bags were really tent bags. The last order for a marquee company facing section-ten, bankruptcy proceedings. But they were green.

The rifles had been a real find. One of the guys in logistics just happened to know the web site of white-supremacist organisation that had been only too happy to supply four thousand, bolt-action rifles, with twelve thousand rounds of ammunition and twenty tons of US military field rations, in return for the eighteen, non-specific end-user, armament purchase certificates issued by the UN.

They had even delivered it all to Gunswale International Airport in a transport plane borrowed from the US military.

Herbert Brewer's Dirty Little Secret

Dereck wondered again what the certificates might have fetched on the open market.

The clothes, twelve thousand green boiler-suits, four thousand pairs of boots and four thousand floppy, green jungle-hats had all been specially made. And don't let anyone ever tell you that Amsarnie didn't take the situation seriously.

Fuckin' stupid war. Who needed it? Not fuckin' Amasarnie, that was for certain.

Dereck had enough crap on his desk without it.

"Did ya get hold of General Mussbiere yet?!"

"I'm sorry sir. There's no answer at Station Good-News."

Mussbiere? Mus' be a cunt, was what he mus' be.

"Try 'is house. And get Snapper in 'ere sometime today."

"Very good. Sir."

How the hell did someone get to be a General in a country that didn't have an army?!

Dereck intended to look into it, and possibly suggest some constitutional changes.

"And get me a fuckin' lager. I'm gaspin'!"

Janet knocked on Gary's door at half past nine.

"Come in!"

The mail, and a re-fill of coffee.

"Thank you very much! Is it lunch time yet?"

"Not even close, but it's heading in that direction. Eleven items of mail."

Spade Braithwaite

"What've we got?"

"Notification of the recent change in the law concerning the transportation of livestock. Large livestock, i.e. cows, horses, sheep, pigs, deer, camels and buffalo, must henceforth hold a Certificate of Humanitarian Conveyance from a licensed veterinarian before being moved more than fifty miles."

"Holy shit! Cancel all leave!"

"Exactly! Similar notification of a change in law concerning the erection of unlicensed radio broadcasting apparatus. Four "Wanted!" packages, for public display. An itinerary and booking forms for the Police Convention in Gunswale. Another one from Ollie Epstein."

"Now what?"

"An unsigned, newsprint-composite confession to the rapes and murders of seven Municipal Electric Company employees. I've checked, none of them exist."

"What's he got against the electric company? D'ya think it's time we pulled him in?"

"Wouldn't do any harm to get a professional opinion. Just in case. And, three very official looking letters with sticky-memos redirecting them into the care of; "Gary Crozier, Chief of Police, Brewer Building, Fourth floor." Three call-up notices?"

"Yeah. Anything else?"

"Harry Melchet's secretary phoned. Could you give Harry a call when you get a chance. What're you going to do with three call-up notices?"

"Federal business. Get Harry on the phone, will you? Cheers for the coffee. Tell me when the next pot goes on."

"I don't like it when you're sneaky. You're no good at it. I'll get Harry Melchet."

"Thanks."

Gary checked the dirt under his nails. None.

Thirty seconds after Janet left, his intercom buzzed.

"Harry Melchet's office on the line."

"Thanks. Harry?"

"Office of the Secretary of the Interior. Can I help you?"

"Gary Crozier, returning a call to Harry Melchet."

"One moment!"

"Gary!"

"Harry!"

"Harry Melchet here! Dazed and confused. Gary, what the fuck 'ave I been hearing about Claust' changin' all their names?"

"We had a council meeting, and we've decided to rename the sewage works, "Fort Melchet", in your honour."

"The very highest honour, I'm sure! But seriously?"

"Well..., there's been quite a bit of spontaneous name changing going on here lately. And, while I know that no one would deliberately evade the call-up, I wouldn't be at all surprised if there was some confusion."

"You know that it's all done by Identification Number? Man, there's big-arse, Federal warrants they can issue for crap like that!"

Spade Braithwaite

"We're all doing our best! And, touch wood, all the right people will be notified of their federal responsibilities, with the minimum of discomfiture."

"Who's idea was this? Not Humner?!"

"Humner's the Health Care Supervisor now. We've got a new Mayor."

"Yeah?"

"A Greek guy, called Herbert Brewer."

"You're puttin' me on!"

"No shit!"

"Okay. I'm sure that you've got this all worked out, but I have to warn you, they're gonna be pissed! An' if they can catch anybody, anybody at all, they'll fuck 'em over badly!"

"I'm quietly confident that we're ready for them. Does it bother you, how much of this story seems to be conducted over the telephone?"

"Well..., maybe, a bit. But that's the nature of it. How else could it work?"

"It's a dilemma, sure enough. I can't help thinking that there could be a bit more descriptive writing. Maybe enlarge some of our character traits a bit more"

"It's supposed to make for a feeling of, "breathless narrative", with the reader left to create their own images. I reckon there should be a lot more commas, but that's just my opinion."

"I guess we'll just have to see what happens. How's the story looking, where you are?"

"It's looking good. I've had half the members of the Cabinet calling me up for a chat in the past three days. I think that everyone in town's heard about your plan, except Cartright."

"What're they going to do?"

"Nothing! Everyone's hoping that it all fucks-up badly so that they can use it to get Cartright out."

"What d' you think?"

"He's way out on a limb. It wouldn't take much."

"That's good to know."

"Gary, can I give you my opinion?"

"Go on."

"This fuckin' call-up nonsense is the dumbest thing he's ever come out with. But, he's a whole lot better than any of the alternatives."

"Hey man, I'm only tryin' to keep my son out of it."

"I know. I'll do everything I can. You take care, mate."

"Yeah. See you at Christmas."

"Take it easy."

Chapter 13

Twenty miles south of Gunswale, at Station Good News, General Aemon Mussbiere checked his watch.

O seven, twenty hours. The loveliest part of the day. Time for a cigar.

"If anybody wants me I'll be reviewing progress somewhere."

"Where?"

"Probably down to the range and back. I'll be half an hour."

On his way out the building, Aemon diverted through the new Trade Hospitality Suite to steal a rasher of bacon and a slice of black pudding from a tray.

Only two miles from the best beaches on the east coast, the morning mist was still head-high and the sun was just starting to get warm.

Aemon had always liked the countryside. Twenty miles out of town and the people were a completely different species. So much friendlier.

The macadam drive ended at the front of the, "House". Behind the House, an avenue of sand snaked between the wooden dormitory buildings and recreational areas, all the way to the palm trees at the bottom of the property.

Herbert Brewer's Dirty Little Secret

Aemon took the cigar out of his shirt pocket and unwrapped it. The smell was better than the actual smoking. He caressed the outer leaves to make sure that it was the same as every other cigar and, reassured, tucked it behind his ear. A pleasure, waiting to be taken.

The soft sand made the walking slightly strenuous, but pleasantly so.

In fact, taking the situation as a whole, Operation Good News made a pleasant change from Aemon's usual routine.

The Good News was that the Government was suddenly injecting an improbable amount of money into Aemon's army.

The bad news was that there was suddenly a lot of interest in how it was spent. A ton of big contracts, most of them bagged before they even left Parliament.

Only forty yards away from the House, Aemon might have been a thousand miles from civilisation. Palm trees looming out of the mist on either side. A few more steps and the square outline of Luke Dorm' slowly insinuated itself into the scenery.

Populace. Aemon's people.

"Gov'ner!"

"Gov'ner!"

"Mornin'! How's it goin'?"

"Lovely job! The main assault course 'll be all poured and hardenin' by lunchtime. Them boys'll be thinkin' that you're their long, lost mother, all the fuss you're makin' of 'em!"

"You chose to be 'ere. They didn't. Remember that."

Spade Braithwaite

    Aemon gave up resisting and lit the cigar from an old zippo. One, two, three puffs. One long drag.

    If only the whole day could all be morning.

    Aemon had started his military career as a civilian, selling stolen meat to a sergeant in the Catering Corp. When Aemon had heard about the approaching retirement of a Corporal in the Procurement Office, he'd made the right bid, to the right person and entered the army with the rank of Senior Corporal, two stripes.

    Since then, he'd enjoyed an exemplary rise through the ranks. Consolidating his influence, cutting out middle men and diversifying into every imaginable branch of criminal activity.

    His last promotion, fifteen years ago had been to the rank of Captain of General Administration. It hadn't been any trouble to lose the, "Captain" and the, "Administration", while keeping the, "General". Amsarnie's army was his.

    If Dereck Cartright wanted a war then Aemon was in a position to sell him one. Aemon's major concern was that Dereck Cartright seemed determined to nobble Aemon's army before it was even conscripted.

    The sun was starting to clear the mist by the time Aemon reached Mathew Dorm'. Aemon wondered, idly, what the Good News Missionary would do if they ever needed to build a new dormitory. They would have Mathew, Mark, Luke, John, and perhaps Acts? Some people just didn't think ahead.

Herbert Brewer's Dirty Little Secret

A spray of marquee tents had been erected in every clear corner to accommodate Aemon's new recruits.

Four thousand, bolt-action, Egyptian rifles, last used during the Suez crises! What the hell was Aemon supposed to do with them? Twelve thousand rounds of ammunition. That worked out as three bullets per soldier! What did Cartright want him to do? Give the soldiers two shots during training and one bullet to take with them, or one practise shot and two bullets for the war!

Aemon often felt that national pride should be a richer currency, in politics.

If he was going to send representation to another country then he was fuckin' well going to let the foreign bastards know that they'd met Aemon's Firm. There were big trade deals to be made in central west Africa and Aemon intended to be on the power-end of them.

A friendly Afghan with huge poppy farms had been asking about rifles so Aemon had given him the bolt-action antiques to get rid of them. At the same time, an Arabian gentleman hoping to relocate to Amsarnie had donated four thousand, modern Kashmirnikov assault rifles and seven hundred thousand, nine millimetre rounds as a gesture of good-will.

Aemon had to smile when he thought about the green boiler suits. They were just fuckin' perfect. Aemon's army would look like a bunch of psychopaths, blundering around the tropics in one-piece uniforms. Exactly the image that he hoped to create.

Spade Braithwaite

At the edge of the main meeting area Aemon paused to meditate on his cigar. The trail of blue smoke and the comforting rasp at the very back of his throat.

The frames of the new assault course rose out of the dirt like dinosaur bones, waiting for concrete to fossilise them.

Two hundred of Aemon's best engineers and procurement specialists had flown out to Bundawa the previous week to prepare for the main arrival. Everything was on schedule for the operations.

"Gov'ner!"

"Mornin', boys."

Zero seven thirty hours and crews were beginning to move. Every soldier in Aemon's army had a trade. Carpenters, butchers, diamond-cutters, card-dealers, film-makers. Aemon liked to keep everything inside the Firm.

The new assault course was a replica of the adventure playground in the middle of the Bisley Public Housing Estate. Forty young soldiers had been in Bisley for the past three days, climbing the ropes and slithering through the whirly-wheel in preparation for the press-release that the video-crew were shooting on Tuesday.

"Alright, Gov'ner?"

"Lovely. What crew are ya?"

"Groundwork. Shuttering, erection and services. All done, bar the shoutin'."

Herbert Brewer's Dirty Little Secret

"Good boy. Have a word with caterin' and hospitality. I think they needed some bodies. An' when they're done you're all on furlough 'til Monday."

"Cheers, Gov'ner! Good one!"

Aemon wandered between the structures, comfortably in control.

Beyond the marquees, in the marshy area, eight truckloads of crushed stone, covered with ten loads of soft dirt, were the bottom of the new rifle range. One hundred yards back from the line of firing.

For contentious situations at closer range, Aemon preferred superior numbers armed with old-fashioned big sticks. It was an old fashioned philosophy, but people seemed to understand what you were saying if you told them, smashed their legs and then told them again.

The world was changing so quickly. In a few years it would be time for Aemon to retire. Maybe get himself a little whorehouse or bar or something, out by the coast. Something to keep him in the game.

Aemon paused for a minute to watch a divet-hawk scan the mounds and then disappear into the trees.

About-turn. Head back to the office.

The last half of the cigar always tasted like old tyres.

Aemon had often flirted with the idea of smoking half a cigar on his outward, morning walk and half a new cigar on the way back but, somehow, it didn't seem right. If you enjoyed the better half of a cigar then you were duty-bound to suffer with it through it's declining inches. That was the law.

Aemon smiled at the thought.

Back in his office Aemon, licked the grease of another rasher from his fingers and settled in for the morning.

"Here Gov'ner. Paperwork for the flight requisitions. They need signatures…, there, there and there. The stock-takes, up-to-month-end, are in. Everything looks good except you might want to have a look at subsidiary merchandise at the Club Mao-Mao. Looks a bit uneven to me."

"Good boy. Any progress with the secrecy notices for that land purchase?"

"Done-deal. Complete security notice, zone-exempted, inspection prohibited. This bloody war is just the best thing! Nobody questions anythin'! It might be worth makin' it a regular thing."

"Now, you know my feelin's about war! Anythin' from Bundawa?"

"Daily report from camp is all encouraging. Everything's pretty-much ready to roll. The private report from Major Schooly should be in your system, ready to download."

"Good boy!"

Aemon loved technology. With all the authority at his disposal, Aemon had the most advanced criminal operation in the world. It had taken two hours and forty minutes to break down Aemon's office in Gunswale and re-assemble it at Temporary H.Q., Operation Good News. Two hours and forty minutes, plus travel time. Travel time had been four hours, including a protracted stop at the Black's Head Pub and a couple of quick stops afterwards.

From Aemon's desk, he could monitor real-time, cash-register transactions at any of the Firm's operations, anywhere in the world. With the touch of a button, he could see tiny areas of profit and loss evaluated, with projections into the next year. He could also get a five-day weather forecast that was accurate at least three days out of ten.

Aemon pulled up Major Schooly's report from Bundawa and matched it to the combination of the cipher programmes that converted it into readable English.

It read:

Category A – Security. TOP SECRET!
21:37 hours, 12th May
Major J. Schooly reporting to General A. Mussbiere.
Status, Bundawa advanced field operations.

Property acquisition and preperation all on schedule. We've got a lovely place, eleven miles south east of central Kinaida. Ground is cleared, catering and admin' are up and running. We dug a load of latrines but I have ordered the digging of a lot more because we've all

got the galloping shits and I expect the boys will get it when they get here.

Bought a second property a hundred miles inland. A disused coal mine. Perfect for that toxic waste idea that we talked about. Three thousand tons, fifty feet below the water table, if we can arrange the transport.

All real transportation is being handled by the British Royal Air Force. We have got handles on a couple of guys there. Set them up with girls, no go. Set them up with boys, bingo. We'll see what pans out.

Sounding out our opposite numbers in the British Army. Load of drunken louts, if you ask me. No real business structure. Too aggressive for any real partnership. Making contacts and trying to find the right people for the big, reciprocal fencing option. We'll keep you informed.

Beer is shite and the whores all got the pox. Might want to consider sending out a company of Women's Recreational Corp. to sort us out. It might get the British coming over to socialise aswell. Just a thought.

Apart from that, nothing much to tell. Take it easy.

Schooly.
End dispatch.

Aemon deleted the message and pulled up an inventory of stolen machinery currently in storage. Three more clicks informed him that stock was expected to increase eight percent over the next twelve months, with warehouse space increasingly expensive and less secure.

It certainly wouldn't do any harm to knock out a few plane loads to Britain, in return for something they could sell on the high-street.

"'scuse me Gov'ner, this might sound like a silly question, but I'm tryin' to get some lectures together, for the induction. Who, exactly, are we supposed to be fightin', in Bundawa?"

"Communist rebels, in the upcountry! I don't fuckin' know. It's all pretty vague."

"Well, it would be nice to have some clear parameters of operation, to brief the lads before they go."

"I don't want any of the new boys doing anything except flexin' a bit of muscle in the background! Give 'em some bullshit about' "shadowy rebel factions", and tell 'em to wear condoms. We should have enough full-time crew out there to handle operations. If we get the chance, it'd be nice to take a few new boys out into the jungle. Let 'em shoot up a few villages and win a few medals. But, I don't want anyone encouragin' the new boys to go anywhere near anythin' dangerous!"

"D'ya think it might come to that?"

"Nah! Schooly's a top-man. We'll come out o' this sellin' time-share to the rebels and protection to the Government. Plus concessions and management. I won't be happy if there's fightin'!"

"D'ya think we should want to be lookin' ahead, and maybe coaxin' some other situations in other parts of the world?"

"You know my feelin's about war!"

"I know, but we could do so much! Without anyone ever…,"

"Hey! War, huh? What is it good for?"

"Absolutely nothin'. But…,"

"Say it again! Yeah!"

War, huh? What is it good for? Absolutely nothing.

Aemon glowered around the room.

"Okay, Gov'ner! I was jus' thinkin'…,"

Chapter 14

At seven o clock on Saturday morning, in the Empire Lounge on the seventh floor of the Brewer Building, a special session of Clausthowlersnauglerbogler's Criminal Court Hearings came to order. The Honourable Justice Jacob Tethers in the chair.

"Hear Yee!"

Judge Tethers tapped his pen on the Judicial Dais.

"Court in session. Gary, how do you want to do this?"

"Your Honour, we have four cases to get through, all pleading guilty. The first two, we can combine. Should be about twenty

Herbert Brewer's Dirty Little Secret

minutes each. I'm the primary witness in one of them. Police Constable Andy Bomar is the primary witness in the others. Shouldn't take long. Janet 'll keep the minutes."

"Let's get to it."

"Okay. First case. Fitzroy, bring the Brewer brothers in."

The Brewer brothers, formerly known as Al and Huey Pheobe, waddled into Court. Constable Kevin Fitzroy herded them, chained, wrist and ankle, towards the make-shift dock with stabs of a chalkboard pointer.

"Ouch! Fuckin' easy, man! Hey Gary, how's it hangin'?"

"Good, thank you. Stand there and shut up!"

"Okay. Will the defendants, please, not be seated until I say so! Gary, what's the charge?"

"Your Honour, the Brewer brothers, formerly know as Pheobe, have been before you a dozen times. I'm getting' bored of showin' their mug-shots to parents and askin' if they were the men. This latest incident involves them hanging around a men's toilet, opposite a popular children's play area, and accosting juveniles for the purpose of procuring illegal, sexual intimacy. They're a menace. I want the fuckers out of town, or I'm going to turn a blind eye to somebody killin' 'em."

"Janet, can that stay out of the minutes?"

"Can what stay out of the minutes?"

Janet smiled. Twenty seven years ago, while she'd been an intern with the council, old Herby Brewer had bought her a few glasses of wine and talked her into coming back to the Building to pose for some nude photographs, draped across the Judicial Dais. Janet liked to imagine that the photographs were still out there somewhere, like lost children that just might come home, someday.

Judge Tethers smiled back.

"Thank you. Call the primary witness."

"Bomar!"

Andy Bomar marched into the Empire lounge, in his best gait and uniform.

"Jake, Your Honour! Andrew Bomar, Senior Police Constable with the Abjure Valley, Regional Constabulary. On the 18th of April, at ten thirteen hours, a.m., in response to an emergency call from our radio operators, I proceeded from my position, outside the Lymington Tavern, to the public toilets, opposite the main entrance to the Burmont Park...,"

"Yeah, I know. What were they up to?"

"In confirmation of the call, and in accordance with my previous...,"

"What were they up to?"

"They were hanging around, trying to get friendly with kids!"

"So what did you do?"

"I apprehended them both, and took them into custody for further questioning."

"Did they give any statements?"

"Indeed they did. Decency forbids me reading it in open court, but here's a copy."

Herbert Brewer's Dirty Little Secret

"We didn't make any fuckin' statement! And we're the Pheobe twins! Not the fuckin', wha' did 'e call us, the Brewer brothers was it?"

"Would the defendant please shut his mouth before I instruct Gary to kick him in it! Janet, please note the entry of a statement into evidence. Andy, give us the gist of their statement. We're all adults here."

Andy Bomar looked nervously at Janet. Janet smiled back, levelly.

"Your Honour, Jake, they told me about a number of previous, non-consensual, sodomous acts that they'd committed against a number of vulnerable people, including an old man in Bishop's yard and a ten year old, blind boy on a piece of waste ground."

"Jesus Christ!"

"You fuckin' liar! We didn't make no statement! We were just bragging about the old guy! He charged us fifty bucks for it!"

"Yeah, and we never laid a finger on any ten year old, blind boy!"

"Shut..., the-fuck up! Gary, what do you think?"

"I'm pretty easy going, but these two creep me out. I don't think that they've done a quarter of what they get blamed for but I want 'em out o' town."

"Okay. Messieurs Brewer. On the charge of aggravated, violent rape, I find you both guilty and sentence you to complete thirty five years of hard labour in a secure, federal institution."

Al Pheobe fainted out cold. Nobody bothered to help him.

Spade Braithwaite

"Wait a minute! Wait a fuckin' minute! What the fuck is all this, "Mis-use Brewer" crap?!"

"Didn't we tell you? We changed your names. As of last week, you're both called Herbert Brewer. Officially."

"What the..., why?!"

"You just are, okay! Gary, what about their pending military employment?"

"Their papers came in last week and they'll be expected to report to the Auxiliary Defence next Thursday."

"Could we defer their sentence until they've completed military service?"

"I suppose we'll have to."

"Okay. Gentlemen, you have been requisitioned by the Federal Government to serve a period, determined at their discretion, in the nations armed forces. I hereby order your sentences deferred until you return to town, on completion of your military duties. The very moment you set foot back in town, you're up shit-creek. Janet, don't write that down. Any comments?"

"Wait a minute, we're in the fuckin' army? We're as queer as pink dog-shit! They'll never have it!"

"Good news, boy! They changed the law. I'm sure you'll make us very proud. If I ever see either of you again, it's all over. Good bye."

"Thank you, your honour. Al! Wake up! We're in the army! Wake up, y' fat cunt! We're soldiers!"

Herbert Brewer's Dirty Little Secret

"Wha'?"

Gary and Constable Fitzroy man-handled Al Pheobe to his feet.

"They've made us join the army instead of prison!"

"I'm dreamin'! Huey, you say we're in the army? Don't fool with me, it isn't funny."

"Yeah, man! And they've changed our names to Herbert Brewer!"

"That ain't funny, Hue. I don't feel so good."

"Come on, sleepin' beauty. You' got five more days in a cell before you go anywhere."

"You got him, Fitzroy?"

"Yes sir."

"Good lad."

Fitzroy goaded the stumbling brothers through the door and back to the elevator.

"Was that okay, Gary?"

"Perfect, Your Honour."

"Good. You didn't actually write any of that down, did you Janet?

"Just for my own amusement.

"Okay, but don't let anyone see it. And I don't want any record of the next two cases. Are we ready?"

"Game on."

Spade Braithwaite

Prime Minister Dereck Cartright liked to work at weekends. The pin-stripes had all gone home and Dereck had forty eight hours to sort out all the crap that they'd caused, before they came back to start again.

Every once in a while his driver, John Sumwun picked up girls that were impressed by high politics and smuggled them in for group sex. That was always nice.

"Mr Cartright!"

(Fuckin'-hell's teeth! He'd have to get a flashing light or a buzzer or something. The intercom was going to give him a heart-attack, one day.)

"What?!"

"Sorry to disturb you, but I've got a Mr Pethey from the Inland Office wanting to speak to you in person. I told him that you don't see people on Saturdays, except for those Special Interest groups that Mr Sumwun organises, but he says that he thinks that you'll be interested. Shall I get rid of him?"

Pethey from the Inland? Pethey. The name rang a bell.

Pethey! Ryan Pethey. Senior Administrator at the Inland. Unelected career man. Good for a lot of dirt during the last election. Sound as a pound!

"Ryan Pethey! Don't be bloody stupid, man. Put a six-pack in 'is hand and send 'im in!"

"Very good."

What could Pethey want, on a Saturday morning?

Two knocks at the door.

Herbert Brewer's Dirty Little Secret

"Come in! Ryan, mate! Good to see you! How's it goin' at the Inland?"

"Mr Prime Minister. Very good, thank you. Your secretary asked me to bring these bottles in."

"Good man! Give'em 'ere. Glass?"

"Ughhm. No thank you. Bottle will be fine. I don't normally...,"

"I know. But we're on overtime. Cigar?"

"Thank you very much. You know I haven't...,"

"I know. But you have to, once in a while. Cheers. Down in one, eh? Cheers! So what's goin' on at the Inland? And I don't mean what's in the reports!"

"Cheers! Well, Prime Minister...,"

"Dereck! D'you mind me callin' you Ryan? I think we've both known each other long enough."

"No! That would be fine, Dereck. Well, I got a note from the Bureau, yesterday, that they'd got an official communication from Clausthowlersnauglerbogler, changing absolutely everybody's name to Herbert Brewer. And all the streets were being renamed Coronation Road. They were asking me if it was legal, or if it was a joke. So I looked up, in a copy of their town constitution, and I found that it's quite legal for their Mayor to change people's names and street names. All they have to do is notify us in writing. Which they did."

"They sent you what, exactly?"

Spade Braithwaite

"Three boxes of computer paper, listing everyone legally registered as an inhabitant of Claust' and notifying us that they'd, hereby, changed their names to Herbert Brewer. And every single road, avenue, cul-de-sac, street, freeway, and even the bypass, was now called, Coronation Road. It's all completely legal, as of last Thursday. I'm only telling you because Claust' is one of the towns involved in the experimental call-up, and I can only assume that it's some ploy to evade their national responsibility."

"The call-up 's calculated by National Identification number! Even if they all changed their names to Doris Day, it wouldn't make any difference! Wha' do you think they're up to?"

"Cheers. I don't know. They've had that freaky Mayor for the last twelve years. Ever since the real Herbert Brewer died. I always thought that he was a weirdo. Something Speelding. Humber, or something. I think he's just weird. Y' know, I like a beer in the morning. D'ya want another one?!"

"Cheers. D'ya think they have a real plan? Or are they clutchin' at straws?"

"I think they're fuckin' ou'-of it! Man! Let's 'ave another beer. Wha' was the question again?"

"Cheers!"

"Yeah Man! I fuckin' love a bit of it, Dereck! Oh man! Y' know, I've got half a dozen scams goin' with those immigration quotas you brought in. I tell ya, man! A man's gotta eat."

"Course he has. It's what we're here for!"

"Yeah, Baby! You don't mind me callin' you Baby?!"

"Nah! All the Cabinet call me Baby. Go on!"

"Cheers, Baby! Them fuckin' ungrateful bastards from ClausthowlerPersianBurgler really piss me off! I'm behind you, one hundred and fifty percent. You know that."

"Thank you, man. I appreciate that."

"I love you, man."

"I know you do. Thanks for the information. Grab a six-pack on the way out, an' take the rest of the day off. I'll book y' the full day."

"I love you man!"

"I know. Take it easy. An' keep me informed."

"Cheers, Baby."

"Next case?"

Judge Jacob Tethers rubbed the Judicial Dais absently. During his first christmas break, as a student at Braithwaite University, he'd gone out drinking with a few of his high school buddies and spoken to Shirley Brown for the first time. Pointy chested Shirley Brown, that always seemed so aloof, three years above him at school. Shirley had finished her degree and was already working full time as the assistant to the Borough Social Advisor.

After the fourth pub they'd paired off and lost the rest of the crowd. With nowhere else to go, Shirley had suggested getting a bottle of wine and sneaking into the Building for a look around.

Spade Braithwaite

Jacob had been terrified, tip-toeing up the fire escape and wandering through the empty offices without switching the lights on.

The Judicial Dais was kept in Herby Brewer's boardroom, in those days. They'd gone into the boardroom because it was the only room on the seventh floor that didn't have an outside window, so they could turn a light on. Shirley had been fairly drunk. Jacob sometimes wondered exactly how drunk she'd been, because it had been her idea to take their clothes off.

Jacob had sobered up as soon as she'd taken off her coat. Then she'd pulled her sweater over her head, unbuttoned her blouse and shown him her strange, jello-mold breasts. That had been enough. He'd thrown her fat arse onto the Judicial Dais, hitched her skirt up and would have fucked her through the fabric of her panties, if she hadn't pulled it aside in time. Her big buttocks planted like a tree while he wallowed. Her beautiful, little tits wobbling, indecisively, with the rhythm.

That had been twenty seven years ago. They hadn't spoken to each other since, outside of their professional relationship.

Jacob rubbed the spot tenderly and decided that he really, really wanted to shag her again, soon.

"Second case. Bring 'im in!"

Chained, young Liam Bourke waddled into court, ahead of Fitzroy with the poker.

"Claust' versus Herbert Brewer. Formerly known as young Liam Bourke. The charges are, habitual, drunken violence, aggravated abduction, attempted murder, the attempted murder of a police man and resisting arrest. Andy Bomar was the arresting officer."

"Do you have anything to say?"

"Who me? I'll wait till you've finished with Herbert Brewer. Sounds like he's really in the shit!"

"I'm afraid, you are Herbert Brewer. We changed your name last week."

"What?! You did wha'?! Hold it! Abduction!? Attempted murder?! Hold on a cotton-pickin'-fuckin'-minute! What the fuck a' you on about?!"

"Call the primary witness."

Andy Bomar marched in as though he was giving his buttocks an isometric work-out.

"Your Honour. Senior Police Constable Andy Bomar. On Tuesday, April 3rd, in answer to a call from the radio operator, I proceeded to the Bourke residence, on the Juno estate."

"What happened?"

"No one answered the door, which shat-me-up badly. 'Cause they always answer the door to cops at the Bourke place. Anyway, the defendant had come home, all pissed-up, and taken his sister in law hostage in the basement. Reckoned he was goin' to cut her throat with some big scissors."

"Bloody hell! What did you do?"

"Well, I did a course in hostage-negotiation, with the Braithwaite police a few years ago. An' that stood me well. I

Spade Braithwaite

reasoned with the defendant until he decided to forgo his threats against his captive and make an attempt on my life."

"Yeah, go on!"

"As soon as the hostage's life was no longer in jeopardy, I arrested the defendant and read him his rights."

"He's charged with resisting arrest?"

"Yes he is! He resisted, in the worst possible way. I was affeared for my life! But I subdued him, as per my training and held him until reinforcements arrived. At which point, I handed over his custody and took the rest of the day off, because I was so traumatised by the whole event!"

"You beat him up?"

"I didn't beat him up! Look at the size o' him! An' look at me! I'm a lover, not a fighter!"

"May the record note that Constable Andy Bomar is, indeed, a skinny, streak-of-urine. Herbert Brewer, formerly called Liam Bourke, the charges against you carry a maximum sentence of forty eight years in federal jail. Do you have any comment?"

"Man! This is fuckin' bullshit! I 'ad a few beers an' I pissed m' brother's wife off a bit! I didn't try to kill anybody! An' why did y' change my name to Herbert Brewer?!"

"We just did. Gary, what do you think?"

"Your Honour. The defendant has been a rash across my arse since he was eight years old. I've arrested him for god-knows how many fights. Last year he beat up a barman at the Juno Tavern and cut one of his fingers off with a broken bottle.

Herbert Brewer's Dirty Little Secret

We never got a conviction because the victim was too scared to testify. I feel that it's only a matter time before the defenendent kills somebody so I'd like to press for the full punishment of the law. Get him off the street, into a federal institution, where he belongs! For the rest of his life! You know it makes sense!"

"I 'ad a few beers an' made a twat o' m'self! We've all done it!"

"Shut up! I choose to hold the defendant's previous bad character in consideration and sentence him to a period of thirty five years of hard labour in a secure, Federal Institution."

"Oh my..., Christ! This is a fuckin' joke, right?! Really?!"

"Do we look like we're having fun?"

"Oh my fuckin..., Hell's teeth. You can't do that. There's civil rights groups, and lawyers and stuff. I can write to the papers. I'm goin' to inherit the family business, one day!"

"Do you remember reading a lot of letters in the paper, from convicted criminals?"

"You can't do it!"

"I have to assure you that I most certainly can. I do it all the time. In this particular instance, Gary has asked me to consider a slightly irregular alternative."

"Well..., go on!"

"Gary?"

"Your Honour. Boy! You ain't inheritin' nothin! None of your family bothered visiting you to tell you that your sister-in-law lost her baby, did they?"

Spade Braithwaite

"Oh my God!"

"Last week, your name was legally changed to Herbert Brewer. I had a word with my friends at the Randolph Bank, an' all your savings, and your pension, have been transferred to your new account at the First Agricultural Bank in Gunswale, in your new name. Everybody changed their names last week, so it's very hard for me to keep track of anyone. By mistake, we're going to find you guilty of supplin' drugs to a minor, and consequently, culpable for that minor's death. We're going to offer you the chance to bargain for a fifteen year sentence, by pleading guilty."

"Fuck off!"

"Then, I'm going to write a little note, and tuck it inside your file, recommending that you be considered for parole after four years. D' you know what I'm saying?"

"Four years?"

"It depends on your behaviour in prison, whether you get the parole or not. I personally guarantee, that if you ever show up in town, or anywhere else, ever again, my constables will be advised to shoot you dead, rather than attempt to arrest you."

"Can I think about it?"

"No. I'm tellin' you what we're doing, not askin' if you want to. Just don't show up in town, ever again."

"When am I goin'?"

"Three days."

"Why?"

Herbert Brewer's Dirty Little Secret

"None of your business. Just be very thankful."

"I s'pose."

"Anything else, Your Honour?"

"I think that that's enough. Next case!"

At Clausthowlersnauglerbogler General Hospital, Dr Payne, the Senior Paediatrician and Official Medical Examiner was far too busy for interruptions.

Daniel Weatherby, an intern, knew that, but couldn't resist.

"Dr Payne?"

"Damn it! What the hell do you want? I've got fifteen course prognostications to write before I even get to look at sick people! What is it?"

"Dr Payne. You're really beautiful when you're busy. D' you remember that stiff we got in a while back, Reuben Schmettz, with the big smile?"

"Yes. Died with one of the Shoop-Shoop girls on top of him. Heart attack. They'll have to cut his erection in half to get the coffin lid down!"

"Exactly! Your white coat makes you look…, so masterful! I haven't had any luck tracking down any relatives, anywhere. God, you're lovely! Do you happen to know what the procedure would be?"

"No distant relatives? Did you try to make his company take responsibility?"

"I did. No dice. If you'll show me your bra, I'll be your slave all weekend! Could we just submit him for a pauper's cremation, and take the money out of his personal effects? He had three thousand dollars in his wallet."

"You'll be my slave for the rest of your miserable life! Here, look!"

Dr Payne slowly pulled her blouse out of her trousers and undid the buttons. Then she pushed her breasts together inside her substantial sports-bra.

"How long's he been there?"

"Twenty eight days. Bounce them!"

"Don't you dare tell me what to do! Stand where you are and take your clothes off. I want to see what a poor specimen you really are!"

"Yes, sir. I had an idea. You know, the town all changing their names, and that? How about, we call him Herbert Brewer and ship him out?! Don't hurt me!"

"They'd ship him back. Have you been rubbing yourself?! You little pervert! I'll bet you think of me when you abuse yourself. Don't you!"

"Yes! But it'd be funny. Sending out a cadaver for conscription. If you show me your panties, you'll own me for the rest of my life!"

"I already own you, from last time! That's a good idea. Phone Gary Crozier to see what he thinks. Look at this and tell me that you don't worship me!"

"I worship you!"

"I know you do. Okay, you may service me now."

"God bless you! I'll phone Gary as soon as I get a chance. I love you!"

"Of course. Not there, you idiot! There!"

"Sorry! It all looks so good!"

"And take your time!"

"Sorry!"

Andy Bomar and Fitzroy carried the Judicial Dais back to storage after young Liam's trial. Andy Bomar had to smile. A few weeks ago he'd wanked-off into the drawer of the Judicial Dais, when no one was looking.

Judge Tethers was happy to be out of the hot-seat.

"How do you want to handle this, Gary?"

"Gently. We'll have a word with him in his cell and see what we can make of him."

Joshua Matenach was reading when they peeped through the door.

Josh looked up and smiled when Gary opened the door and led Judge Tethers into the room.

"Good morning Josh. How are you?"

"Fine."

"You know you can come and go on this floor as much as you like? There's a TV in the common room."

Josh nodded.

Spade Braithwaite

"Okay. Josh, this is Judge Tethers. You might know him."
Josh stood up and shook Jacob's hand.

"We've been having a very special court session this morning and we think we've found a fair solution for you. You understand that Ernie Bishop has threatened to shoot you dead, and a lot of people are waiting to see what happens you. Well, we think we've solved it."

"Gary tells me that there's a lot of doubt as to whether you actually gave the drugs to Rupert Bishop, but you understand that we just can't put you back on the street."

"But here's what we've done. We got someone else to go to jail for you."

"Who?"

"Young Liam Bourke. He was facing forty years so he was only too happy to take your sentence instead. So he's going to jail in your name. We need to get you out of town for a while so I've had a word with a few mates in Precaria, on the coast, and I've got you an apartment above a shop and a nice little job driving a fork-truck for a construction company. If you decide that you want to come back then, in a year or so, you can grow a beard and cut your hair short and turn up with no one the wiser. We'll get your B.S.A. shipped out there and we can give you a thousand dollars out of the funds to get started. After that, you're on your own. What d' you think?"

"I want to join the army."

"You don't have to! We've sorted it out so that you'll have a nice place and a nice, new job, ten minutes from the port. Your old company said what a good worker you were."

"I want to! I want to join the army."

"You can if you want. I don't know how long you'll be gone but you won't be able to come straight back to town afterwards. But, we can make that work. If it's what you want."

"It is."

"Fine! Be ready to fly out next Thursday. Oh, and by the way, your name's Herbert Brewer. You never heard of Joshua Matenach, or anybody else not called Herbert Brewer. I'll have Shirley call by and explain it all to you. Good luck, mate!"

"Thank you."

Chapter 15

On Sunday morning, nothing much happened in Bundawa. Upcountry, while the heat began to creep, life-hardened villagers licked their wounds, contemplated their religion, drank toddy or rum out of dirty coke bottles, berated their spouses and children, played dominoes, cleaned house or just slept.

Spade Braithwaite

Eleven miles south east of central Kinaida, Major J. Schooly, the Supreme Commander of Amsarnie's Forces on Assignment lay in a hammock sipping vodka, contemplating his career and directing his campaign.

"Make a note to get a fuckin' ice machine shipped out. An' a few cases of tonic. I 'eard that tonic water was good f' malaria. Christ, it's fuckin' hot! Did y' get anything sorted out, fo' tonight?"

"We met a few guys. There's a few clubs in Kinaida that'll be geared up for us, if we turn up. Some geezer wanted to send a few buses to take us to 'is casino. Reckoned he 'ad some serious boxin' lined up."

"I think a night just hittin' all the bars might be the ticket. What else do we have to do?"

"Not a whole lot. Transport crew want an area. Tools and lifts and stuff are all there, we just need to pour a concrete pad to put them on. That'll take ten bodies half a day, plus finishin'. We got hold of enough DDT to clear a thousand yards around the fence."

"Good lad. Put odd-numbers on a twenty four hour furlough from noon. Evens tomorrow. I'm lookin' forward to havin' a stroll round town. 'Ave we made any friends with the British yet?"

"They're all Scottish. We can't understand a fuckin' word they say! One of the Patels reckons he was with a Scottish regiment once, so we've 'ad 'im on it, full time. I don't think they actually have a business structure, as such."

Herbert Brewer's Dirty Little Secret

"Find the individuals and coach 'em. They're devious enough."

"But they're nasty, with it. They seem more interested in the fightin' than the opportunities! We'll sort somethin' out, an' make it work."

"Good lad. I like this country. It's got a good feel abou' it. Like, frontier country! Brave men with guns could do well in a country like this."

"Do they actually expect us to do anything, while we're here? I mean, fighin' an stuff?"

"They'll be disappointed if they do. Have we got any leads on the rebels?"

"No. We know who they are and we've tried approachin' their families but we can't find anyone. I'm not sure how to get in touch with 'em."

"The local mob's gotta be in with it!"

"Not as far as we can tell. We'll make the enquiries."

"Good boy. I don't want to antagonise anybody, but I'd like 'em to know we're here. See if they need anythin'."

"We're doin' our best."

"Good boy!"

In down-town Kinaida the pace was a bit quicker. The markets and the vendors traded seven days a week. Abraham Unduwe, leader of the Bantu Nation Redeemist Guerrillas

Spade Braithwaite

walked amongst the hawkers as though he was looking for something really special, at the right price.

Cricket bats, carved from old, fork-truck bearers. Pressed steel cooking implements, cut out of oil drums and beaten into shapes. Hot, spicy fried chicken with mysterious ribs and eight inch drum-sticks. Wrought chains and cast padlocks. Used moped tyres. Every type of clothing with a Chicago Bulls motif. Shoe laces. Second-hand school books and National Geographic magazines.

One of the magazines caught Abraham's eye. The cover showed an Asian child posing, proudly, next to the body of a government soldier hanging by his feet from a home-made snare.

"Combiah?"

"Thirty."

Abraham dropped the magazine with feigned disgust and walked on.

Two small children, naked except for dirty vests, begged a franc and tried to rifle Abraham's tool bag.

"Bakshees, bwanah?"

Abraham slapped one, playfully around the face and kicked the other's arse.

"Y' thievin'! M' tell y' mam on you!"

And one day I'll teach you to read and write. Give you a bit of dignity, just see if I don't!

Holy-hell, but the game was on!

Herbert Brewer's Dirty Little Secret

Abraham had two more bombs to plant. One for the Monument to the Unknown Rapist, as Bundawa's Civil War Memorial was commonly called. The other, to blow the gates right off the Presidential Palace.

Beyond the market, Abraham paused for a moment to get back into character.

Through Whitehall Terrace, Abraham cut across the Presidential lawn and marched right up to the military booth designed to protect the Leopold Avenue approach from attack by small groups of unarmed house-wives.

Two soldiers manned the booth around the clock.

"Halt, man! Why be to?"

"M' telephone man! M' be settin' y' relay into government settin's. ' Be all accordin' t' reg'lation. Y' m's 'ave m' paperwork?"

"Nah! We b'w'nt 'eard nothin'!"

Abraham hustled his way into the booth and opened the service box beneath the counter.

"M' Lor'! Let m'ave a look! Ooh me Lor'! J' fuckin' cobweb like a blanket! Give me a minute. Put tha' fuckin' stool here, man."

"Y' want a drink?"

"Y've rum?"

"Yeah, fuck!"

"M' be a minute. N' more. How th' phone soun'?"

Spade Braithwaite

One of the soldiers picked up the ancient handset and cranked the booster

"Wait. Hello? Hello? Command Centre One? Y'm be b'wiss'n't Harvey an' Cedric, on Leopold Avenue. Y'm be hearin' it all good? Okay. T'anks."

"What be say?"

"The phone's good as ever! Wha' be to?"

"M' be updatin' the network f' the inclusion o' internet. M' not tell y' the whole lot, but Silus Mantè wantin' to order Levi-Straus copper riveted pants, online. It all hush-hush."

"W' bein' the soul' of discretion! Internet? M' we be getting' internet here, in m' booth?"

"M' see n' reason why not. M' cousin be sellin' y' a good Wamaculum 80 processor, with keyboard and monitor f' three thousand franc."

"T'anks, anyway. Hurry up an' be from!"

"M' be rushin! M' be goin' now. T'anks boy. An' remember, y'nam be sayin' stuff!"

"M' be the secretist man in the squad. M' hardly tell anyone!"

"That's the spirit!

Abraham closed the box, put his tools away and wiped the cobwebs from his hands.

"It all good now. M' be headin' on. The kitchens o' the Assembly be needin' internet so that Silus can e-mail his chef w' orders. M' see ya. Bwye!"

"Bwye! Take i' easy, man."

Herbert Brewer's Dirty Little Secret

Abraham walked away and tried not to smile too much. It was all too easy.

The Bantu Nation would phone in a warning, the area would be cleared and Abraham would enjoy the pleasure of detonating this one himself.

When he was fifty yards away one of the soldiers opened the service box to have a look at their new internet connection.

"It ain't connected to nothin'! It jus' be sittin' there, behin' all the wires an' stuff. With a wire danglin' out, no' screwed into anywhere!"

"J' reckon it worth money?"

"Prob'ly."

The two soldiers paused to consider the options.

"W' never sign nothin'. It his word against ours."

"M' cousin peddle car aerials 'n stuff. Maybe m' take it there after work 'n see if he can sell it."

"Good thinkin'."

John Shutu and his deputies called in at the Jamaa Company works cafeteria on their way upcountry.

Maintenance and Engineering worked Sundays so the cafeteria opened with a skeleton staff.

As soon as John walked in, the half dozen customers, spread throughout the dining area, quickly finished their meals and cleared up.

Spade Braithwaite

Everyone knew what John Shutu and his deputies had been up to lately.

The cafeteria manager bustled out to greet them, terrified that he, himself might be the subject of today's raid.

"John! Nice t' see ya! Why be to, with y' boys, of a Sunday?"

"M've got a final clue as to the whereabouts o' them scoundrels that's been causin' all de trouble! We fin'lly goin' upcountry t' sort-out them acquereur bastards, once an' f'r all!"

It was true. Under mounting pressure from Kinaida, John Shutu had decided that the time had come for him to kill all the rebels and get back to policing. It was a shame, but what could a poor, rural policeman do?

The cafeteria manager crossed himself and thanked god.

"Thank god! Thank god y' gonna sort it out! M' 'ave some't special. An' English pork pie! One o' engineers order a box 'n 'em, an' w' be findin' a few gone stray. English all mad for it! 'Im say it a delicacy, in England!"

"Bring it on! An' eight breakfas'. D' full monty!"

"Comin' up!"

John was sorry to have to end the civil strife. It' had been a hell of a good time and, in some ways, he was disappointed that he'd survived. Maybe the magic wasn't in him.

The cafeteria manager and a kitchen-boy came straight back out with eight frosted mugs of Belgian lager and a pork pie on a china plate.

Herbert Brewer's Dirty Little Secret

Managing the cafeteria was obviously a very good number. John made a mental note to come back and visit the manager as soon as an opportunity presented itself.

"Thank y', m' forget y' name?"

"Carlo! M' Carlo, sir. Thank you very much. Enjoy y' pie, sir."

The moment John left Carlo intended to run home, dig up his passport and his assets and be on the next bus to Kinaida International Airport.

"What it all wrapped in? Cardboard?"

"That pastry, sir. That how the English like it."

"Hmm...,"

John took a big bite, expecting the crust to melt in his mouth but it didn't. If fact, if it had been cardboard, it might have tasted better.

He opened his mouth to roar at the manager and sucked a big lump of impact-tested, English, suet-crust pastry deep into his oesophagus.

Anger, never far from John's emotions, erupted inside him with terrifying violence.

He tried to shout obscenities but nothing would come without air.

Gun! Where was his fucking gun?

He slapped the spot on his belt where it would be if he hadn't left it in the car.

No gun!

Spade Braithwaite

He kicked the table over and tried desperately to breathe.

Seven deputies stood and watched, more surprised than worried.

The cafeteria manager held his face in absolute horror.

For five, full minutes, John thrashed and wretched and spasmed on the floor until he realised that, this time, ferocity wasn't going to save him .

Calm! Got to be calm. Take a deep…, Fuck! Just, cough it out, and then kill that fucking Carlo! Take a deep…,

It was going to kill him. Good ol' John Shutu, heir to the Devil himself, was going to be killed by a fuckin' English delicacy! What kind of a death was that, for people to write songs about? It couldn't happen like this.

John picked up a butter knife and stabbed the manager in the throat before sinking to his knees and blacking out.

For a full five minutes no one spoke.

"What, 'im all dead?"

One of the deputies felt for a pulse. He'd never really known where to look for a pulse but John's uncharacteristic silence told everyone that John was dead.

"Yeah, 'im dead!"

The cafeteria manager had passed out and died, clawing at the door of the ladies' toilet.

"M' reckon tha' maybe why Mohammed recommend agains' eatin' pork!"

"Could be."

Herbert Brewer's Dirty Little Secret

"What now?"

"Dunno."

"M'either. M' reckon, after breakfas', w' go an' see where he kep' his money."

"M' reckon."

"Wha' 'bout they rebel?"

"Fuckit!"

"Yeah, fuckit all! Live 'n let live, m' say!"

"Yeah, boy! M' think 'e put money in m' Station, somewhere!"

"All i' favour o' havin' a look in d' Station, 'n blamin' it o' rebel? Carried! Game on!"

(Author's note: Another scene with a lot of one-off characters that you'll probably never hear of again. If you're finding it hard-work then you're trying too hard.)

Francis Van Der Schmee examined the three items in front of him carefully.

He got a lot of valuable loot from the children, very cheaply, because they rarely knew what it was that they'd stolen. This time, Francis himself was stumped.

"Why y' say it come fro'?"

"We foun' it!"

"Foun' it, fuck!"

Three, grey steel boxes the size of transistor radios. Each, with a pokey, little, electrical gizmo fitted into the top and an unconnected wire dangling out of the side.

Spade Braithwaite

The yellow lettering didn't give any clues. Maybe the electrical bit had something written on it. Francis reached for his pliers and then thought better. Maybe they were computers that would break if he pulled the chip out. Maybe this was what computers looked like.

"Tell m' where i' stole, 'n I migh' be wantin' some!"

"W' no' stole anyt'in'! W' follow a man 'n he lef' 'em all over town!"

"Li' Santa Claus! M' n' think!"

"Hones'! 'im lef' one insi' a man-hole on d' Rue D' Independence. 'im lef' one wedge behin' f' bill-boar' bwye John Lennon Circle! M' reckon mus' be a mad-man, 'r somet'in'!"

"Wha' y' reckon i' be?"

"M' naa! M' reckon it cos' money!"

"Fifty franc."

"Each?"

"Fuck! Fifty franc f' three."

"Fuck y'all! It be state o' art, electronic wonderment!"

"Y' tell m' wha' t'is, an' I'll tell y' it worth more money! Fifty franc, yes, o' naa?"

"Give it! Y' fuck! Y' want more, if we fin' 'em?"

"Nex' week, maybe."

Bantu Nation younger brothers, Dominic and Elijah sat on the pavement outside the Kinaida Hilton and tried desperately to think in real-time.

Herbert Brewer's Dirty Little Secret

"What time is it?"

It had to be past lunchtime. Elijah was hungry enough to eat street food.

Dominic stared at the reflections coruscating off an office window and tried to remember what he'd been meaning to ask.

"Didn't we buy a bottle?"

"Here, man."

Elijah passed the bottle to Dominic and thought some more about food.

"Weren't we going to lunch somewhere?"

Oh, fuck! That was it! They were supposed to be touring Kinaida, pretending to be part of a group from Jamaica. It had been Abraham's idea. They had been trying to do something about their accents but there just happened to be a large party of Jamaican tourists arriving that day so it had been decided that younger brothers Dominic and Elijah would do better to tag along with the party and plant bombs wherever they got the chance. Abraham had given them two bombs.

The group from Jamaica had all turned out to be white businessmen, with Dominic and Elijah tagging along like pimps at a Mormon picnic. What a fuck-up.

It had been Elijah's idea to score some grass, just to prove their Caribbean credentials.

"Yeah, mon!"

Bombs. Oh man! Bombs!

"Where's the bag?!"

Spade Braithwaite

"We told her what we thought in that last place."

"No, man! The bag with the gear!"

"I got it in my shirt. I'm goin' to roll another one, as soon as my eyes stop twitchin'."

"No man! The bag that Abraham gave us! With the petards!"

"Wait a minute! Wait a minute. It's all coming back. We're supposed to be planting bombs! Where are they?"

"We had 'em in a bag! Where did we leave the bag?"

"Oh shit! I think I swapped it for the brandy."

"Did you tell 'em what they were?"

"I think I told 'em they were special, intercontinental, silent, laughing bombs, signed by Charlie Chaplin."

"Yeah, we swapped the bombs for a bottle of brandy. It was funny-as-fuck, at the time. What d' you think we should tell Abraham?"

"We planted them at the Museum and opposite the police headquarters! If some stupid fuck stole 'em, after we planted 'em, and blew himself up then it serves him right. D'you think we could smoke another one, and keep the story straight?"

"Don't see why not. Give me the fuckin' bottle! Man, I haven't laughed that much since I was a kid."

"Yeah, mon!"

"Don't! Don't get me started!"

"Yeah. Mon!"

"Don't, you fucker! My face is ready to fall apart from laughin'! Don't even go there again! What was the question?"

Herbert Brewer's Dirty Little Secret

"Yeah, mon!"

Chapter 16

The day arrived. Thursday, the day of the call-up.

At six thirty a.m., Prime Minister Dereck Cartright met General Aemon Mussbiere for the first time, in a secure conference room in the basement of the National Assembly Building.

Aemon brought three members of his Senior Staff, all of whom looked, to Dereck, more like tobacco-lobby attorneys than soldiers. Dereck ushered them in and shook their hands without comment.

Dereck's advisors, Ryan, Nobby and Barney-the-Minute-Man, all smiled without getting up.

Dereck opened the meeting with a minimum of ritual.

"Gentlemen! Thank you all for coming in so early. We've all got a busy day, I know. General, I'm pleased to meet you at last."

"Sir. Likewise. My guys, Cyril, Kevin and Geoff. All top-men, at your service."

"Lovely. Barney, can we get some drinks in 'ere? I'm fuckin' gaggin'. Drinks, gentlemen?"

"Bit early, maybe a vodka. Drink, boys?"

"Beer."

Spade Braithwaite

"Yeah, beer, please."

"Cheers."

"Cigar?"

"Cheers, mate."

"Good one!"

Against his better judgement, Dereck found himself liking General Mussbierre and his staff.

"Barney, get a couple o' cases and a bottle, and stuff, sent down. An' breakfast. Good lad! So, General, I've read the reports but can you tell me, yourself, what's goin' on today."

"Sir. The parameters of the mobilisation were all calculated by your new War Department. May I ask if they're represented here?"

Aemon studied Dereck's advisors, unsympathetically.

"The War Department are a bunch o' tossers! Don't ever tell 'em anythin' important."

"We'd arrived at that policy ourselves. Anyway, as per their notification from the War Department, fifteen hundred young men will be joinin' the army today. Five hundred from each of three towns, chosen by you. Pershing, Haipnath and Clausthowler-whatever-it-is. We've chartered six DC9's for the day. We fly in, identify 'em, tick 'em off and ship 'em back to Gunswale. They should all be arriving at Gunswale International between three and six this afternoon. We've borrowed some buses to ferry the boys to station Good News. They'll get a week's training before the British Royal Air Force flies 'em out to our camp in Bundawa, and then we repeat the process with fifteen hundred new recruits."

"You've got 'em all catered for, at Good News?"

"We have. I took the liberty of asking the War Office to include a note with their draught notices, telling 'em to bring a sleepin' bag, socks an' underwear and at least one change of clothes. Your Cabinet farmed out the food contract so we slapped a secrecy notice on it an' bought it back. Lucky for us, a restaurant that we do business with was closing three outlets, so we picked up the kitchens, dirt cheap. Our chefs 're lookin' forward to the challenge of feedin' the boys."

"What about in Bundawa?"

"Local caterers, under supervision. My boys tell me the food's top notch, very spicy and relatively wholesome. We're shippin' incidentals, booze an' toilet paper an' stuff, out every day, as per requirement."

Dereck was impressed. At last, he'd discovered the branch of Federal Government that functioned inside its budget without moaning.

"What trainin' are they going to get, in the week at Good News?"

"Very basic, basic trainin'. How the guns work. Appropriate behaviour. How to avoid situations when they're on the town. How to handle foreigners, should situations arise. Basically, how to stay ou' of mischief."

"Whad'ya think o' them rifles we got ya?"

Spade Braithwaite

"With all due respect, we had to loose 'em. I called in some favours an' kited our boys out with the real thing."

"I don't want any fightin'!"

"No more do we. But we felt that the local crew ought to appreciate that if there was any fightin', we'd be doin' it. We got the proper gear. We're goin' to try to organise a few outings, for the boys to shoot-up the jungle a bit. In safe areas, removed from any conflict."

"Good man!"

"Make some noise, 'ave a bit of fun. You can award some medals, if y' like."

"Lovely, Aemon! I'm glad you're in charge. It sounds like you've got a handle on the situation. Have you heard any rumours, out of Clausthowlersnauglerbogler?"

"Indeed we have. We heard that they all changed their names to try an' get out of it. Claust' is a funny ol' town. We don't 'ave one, single connection in Claust', so we sent a couple of operatives to reconnoitre, incognito."

"What've they found out?"

"Slightly less than we already knew. Cyril's headin' out there with the first plane, today. I'm not sure 'ow you want to proceed but we can be as heavy, or as gentle as you like."

"Sadly, I'm only an elected official. So, gently does it. Nobby, what's the official line?"

"Dereck, we've read their Charter half a dozen times, an' we don't see anything they can do. A Federal crime is a Federal crime. The warrants don't expire. They can change their names to Albert Einstein if they want to, but if they don't answer the draught then they're still "life-ers".

Barney reappeared, pushing his way backwards into the room, carrying a crate of Tiger beer, a bottle of Absolut and a stack of paper cups.

"Cheers Barney. I'll 'ave a bottle an' a shot. Pass it round. Cheers. So, their angle, we assume, is massive civil disobedience to provoke a confrontation, and then try to make the draught unworkable so that I'll have to negotiate an alternative to avoid humiliation. They know that the call-up's goin' to be in every paper in the country, so they know that we're goin' to want to play-down whatever it is that they're up to. That means that we can't shoot anybody. They must also know that I can declare an Emergency Situation and replace all federally appointed personnel."

"Who would that be?"

"Ryan?"

"The Federally appointed personnel are, give me a moment…, Chief of Police, Gary Crozier, Senior Court Magistrate, Judge Jacob Tethers, Defender of the Flag of Honour, William Letter, who, if he's still alive, is a hundred an' seventy four. We suspect that they just never bothered re-selecting that one. And, Highway Sheriff, also William Letter."

"You can replace the Chief of Police and the Senior Judge? That's interestin'."

"I might threaten to, but I wouldn't do it. Between you an' me, most of the statistics I quote every year come from Claust'. They run a pretty tight town. I'm actually quite sorry that we picked 'em f' this fuck-up. The fuckin' War Department figured that Claust' had such a low crime rate that they'd go along with it, no bother. Nobby, can we do anythin' about their postal service?"

"Sir, it is a federally regulated service. If there was evidence of serious mismanagement or hanky-panky then we could appoint an Acting Situation Controller, with authority senior to that of the Head Post-Master."

Dereck absently rolled up his ear lobe and tucked it into his ear.

"Might be worth thinkin' about…,"

Aemon stared into his paper cup and tapped it with a finger. Tiny ripples reciprocated through the spirit more quickly than they would in water. Something to do with surface-tension, someone had once told him. Aemon knew that it was a good brand of vodka but, quite honestly, he couldn't tell the difference. He'd always regarded good taste as a weakness.

"Mr Cartright, how would you feel about creating a Military Secret Service?"

Dereck shifted in his seat.

"F' what?"

"Security situations like this. An' anythin' else that you needed taken care of."

"I do my own dirty work. How much would it cost?"

Herbert Brewer's Dirty Little Secret

"I'm confident that it could generate its own provision, and turn a profit that we could all rely on, in our declining years."

"You want to create a security service, for dirty tricks, an' spyin', an' stuff?"

"Fuck-me no! We already have that covered."

"What do you want?"

"We'd like to put a man in every one of our foreign consulates. No questions asked. And we want to build an airport an' buy a few of our own planes, the comings an' goings of which would be a state secret."

"What's my angle?"

"You'd be in the Firm. On the inside. That would mean absolute, political security, and very large amounts of money, in different currencies."

Dereck contemplated absolute, political security and experienced a small blood-rush to the crotch. An hour too late for any practical purposes.

"D' you think that you can sort out whatever's goin' on in Claust'?"

"No problem. It's what we do."

"What about my boys, here?"

"They can be involved, under your supervision. Or they can leave the room now. Your call."

"I think I'll keep 'em. For the time bein'. Go on...,"

Spade Braithwaite

Meanwhile, in Clausthowlersnauglerbogler, first-shift was struggling to start the day. Third-shift was scoring gas station sandwiches on their way home. Second-shift was sleeping in.

Four hundred and sixty three of the most unlikely soldiers in the world had woken with the dawn and were feeding cats, changing their wills, spring-cleaning, writing to newspapers and all the other mysterious things that the aged and infirm do at unnatural hours of the morning.

Mama Jen slapped her alarm clock from the very depths of a righteous sleep.

"Fuck off!"

Eight minutes later, at six forty five. Left handed, without disturbing another muscle.

"Bloody thing!"

People sometimes assumed that Mamma Jen didn't need much sleep, because of her age. They were dead wrong.

Six fifty three.

"All right! I'm coming!"

Mamma Jen threw back her quilt and allowed the morning air onto her body, hoping that it would magically wake her up.

It didn't but, after a few minutes, she rolled off the bed and staggered into the shower.

It was going to be a busy day. Buses would begin picking up the recruits as soon as they'd finished taking children to school.

The first event of the day was a bingo breakfast at Snaugler High School gymnasium.

Herbert Brewer's Dirty Little Secret

Mamma Jen had considered ordering a taxi but had decided against it. It would be good to ride in the buses with everyone else.

God bless hot showers and strong coffee.

The radio weather forecaster informed her that it was going to be a hot, sticky one, with twenty percent chance of a late afternoon thunderstorm.

Mamma Jen opened her wardrobe door all the way. Dignified but cool. Not bright red. Not court-room grey. Cotton, off-white, short-sleeved dress with white sneakers. Big white hat. Perfect.

She laid them out on her sofa.

The note had said to bring, "socks and underwear and a change of clothes".

Mama Jen had a case of lingerie at the back of the wardrobe that hadn't seen daylight in long enough.

The note also said, "sleeping bag," but Mamma Jen wasn't sure if that meant a bed-roll or condoms.

Mama Jen slipped three, ancient prophylactics into her purse, just in case.

Then she made the bed, cleaned the kitchen and cleared her mind in preparation for half an hour of tai-chi on the roof.

The bus would be out front at ten past eight. At eighty three years old Mamma Jen enjoyed the sleep patterns of an eight year old but she had to be up and moving for at least an hour, in the morning, before she could think of taking a crap.

Spade Braithwaite

Old age was a trade. Your body lost all its hormones but that wasn't wholly, a bad thing.

Seven twenty two. Five minutes for Puccini and another coffee before she greeted the day.

In Scotland, they advise no man to say he's happy 'til he's six feet underground. Mamma Jen was confident that she was fairly happy.

Mayor Charles Andropolous wasn't completely unhappy.

Jane Charlotte, the recently divorced ex-wife of Stavros Andropolous had insisted on cooking him a vegetarian nudie-breakfast before she left. Tomatoes, mushrooms, toast and humus. Turkish coffee that would rot the teeth off an excavator bucket. Tantric-sex under the kitchen table. Lino-burns and crumbs up his arse.

There was a lot to be said for the holistic life-style.

Jane had finally dressed and left at quarter past eight, leaving Charles quarter of an hour for a hot shower and a large, holistic brandy.

At eight twenty eight, in blue jeans and a green sweater, Charles had walked to Gallipoli Street, sweeping the pavement with a borrowed white-stick. Scarcely able to see the pavement through his dark glasses.

The bus stopped opposite Sherwin Park at eight thirty six. Charles groped his way up the steps to the aisle.

"Good morning, citizens!"

"... to see the Wizard! The wonderful Wizard of Oz! If ever a Wiz of a Wiz there was, the Wizard of Oz, is one because, because, because, because, because...! Because of the wonderful things he does!"

Shirley Brown was at the back, bolt upright in a window seat, tweaking her sweater hem and smoothing out each of the five pleats in her skirt.

"Shirl'!"

"Charles."

"Paranoid schizophrenic?"

"Autistic."

"Good job!"

"Do you think they might give us a hard time?"

"Probably."

"Seriously?"

"What can they do? Every newspaper in the country's going to be watching the arrival at Gunswale. The last thing in the world they need is photographs of us spazies, rollin' off the plane to start our national service. They can't afford to take us to Gunswale."

"But they could take us somewhere else! And hold us! Technically, we're federal criminals!"

"No, technically we're not. We received call-up notices and we're co-operating fully. They don't have anywhere to take us. Whatever they do, they can't draught us. Be calm. If something unexpected happens, pretend that you were expecting it."

Spade Braithwaite

"I'm autistic, I'll throw a fit. I might even need restraining. Mind y'ur fingers or I'll bite 'em off!"

"Good one!"

"No one had better mess with me today. When were you born?"

"Twenty fifth of May, nineteen sixty two."

"That was a Thursday!"

"Saturday, but you were close. Who's going to win the Empire Derby?"

"I'm autistic, not bloody psychic! Don't mess with me today!"

Gary had taken the day off work. He had an idea that he was going to be the very first person that the army tried to contact when draughtees started reporting, so he had booked a vacation day just to make things a little bit more difficult for them.

At nine thirty Bo-Bae had caught him rubbing himself in the shower. Idly soaping a semi- erection with no bubbles anywhere else on him.

It had taken half an hour to prove that he had been thinking only of her and he couldn't imagine a better way to use thirty minutes, on his day off, in the shower.

At ten thirty he called in at the office to make sure that everything was running smoothly.

"Janet. How's everything?"

"Gary! You're out today! It says so on my calendar. What do you want, damn you?"

Herbert Brewer's Dirty Little Secret

"My, but you're looking particularly attractive today, although I have eyes for no one except my lovely young wife. What's going on?"

"Everything's good. No trouble with any of the buses. The bingo's going well. Constable Fitzroy wants to know if he can keep the exercise bike, even though he's on duty and it was a complimentary bingo-card."

"Why do we have to hire them all? Can't they get jobs anywhere else? What else?"

"Nothing. It's like a criminal armistice. Two thirds of officers on duty and not so much as a squawk over the radios."

"An average Thursday. How are our lovely guests doing?"

"Al Pheobe keeps throwing tantrums, wanting to know why he can't have his underwear."

"I thought I left a note for you to take out of petty cash for socks an' underwear, an sleeping bags for them?"

"You did. Fitzroy bought them a six-pack of socks and Y-fronts, and a sleeping bag each, from the Army Surplus. Al keeps saying that he's spent a fortune on underwear, over the years, and if he's going to join the army then he needs it now more than ever."

"Did you suggest to Fitzroy that he go over to the Pheobe's place an' pick up their underwear?"

"I did."

"What did he say?"

"You can imagine."

Spade Braithwaite

"I wish I'd been here to see it. I can't ask a bloke to do something that I wouldn't do myself. Did Josh get his stuff sorted out?"

"Andy Bomar took him home last night. Josh should've caught the bus this morning with everyone else. He's a nice lad, he really is."

"I know. I'd love to see you naked. Anything else that really needs my attention?"

"I heard that! Go home, you sad pervert!"

"Who are you calling, "sad"?"

"Where's Jim? You know that that's the first thing they're going to ask."

"A father's legal obligations towards his progeny disappear as soon as they leave school. I know not, and less do I care! He's with his mate Lizzy, at her aunt's place on the Juno estate, well out of the way."

"Sounds good. Now go home, and stay out of mischief."

"Okay, boss. See you tomorrow."

"Just go! Go on! See you tomorrow."

At Clausthowlersnauglerbogler General Infirmary, Intern Daniel Weatherby was adding the final touches to the corpse of Herbert Brewer, née Reuben Schmetz, before it was sent to answer its patriotic destiny.

Commonly, in the health industry interns tended to avoid morticiary but Daniel found it strangely therapeutic.

Herbert Brewer's Dirty Little Secret

The usual extent of his involvement was sowing the heads back onto motorcyclists and tidying-up cadavers before they were sent home, so Reuben was a rare treat. It was only a shame that it already looked perfectly ghoulish, before Daniel had even touched it.

When the ambulance had brought it in, dead for less than twenty minutes, it had already contracted into a hunch that looked like the later stages of sun-ripened rigor-mortis. With the eyes rolled back and the mouth frozen in a hideous grin.

All Daniel had needed to do had been to dress him and put a little powder on his cheeks.

Daniel wondered about the erection. Reuban had died of a heart attack, shortly after ejaculating. Daniel would have supposed that it would have contracted with the loss of blood pressure but, apparently not. Cause for hope in an unsure world.

"Beautiful! Beautiful."

Daniel pinned the call-up notice to its lapel and arranged its hands so that it clutched the bag containing its change of clothes and its sleeping bag.

"Good to go!"

"Morbid fucker!"

The driver and an orderly guided the gurney down the ramp to the morticiary-vehicle.

"I'll want to know all about it when you get back!"

Spade Braithwaite

The driver and the orderly paused to scowl, incredulously at each other.

"Morbid fucker!"

"Yeah!"

Two hours out of Gunswale, thirty minutes from Clausthowlersnauglerbogler, Cyril was summoned to the flight cockpit for a radio briefing from Camp Good-News.

The stewardess introduced him to the flight crew and gave him another beer.

"Cheers love! What do I do?"

"You can put the head-set on, if it's secret. Or else it's on speaker-phone. Press this button when you want to speak."

"Lovely. Gov'ner?! Are y' there?"

Aemon crackled through, as clear as spring-time.

"Cyril?"

"Gov'ner! What's up?"

"We've finally got some intelligence reports from Claust'. We've changed the plan, ever so slightly. 'Ave you got your lap-top there?"

"Yeah boss. Always."

"Plug it into the mike-jack an' download. Code-five cipher programme. It'll tell you the crack."

"Everything alright?"

"Lovely! New orders of operation. Nothin' serious. What're the hostesses like?"

Herbert Brewer's Dirty Little Secret

"Gorgeous!"

"She sounds like a cutie! Free booze?"

"We're getting' our money's worth!"

"Top-man! "Ave a read, an' proceed as per. Over an' out."

"Sure thing, boss."

Cyril plugged his lap-top into the mike-jack and downloaded.

Two minutes later, back in his seat with a fresh beer, he matched the report against code-five cipher programme and let the random characters transform themselves into sentences.

They read:

Category F – Security. SECRET!
12:50 hours, 19th May
General A. Mussbiere revising orders to Colonel Cyril Neff.
Latest intelligence from Clausthowler –whatever-the-fuck-it's-called.

We've finally heard from our blokes in the field. They confirm that you can expect five hundred non-serviceables to report for the draught. Re-affirm, do not bring non-serviceable personnel back to Gunswale. However, after extensive attempts to contact local, criminal structure, we are lead to believe that the big-boss is an elderly Asian lady, name of Mamma Jen, likely to be among non-serviceable draughtees. We have dispatched a courtesy jet to be there before you.

Spade Braithwaite

IMPORTANT! Identify Mamma Jen and facilitate her return to Gunswale on courtesy jet. DO NOT instigate confrontation. Be all things, pleasant and charming.

Also, heard a rumour that Claust' intends to empty their jails into the army. Keep an eye out for any obvious likely-lads and bring them along too.

Play it by ear. Have fun. Keep us informed. Take it easy.

The Governor

Chapter 17

Senior Career Officer Laurence French, reluctantly representing the National Office of Domestic Security, was the first to arrive at the airport.

He got there at five minutes to nine, ten minutes ahead of the bus that brought the check-in staff, air-traffic-controllers, security personnel, concession vendor and cleaning lady.

Laurence followed the signposts into, "International Long Stay Parking", and parked. "International Long Stay Parking",

Herbert Brewer's Dirty Little Secret

contained a total of nine parking spaces, fifty yards from the main terminal building. There were no other cars.

A set of doors opened automatically as Laurence approached the terminal.

The team of Dutch architects that had designed the airport in nineteen seventy seven hadn't even considered putting locks on the doors and, in the twenty five years since, no one had found an easy way of switching the climate control off at night.

If Laurence had been a stranger to Claust', or if he hadn't been up till one in the morning, drinking beer and discussing the draught with Gary Crozier then he might have thought he'd arrived on the wrong day, at the wrong time.

The toilets at Clausthowlersnauglerbogler International Airport rivalled the best of the very best. Laurence had never been abroad but he'd seen enough James Bond movies to know that the first thing international jet-setters craved after a long flight was a shave and a change of turtle-neck sweater.

Laurence made a mental note to bring a turtle-neck sweater if he ever flew into Claust'.

The airport-staff bus arrived at five past nine. The airport didn't usually open at all on Thursdays but today was a special day. Three charter flights were expected from Gunswale. Two DC9's for the call-up and one mysterious lear-jet. Clausthowlersnauglerbogler International Airport had never received a passenger charter flight before. The Order of the Knights of Queen Fatima had booked one, once, for a World Cup soccer qualifier in Gunswale but the travel agent had struck a deal and crammed them into the mail-plane for half the price.

Amsarnie had been knocked out of the World Cup by Bangladesh. No one had chartered a plane since.

Laurence was nosing around the VIP lounge when he heard the staff arrive. Everybody going straight to their part-time positions.

Mrs Sidcup, the cleaning lady came into the lounge for her trolley of tools.

"Good morning."

"Yaaghh!!"

Mrs Sidcup clean-jumped a yard into the air and two yards backwards. She landed, sobbing like an evangelist, clutching a new light-bulb changer and her badly shaken heart.

"Bloody Nora! Who the bloody hell are y'?! Scarin' old ladies! Get out of 'ere, go on! Jesus Christ!"

"I'm sorry! I was just havin a look."

"Took ten years of m' bloody life, is what you did! Go on! Get ou' of here. Sneakin' around scarin' people! Go on!"

Laurence apologised again and went looking for the airport manager.

At ten forty seven a lear-jet radioed its approach to Clausthowlersnauglerbogler International Airport.

Herbert Brewer's Dirty Little Secret

"Clausthowlersnauglerbogler ground control. Alpha – Mike Romeo Mike Romeo. Heading two niner three. Requesting permission to join Clausthowler' circuit for final descent."

"Claust' control. Alpha – Mike Romeo Mike Romeo, wherefore art thou, Mike Romeo?"

"Repeat?!"

"Just messin' with y'. Yeah, come on in. Runway zero niner."

"Anticipated arrival seven minutes. How many ahead?"

"Don't be a wise-arse, Mike Romeo. Anytime you're ready."

"Roger, Clausthowlersnauglerbogler. Mike Romeo turning base-leg. Clear for finals?"

"Yeah."

"Clear for finals?"

"Yeah-per!"

"You guys are somethin'! See you in a few minutes."

The first of the draught coaches arrived at the airport at twelve ten. Mamma Jen was the twelfth person off the bus. Colonel Cyril Neff was waiting for her.

"Senõra Herbert Brewer!"

"Si!"

"Mamma Jen?"

"Perhaps, who wants to know?"

"Colonel Neff, first class, at your service. Would you care to follow me. It's not a bust. More of a peace mission. I guarantee your personal safety and well-being. I trust that you're not armed?"

"Young man, you do me a compliment."

"Thank you. We've cleared the VIP Lounge for a few hours. I assume that you have people nearby that you would want present at any negotiations?"

"Indeed I have. Messieurs Herbert Brewer and Herbert Brewer. No names, no pack-drill. I believe they're on the next bus."

"Bring 'em on."

"And, five hundred recruits, turning up as instructed."

Sixty other unsteady citizens struggled to alight the first bus. Mamma Jen coached them into a group.

"Ladies! Gentlemen! We have an Indian lunch booked at twelve thirty in the observation lounge! I have been invited to negotiations at the highest level. Stick with the game plan, don't tell anyone anything and we'll have this debacle wrapped up before the weekend. Bingo or bust!"

Colonel Cyril Neff watched them clambering off the bus and was reminded of a film he'd once seen about the liberation of Auschwitz.

"Mama Jen, I have to tell you that you're about the damnedest operator that I've ever dealt-with. Full marks for style. I think we can call a truce, for now. Get y'r crew and we'll go."

Herbert Brewer's Dirty Little Secret

After thirty seven verses of the song, "The Lady of Nantucket.", Charles was ready to get off the bus.

He retrieved his cane from the rack and stood in the aisle to exit.

Old people moved so slowly. Nothing to do with infirmity, they just seemed happy where they were. Chatting and swapping grand-child photos.

"Okay people, seven more buses after this one! We've got a lovely lunch for you! Move along the bus, please!"

Shirley Brown was right behind him.

"Excuse me! Is there a toilet?!"

Seventy pensioners snapped to attention and filed, smartly out the door.

"Shirley! How did you do that?"

"Trick of the trade. Old people always need to pee. You just have to remind them, sometimes."

"You live and you learn. Well done!"

The bus let them off them right outside the main terminal doors. International Arrivals and Departures, Maximum Stay - Twelve Minutes.

Jenny Won was waiting. With her was a man in expensively modest, casual clothes, late thirties, with a comfortably athletic smile. Charles guessed him to be an executive-level, serious hard-case. A man to be taken seriously.

"Herbert! And Herbert!"

"Herbert."

Spade Braithwaite

"This is Colonel, First Class, Cyril Neff, representing the Military."

"Colonel Neff!"

Charles shook his hand firmly enough to convey security. Not so firmly as to betray wariness.

Colonel Cyril Neff reciprocated the gesture with a slight bow.

"Mister Brewer! And Mizz Brewer. I'm very pleased to meet you. I hope that we might be able to work together. If you'd like to follow me to the VIP lounge, we have time for a cocktail before we fly back to Gunswale. I think we've booked you in at the Paradigm, but if you would prefer somewhere else then I'm sure that we can accommodate you."

Mamma Jen presented Cyril with her luggage and led the way.

"Colonel Neff. I'm sure that the Paradigm will be fine. I don't know about anyone else, but I'm about ready for a bloody-big whiskey."

Cyril chuckled and shook his head.

"You've got a lot o' class, Mamma Jen! Maybe I'll come an' work for you!"

Senior Career Officer, Laurence French had practised the phone call for four days. Charles had coached him on pauses, emphasis and an appropriate amount of indignancy.

Herbert Brewer's Dirty Little Secret

Laurence made the phone call from the Airport Manager's office. Sam Snelly-Snell, the Airport Manager had shown Laurence how to use the phone before he went home.

Hash-nine-three to unlock it. Nine for an outside line. Area code one-seven-three-seven. Exchange two-one-five. Local number five-zero-double two.

"National Office of Domestic Security! For an up-to-the-minute media briefing, press one! For information on specific...,"

"Extension one eighteen, please."

"Hold on! Give me a minute. One eighteen, y' say?"

"Thank you."

"Extension one eighteen. Puttin' y' through... now, there we are! Have a nice day!"

"Thank you."

Three rings.

"Office of Domestic Security! Mellisa speaking!"

"Mellissa, its Lozzer here. Clausthowlersnauglerbogler. Something terrible's happening! Everythin' was goin' great, but now there's a whole load o' spazzies turned up f' the draught! They all swear-blind that they got the call-up notices in the mail! They're all cripples, an' old bastards, an' every type o' freak you can imagine!"

"Hold on Lozzer! Don't get y' shreddies in a fankle! I was told you might call. I'm transferring you to the Office of the Inland. Hold on...!"

Spade Braithwaite

"Office of the Inland Attorney. Samuel…, Samuel Gwu-wirth-ji's office. How can we help you?"

"It's the call from Clausthowlersnauglerbogler that we were expectin'."

"Put it through."

One ring.

"Yes!"

"Mr G., the call from Claust' that you've been waiting for."

"Got it! Hello! Is that Mr French? Samuel Guarthje here. Inland Attorney. What's going on?"

"Mr Gwor-earth-joy. Laurence French here. It's all gone nasty! I've been officiating the call-up, in Claust', and everythin' was goin' well. All the school-leavers seemed happy enough about it, and I interviewed everybody else on the register in previous years. So it all seemed good, but the papers must have got mixed up at the Post Office, or somethin'. I've got bus-loads of thalid's an' grannies turnin' up, thinkin' they're in the army!"

Samuel smiled to himself. Laurence French was obviously involved in the scam over the top of his boots. That was good to know.

"Oh my God! How do you think this happened?"

"Christ knows! The army's turnin' them away. Not even sendin' them to Gunswale for processin'."

"I must tell you, Laurence, that we heard a rumour about this, and I spoke to Mr Cartright himself. As of now, you are the

Herbert Brewer's Dirty Little Secret

Official Federal Emergency Governor of Clausthowlersnauglerbogler!"

That wasn't supposed to happen. Charles hadn't coached him for that.

"Do what?"

"I have Mr Cartright's signature on a directive ordering that, in the event of a problem in the process, you were to be appointed Emergency Governor, with powers superior to all other Federal employees in Claust'."

"Wait a minute. You're not supposed to say that. What do you want me to do?"

"Put a bit of stick about! Kick arse! Get it sorted!"

"Okay..., who are the Federal employees in Claust'?"

"Chief of Police...,"

"Gary Crozier."

"And Senior Magistrate, Judge Jacob Tethers."

"I'm a Career Officer! I do the Registration every year because it's a formality. I don't do Emergencies!"

"You do now! Dereck Cartright signed the papers himself. We all have to adapt, in wartime. I'm sure you'll have it sorted out in no-time."

"Can I book a room at the Blandford?"

"Whatever it takes."

"What do you reckon I should do?"

(Kiss your pension goodbye, for starters.)

Spade Braithwaite

"I've taken the liberty of appointing an advisor for you. A trouble-shooter. She'll be arriving tomorrow, at ten thirty six, on whatever plane gets in at that time. Miss Alison Dawa, if you could arrange to have her picked up. She'll help you get to the root of the matter. I suggest that you find out why the Post Office delivered all the notices to the wrong people. If you find any evidence of prevarication, fire everybody and re-hire from scratch."

"Hire an entire postal system?! In a town like Claust'?! Jesus wept! Then what, declare myself Emperor?!"

"This is a wonderful opportunity for you! Sort it out and you'll practically be able to name your own Quasi-Autonomous Fact Finding Mission. Huge pensions!"

"You're tellin' me I'm fucked, aren't you!"

"Basically. But that's politics! Get it sorted within the week and you'll be a Social Service legend! Otherwise...,"

"You're a fuckin' piece of work! You really are. Thanks, buddy!"

"I wish you luck. I really do. Goodbye."

"You greasy, little..."

Samuel pressed the button to disconnect.

It was amusing to deal with provincial staff, every once in a while. Not too often.

Samuel pressed another button to speak to his new secretary.

"Miss...,"

"Siva Amritanandaprakesh. How may I help you?"

"Miss… Siva. Could you have a look in my rotodex, find the number for Charley Weber, call him and tell him I'll meet him for lunch at the Fat Ox in Wheat Street at one thirty. Thank you."

"Excuse me, sir, there's nothing in your rotodex under Weber."

"Look under, 'N', for National Clarion. Or, 'P' for Press Leaks."

"Got him! 'N', for newspaper!"

"Good girl! Let me know that you've sorted it. Thank you."

"Thank you, sir."

Joshua Matenach was last off the last bus. With his spare underwear, change of clothes and sleeping bag in an Italian military ruck-sack, he imagined himself to be Clint Eastwood, the Man with No Name. Or, more accurately, the Man with Exactly the Same Name as Everybody Else.

The driver was struggling to clear old people out the way to retrieve half-dozen oversize suit-cases from the luggage lockers.

"It says I 'ave to 'ave m' thermals, and m' sleepin' bag. It says!"

The driver shook his head, almost patiently,

"They're not takin' y'! You'll be back on the bus in an hour! Get out the way! I told you to line up outside the terminal! Over there! Jesus Christ!"

Spade Braithwaite

Josh scratched his chin, where stubble would have been if he hadn't just shaved, and ambled past the scattered queue towards the terminal.

A sign on the terminal door informed Josh that the airport was a smoke free zone. With exaggerated sloth he pulled a packet of Kempdown non-filters from his shirt pocket, tapped one out and sparked-up from a plastic lighter.

Sensors caught the movement and opened the terminal doors.

Josh took a long drag and squinted distantly towards the freight lock-ups on the eastern edge of the airport perimeter.

The doors stayed open. Conditioned air spilling into the atmosphere. He sucked in a quick lungful and flicked the rest of the cigarette into a gully pot.

As he entered an old man took his place to smoke a cigar, keeping the doors open behind him.

A big sign made of blue letters printed on white vinyl welcomed soldiers and directed them to sign-in at Boarding Gate One. A smaller paper notice informed non-soldiers not to bother, but to go directly to their Indian Lunch in the observation lounge, second floor.

Josh had been to the airport only once before when he was twelve. It had seemed terrifyingly chaotic back then.

Being Clint Eastwood was a good defence against terrifying chaos.

Herbert Brewer's Dirty Little Secret

Josh scanned the room without looking directly at anything. There were big signs everywhere, informing people where things were. Boarding Gates One through Three, (Domestic Departures), were signposted down a wide corridor. Josh pictured a gate with a latch and tried to equate it with airports that he'd seen in films.

Fifty yards down a big, clean, white tiled walkway, Gate One was actually just a big room with seats and a shop counter blocking doors that led onto the airfield.

Two men sat near the door with their backs to Josh. Two other men stood at ease behind the counter.

The older of the two standing men opened a big ledger, somewhere near the middle and sighed.

"Good morning, sir!"

"Hello. Is this were I join the army?"

"It certainly is. May I ask your name?"

"Ughmm…, Herbert Brewer."

The seated men turned to give Josh two thumbs-up. Fat, leery, scary-lookin' bastards with Cheshire-cat grins. Josh recognised them from the other cells at the police station.

"Of course it is. National Identification number?"

"No names, no pack-drill. I'm sorry, I'm not allowed to tell you."

"You will be required to later, if you want to stay in the army. But I won't push it, here. Three, so far. Any idea how many we can expect, all together?"

Spade Braithwaite

"No. Sorry mate. I've been…, I've been on vacation for a couple o' weeks so I don't know what's goin' on."

"' Course you 'ave. I think we might as well get on the plane an' fuck off."

Two ambulance drivers followed Josh into the room pushing a gurney bearing a grotesquely contorted corpse.

"Herbert Brewer! Here f' the call up. Where d'y' wan' 'im?"

The older soldier shook his head and smiled.

"Go on! Let's 'ave a look!"

The ambulance drivers wheeled Reuben to the counter for inspection, trying not to smirk.

The five other men in the room stared at Reuben's erection with quiet awe.

"So what did he die of? I'll do 'alf a line!"

The drivers gave Reuben his minute and then turned him around to leave. The soldier stopped them with a bark.

"Name?"

"Wha'? Herbert Brewer. We told you!"

"National Identification Number?"

"Phhh! Best ask 'im."

"Bring 'im round to the doors. We're takin' 'im!"

"What?"

"I said, we're takin' 'im! Thank you gents! Good bye."

"You're takin' 'im?!"

"He's been called up. He's goin'. Thank you again, gents. Good Bye."

Herbert Brewer's Dirty Little Secret

Huey Pheobe had controlled his excitement for too long.

"I'll carry him!"

"Shut up! An' sit down. I don't know why you two where in the Nick, but it creeps me out, thinkin' about it. Leave 'im here. We'll take 'im. Good bye. Right! Let's get back on the fuckin' plane!"

"Is he freight, or a passenger?"

"Passenger, economy class, non-smokin'. Book 'im a kosher meal. We're goin'. I've 'ad enough. Come on! Let's go!"

"You're really takin' him?!"

"You've got a lot to learn about the army, boy. He's comin'."

What the hell. The Gov'ner would get a laugh out of it. And a few other people.

At one thirty five, Samuel Guarthje, Inland Attorney entered the public bar of the Fat Ox on Wheat Street.

With three national newspaper offices within two hundred yards, the Fat Ox steadfastly refused to redeem Luncheon Vouchers for alcohol. Samuel was confident that Charlie Weber would be able to find it and that no other journalists would be there.

Charlie Weber already had three, "Entertainment Expense", receipts in front of him when Samuel found him in the lower Public Bar.

"Chas! Mate!"

"Sammy! Lager? Two lagers, an' two large shots of tequila."

Spade Braithwaite

"Game on, boy! Please Miss, put it all on my bill, Thank you."

"Good boy, Sammy. So what's the scoop?"

"Charles! The strangest thing has happened!"

"Doesn't it always!"

"No, seriously! You know about the draught? Fifteen hundred kids from Pershing, Haipnath and Clausthowlersnauglerbogler?"

"I must admit I've heard something about it."

"Well, Claust' are avoiding it! They've changed everybody's names to Herbert Brewer, who was their only real politician, and they're not answering the draught."

"They're bunking out?"

"They're sending the wrong people. Old age pensioners and cripples."

"That's a Federal crime! It's all worked out by National Identification Number. What's the Government going to do?"

"We've appointed a Federal Emergency Governor, with all the authority he needs to sort it out. I have to admit that I foresee a fuck-up that might very well bring Dereck Cartright's Premiership to an undignified end."

"Why?"

"It's about the only chance that the opposition stand of beating Dereck. When it all goes nasty, I'll call for a vote of confidence that will be un-forthcoming. The opposition 'll take over for eight months until we precipitate another vote of confidence and call another General Election. I wouldn't be surprised if the party regained power with one of us in charge."

"Any speculation who the runners might be?"

"Mr Bernard Kent, the Foreign Advocate, has done a fine job, with a poor grasp of domestic economics and a wife that yearns for her roots on the trailer-park."

"Go on…,"

"Charles Mintion, in the Cabinet Office, has dreams of high office, but he has a closer-than-passing aquaintenship with the three-dollar-bill, if you know what I'm saying?"

"Queer as a three-bob note. Got'ya! So who do you predict, for the top job?"

"That's a difficult question! There are so many worthy candidates. And I, myself, would be honoured to accept the challenge…, should it be suggested. God knows I've got the background."

"Got'ya! Would I be on the inside, if we make it happen?"

"Charles! You insult me! My press office would be accessible to all the media. Any secrets that leaked themselves to yourself would be very regrettable, but inevitable. "

"Game on! How about, "Samuel Guarthje's Crusade against Constitutional Crisis!"?"

"I think that it might be a bit early for headlines. But if you could include my name amongst some conservative reservations about the call-up, it couldn't do any harm."

"Job done! How about, "Mr 'G',s Secret Call-Up Fear!"."

Spade Braithwaite

"No."

""Sammy's Soldier Locker Shocker!"?"

"No."

""Clausthowlersnaugler-bugger-the-rest-of-us!"?"

"Getting better. Let me know before you go to copy. Would you care for another drink?"

"Does the Dalai Llama smile a lot? Go on, boy, you know it makes sense. How about, "Cabinet Back-Room Generals Anticipate Disaster! "."

"Good enough. Mention me in paragraph three."

"Name?!"

"Longdon, Charles David."

"National Identification Number?!"

"Wait a minute...,"

The boy scrambled in his pockets, terrified.

"Here it is! Oh three seven, dash, forty one, dash...,"

Sergeant Gil Kelly watched the exchange with mixed feelings.

The boy identified himself to the satisfaction of the reception party, hoisted his bag and climbed onto the bus. Bus number five. Gil's bus.

Gil had driven a bus for the first time only three days before. For half an hour.

Now he watched while he waited to shuttle his first load back to Good-News.

"Name?!"

Herbert Brewer's Dirty Little Secret

"Herbert Brewer."

"National Identification Number?!"

"Sorry mate. No names, no pack drill."

The boy smiled, not provocatively but warmly.

Gil's attention focused in. Appalling, suicidal tenacity. Worth a few minutes of morbid interest.

The Corporal behind the desk vibrated for a moment while his temples turned purple. Then, like the change of a slide-photograph, the Corporal's face turned white and his eyes opened like oysters.

It was a face that Gil recognised. Once upon a time it had won Britain her empire and scared the crap out of the bravest, shag-nastiest warriors that ever pitted themselves against it. It was the face that an Irishman makes just before he paints the world with the blood of his sworn enemy. A strange, happy face.

The Corporal smiled, horridly.

"I beg your pardon, boy?"

Gil shuddered but couldn't look away.

The boy's face showed momentary re-evaluation but never once a trace of fear. In the same way that people who witness great disasters often notice minutia while missing the big-bang, Gil saw the Major seated next to the Corporal recoil from the area of imminent eruption.

The next few moments flowed like cold ketchup. Gil eventually retold the story, as he remembered it, a hundred times without ever really understanding what occurred.

Spade Braithwaite

The boy's expression became pointedly serious, even conspiratorial.

"My people's rules. No names, no pack-drill. I'm Herbert Brewer, here to join the Army. That's all I can tell you."

The Corporal flashed shades of iceberg blue.

Conflict-hardened veterans backed away, clutching their coffee and their clipboards. Brave men crossed themselves and big dogs stopped barking.

Then a strange thing happened. A previously inconspicuous, plain-clothed Colonel from Admin' stepped forward and had a quiet word in the Corporal's ear.

The Corporal morphed through azure back to purple and started to vibrate again.

He swayed back and forth for a full twenty seconds and then smiled, even more horribly than before.

"Okay, boy. Good enough, for now. How many with you?"

Gill saw the young man's countenance break for the first time as he shrugged towards the two fat, ugly men behind him in the queue.

"Two. And a corpse. Nothing to do with me."

"Lovely! Next?!"

The Corporal snapped off a table leg as he struggled to maintain bloody-minded composure.

The young man shouldered his backpack and got on Gil's bus. The fat, ugly pair, obviously brothers, smiled nervously to the Corporal and followed him up the steps.

There was a moment of silence while everyone digested what they'd just seen.

Gil had seen action in a dozen campaigns including the Turkish-Mafia Amphetamine Foray, but in fifteen years of violence he'd never seen cold-blooded bravery that approached what he'd just witnessed. If the Corporal hadn't still been sitting there, grinding his teeth and distractedly folding the table leg into a cube then Gil might have led an ovation.

Instead, Gil shook his head awake and got back on his bus.

Chapter 18

Shirley Brown woke up in the biggest bed she'd ever seen and, apart from a slight hangover at the base of her neck, she felt wonderful.

Crisp white linen and a four-inch-thick quilt that felt like coal-fire glow all over her body. Until now, Shirley had never even suspected that waking up in a bed could feel so good.

Charles and Mama Jen had acted as though they always stayed at expensive hotels when they travelled. Shirley had taken a lead from them and pretended not to be knocked out.

Five more minutes and then she'd get up.

Outside, in the corridor, Charles intercepted the breakfast steward and knocked on Shirley's door.

"Good morning! Breakfast."

Shirley found her glasses on the bedside table and squinted at the clock. Eight twenty eight.

"Come in. It's not locked. Charles! Good morning. I could get used to this."

"Good morning. You really should lock your door. English breakfast and newspapers. Enjoy your breakfast because I suspect that the honeymoon's over."

"What's up?"

"Have a look at this."

Charles handed Shirley a crisp copy of the days National Clarion.

The headline read:

Dereck's Call-Up goes Tits-Up!

"Who the hell do they find to write this shit?!"

"More worrying, who do they find to read it?! It's the country's third biggest selling national daily. Read the story."

Clausthowlersnauglerbogler humiliates Prime Minister Cartright.

In what appears to be a deliberate snub to Prime Minister Cartright, the town of Clausthowlersnagleburger (believed to be somewhere in the western desert) sent five hundred disabled pensioners to join Mr Cartright's new army, in place of the young men chosen by Mr Cartright for their expendability.

Herbert Brewer's Dirty Little Secret

```
     This comes as a serious blow to Mr Cartright's
credibility at a time when even senior Ministers are
questioning the wisdom of Mr Cartright's actions.
```

"How many times can they mention Dereck Cartright's name in a negative way?"

"It doesn't get any better. The article goes on to state that, let me find it…"

```
... Claustellersnowglerbogler's actions might even provoke
a Constitutional crisis, leaving the Prime Minister's
leadership of the country open to question. It is
generally accepted that Dereck can no longer rely on the
support that he once enjoyed.
```

"Garbage rag! I wouldn't wrap fish 'n' chips in it."

"Quite. The editorials are caustic enough to wipe the smile off a two-dollar coin. I, myself, wouldn't wipe my arse with it in an emergency, but the circulation number on the front page says that it sold over seven hundred thousand copies yesterday. So the other Nationals won't be far behind. I think we should prepare ourselves for a rough ride, from here on in. Eat your breakfast. Save the sausage till last. It is the stuff of heaven."

"So, what do we do?"

"We stonewall. We're hard-nosed professionals. And we have a good hand to play. Let the games begin."

"I think you should phone Gary. Maybe warn him."

"I did. He says that Claust' is wound up, "Tighter than a Parson's arse." So bring it on."

"Realistically, can we pull it off?"

Spade Braithwaite

"It's a fuckin' walk-over. We can eat these clowns for breakfast. Talking of which, can I have your marmalade? It's sex on a plate."

"Help yourself."

"Thank you. Game on!"

Prime Minister Dereck Cartright read the article with his nine o clock libation.

The first time he'd ever read about himself in a newspaper he'd been really upset. Since then, his heart had been broken by experts. Dereck had long since evolved a creed recognising that, while sticks and stones might break his bones the newspapers had, so far, been unable to get rid of him.

The way to deal with newspaper campaigns was to encourage them into an extreme position. To provoke outlandish exaggeration, while quietly disbarbing the substance of their attack. Then, to throw the situation wide open and personally accept ultimate responsibility for a situation that obviously wasn't a quarter as bad as the newspaper had led everyone to believe.

It was a complicated strategy that involved playing a lot of hands against each other but, fortunately, newspaper reporters were mostly shit-thick.

More sinister than the story itself was the knowledge that the National Clarion's entire staff of investigative journalists couldn't have found the Parliament Assembly Building on a map, if their lives depended on it.

Herbert Brewer's Dirty Little Secret

Somebody inside Dereck's own camp must have planted the story.

The opposition wouldn't do it. Their party was in such a mess that they wouldn't dare try anything that might cause an election.

No one in Dereck's Civil Service would have done it. Dereck knew the game too well to let capricious career-men anywhere near the facts.

Dereck found a water-cooler cup in his stationery drawer and poured himself a medium Scotch.

A feeling in his bladder told him that Inland Attorney, Samuel Guarthje was the culprit.

Dereck had mixed feelings about his bladder because it woke him up three times a night, but it was almost never wrong.

The Constitution dictated that Dereck had to have twelve members on his Executive Cabinet. Not one of whom, Dereck would have trusted to look after his beach-towel for half an hour. And recently, a few of them had been sporting, "You're-my-bitch" smiles.

Dereck couldn't have told you what made him know, but he knew. Samuel Guarthje had better slick-up his little ring-piece with vaseline because he was about to get shafted.

The first call came at ten past nine.

Baarppp.

"Fuckin' hell! Hello?"

"Mr Cartright? I've got Mrs Ogden-Smith on the phone, from the League of Women Voters, in Braithwaite. They donated a thousand dollars in the last election. Remember to ask about Braithwaite's Beer-for-Bums project."

Dereck wiped his brow. In the United States, lobby groups donated tens of millions and President Sharpton phoned them back when it was convenient. In Amsarnie, you could throw a dollar in the pot and they'd give you Dereck's home phone number. Something was wrong, somewhere.

"Go on. Put her on. Mrs Ogden-Smith! I've been meaning to phone you. How's the Beer-for Bums project going? A cause close to both our hearts, I know."

"Mr Cartright! Is that you?"

"Of course, Mrs Ogden-Smith! My staff has orders to put you through immediately, if I'm in the office. How can I help you?"

"Mr Cartright! Have you seen the National Clarion today? Is it true? Are you, "besieged by doubts to [your] leadership. With Clowstvowlersneglerbogle's challenge to [your] authority coming at a time, when [you] can ill-afford political dissension."?"

"I'm happy to be able to tell you that it's a whole load of fart-gas. I'm afraid that my Oath of Office prevents me telling even you any of the specifics, but I can tell you that we've had to deploy an, "Unseen Initiative," an' those cock-suckers at the Clarion just couldn't wait to jeopardise the lives of our boys in the field."

"So the report's just a big piece of cow-poop?"

"Grand-dad's camel-shaggin' story!"

Herbert Brewer's Dirty Little Secret

"You certainly reassure me, Mr Prime Minister. Keep on doin' the Lord's works, and I'll try not to over-react so much next time. You know, the gals wonder if you might have an hour to talk to us, we-all do admire you so much."

"I'm sure I can fit you in, somewhere..."

Dereck remembered the League of Women Voters in Braithwaite and reflected that he really would love to fit them in. A room full of rich, neglected wifeys, with expensive lingerie and hormone-replacement-therapy. What could possibly be more important than that?

"Speak to my secretary and pencil me in for sometime in July."

"You are the sweetest man!"

"You know, I think I might be! You take care, y'all!"

"Bye now!"

"Bye!"

Dereck pressed the button to release.

Scotch was a damn good drink, in the morning. One small cup had taken him right back to the best part of last night. After the restaurant and before the punch-up. Dereck made a note to speak to John Sumwun about the punch-up. Dereck suspected that, when President Sharpton's life was threatened his bodyguards didn't shout odds of nine to seven, Queensbury rules in the back bar, ten dollars a head to watch.

Dereck sipped the whiskey and rubbed his aching ribs. A big red button got his secretary's attention.

Spade Braithwaite

"Sir?"

"Get me a couple of bacon an' egg sandwiches, will ya? An' some coffee. Don't tell 'em it's for me 'cause they prob'ly spit in it. Find John Sumwun an' tell him he's sacked. An' tell 'im the Domestic Revenue are investigatin' his chaperone business."

"Mr Sumwun's been fired?!"

"Christ, no. But try to put the shits up him a bit. An' find Snapper."

"Snapper?"

"George Snapper, Minister for Allied Stability. He's supposed to be in my Cabinet but I have yet to actually meet the fucker. Also, track down General Mussbiere."

"General mus' be a ...?"

"Exactly! Head of the army. Find out why I'm getting' crap in the newspapers when he promised me silk knickers."

"Find out why you're getting crap, when he promised you silk knickers!(?)"

"Just get the fucker on the phone! The man himself. Accept no substitute."

"Will do! Would you like brown sauce with the sandwiches?"

"Your'e a good lad! And a big, black coffee. Thank you."

General Aemon Mussbiere was genuinely pleased to meet Mamma Jenny Won Baker at last.

Herbert Brewer's Dirty Little Secret

During fifteen years of top management he'd bought and sold the politicians of every township in the country except Clausthowlersnauglerbogler.

The few forays he'd sent into Claust' had all come home empty-handed, causing him to assume that the town already had an invisible syndicate in operation. Since then, while quietly admiring their subtlety he'd left them alone.

The limousine arrived at Camp Good-News shortly after breakfast. Aemon and an Honour- Guard were ready for them.

Colonel Cyril Neff jumped out to help the ladies and make introductions.

"Gov'ner!"

"Colonel Neff."

"Gov'ner. I'd like you to meet Shirley Brown, Charles Andropolous and Mamma Jenny Won Baker. Ladies, Charles, I'd like to introduce the Supreme Commander of National Defence, General Aemon Mussbiere."

Aemon shook hands as they stepped out.

"General."

Charles was exactly what Aemon had expected. Mama Jen and Shirley Brown were very close to exactly not what he'd expected at all.

"Please, call me Aemon. Ms Brown, Mr Andropolous, Mamma Jen, I'm very pleased to meet you. I trust that we have enough areas of common interest to create something positive out of this situation."

Spade Braithwaite

Mamma Jen treated Aemon to a dangerous dose of her subtlest, deadliest smile.

"Aemon, everything that I've heard about you leads me to expect uncommon acumen. I'm sorry we have to meet across a division of circumstance but I have no doubt that we can sort out this conscription fiasco between us. I suggest that we enjoy an accelerated review of the facilities and then discuss our options over lunch. I assume that you have some proposals?"

Aemon, like a thousand men before him was charmed off his feet.

"Indeed we do, Mamma Jen. Lunch will be ready when we are. If you'd care to follow me, I think that you'll be pleasantly surprised by our organisation. We see ourselves more as a family, than an army. Please notice the large areas of open ground. We encourage all outdoor activities including team sports, athletics, tai-chi, yoga meditation and quiet contemplation."

Mamma Jen slipped her hand into the crook of Aemon's arm and allowed herself to be shown around.

Charles and Shirley Brown followed in the objective periphery.

Flight BU113 landed at Clausthowlersnauglerbogler International Airport shortly before eleven. Of all the passengers on board, the least important was probably Turkman Khan, visiting Claust' to learn the retail business from his uncle.

Herbert Brewer's Dirty Little Secret

The most important, in her own eyes at least, was Alison Dawa, anxious to execute her mission of Assistant to the Emergency Supervisor.

Recently appointed Emergency Supervisor Laurence French was there to meet her with a rented car.

Nobody was more upset than Laurence when Alison Dawa was detained, having been found transporting a condom full of heroin inside her bottom.

And Laurence was mortified when the elevator, transporting Alison to the second floor became stuck between floors, what with the emergency repair crews unavailable until Monday.

Poor Laurence fairly beat his chest with self-reproach.

Nobody was more pleased than Laurence when they finally managed to lower a bargain-bucket of fried chicken and a potty through the escape-hatch to poor Alison, stuck between floors.

You would imagine, in a society that can put a man on the moon, that rescuing a young lady from an elevator, stuck between ground level and Air Traffic Control would be a simple procedure. But no.

Anything involving hydraulics was union, and the union employee wouldn't be back until Monday, at the very soonest.

Laurence beat his chest some more and retired to the bar-restaurant for a soul-tonic. Didn't shit just happen, though! Oh yes.

Poor Alison.

Chapter 19

Clausthowlersnauglerbogler was quiet.

By half past twelve Gary Crozier was bored witless. Janet caught him on his way out the office.

"Lunchtime, already?"

"Actually, I have a meeting to discuss a liquor licence."

"Elaine's Diner?"

"Maybe, but damn your impudence!"

"Bring me back a slice of walnut cake. No cream."

"I'll be stopping on the way back to review an entertainment licence."

"I can wait. Have a pint for me."

"Get back to y' work, woman, before I have you fired and thrown in the street! I like your blouse."

"Thank you. Stop leering at my chest!"

It was another lovely day. Gary drove out to Elaine's Diner, quietly cursing everyone and everything.

Elaine's Diner, just off Morecombe Boulevard, was the tonic for a tired man.

Gary found a seat at the counter and studied the menu.

"Gary!"

"Jane! You must get hundreds of men telling you how hot you look in your little, waitress pinny!"

"Ughmm .., not really. How's your lovely wife?"

"Lovely. Do me a favour. Pretend, for a minute, that I'm an attractive bachelor and flirt with me."

"Gary! If you were a bachelor, then you wouldn't be a bachelor 'cause I'd 'ave snapped you up!"

"I love you, Jane. Can I have a big, greasy, illegal breakfast, with extra greasy stuff and a black coffee."

"For you, my darlin', the world!"

Sam Snelly-Snell, the Manager of Clausthowlerbogler International Airport was glad to see Gary in Elaine's. It saved him a phone call.

"Gary, mate!"

"Sam. How's it goin'?"

"Brilliant! I was goin' to call you. We've got the Government hatchet-woman locked up at the Airport. I was goin' to ask you what we should do with her."

Gary rubbed his eyebrows and looked around for a source of alcohol, or nicotine.

"I'm sorry, you have what?!"

"Laurence French told us there was a Government Trouble-Shooter coming in to town, so we held her up."

"You robbed her?!"

"No! We did a random drug search and we found a Johnny full of white powder stuffed up her chuff."

"You're still holding her?"

"No. She's been stuck in a lift, between floors for the past hour."

Spade Braithwaite

Gary tried to recount all the books of the bible, in order to prevent himself turning critical. He'd seen Ronald Reagan do it in a film, once, and it had seemed to work.

Genesis, Exodus, Leviticus, Holy, Jesus, Fuckin', Christ, Almighty! It didn't work!

"Was this Laurence's idea?"

"No! Honestly! I thought up the drug thing but the elevator just happened."

"You put her in an elevator, up to the Control Tower?!"

"Yeah."

"And it just got stuck?! Get her out, as quick as you can. I'll have someone pick her up in ten minutes."

"What about the drugs?"

"Drugs?!"

"Icing sugar. But it looked like heroin!"

"Tell her that you're very sorry, and Handshake-Harry-Houdini has admitted planting drugs up her bum. Then kiss her bum like you've never kissed before!"

"But she's the bad guy!"

"We've already got a plan! And it's good enough that we don't need concerned citizens free-lancing their own agendas. What's she like?"

"Not my type, but quite attractive, in a six foot tall, stern, austerely handsome kind of way."

"But not your type?"

Herbert Brewer's Dirty Little Secret

"Well, exactly my type, now you mention it. Damn good-looking woman. But I promise that the search was conducted according to Federal guide-lines"

"Oh christ! Don't tell me, Bridgett and Caroline…"

"I think it might have been…"

"Fuck! Get her out of the lift, offer to commit suicide for her personal amusement and if she refuses do it anyway. I'll have a car there in five minutes. You fuckin' pillak!"

"What?! I thought you'd be pleased!"

"Next time, don't think. Spare me the grey hairs."

"Okay! Sorry if we fucked up!"

"Don't worry about it. Just get 'er out and sweeten 'er up. Quickly! I'll phone Laurence."

"If that's what you reckon. You're the boss."

"Thank you."

Inland Attorney Samuel Guarthje made a dollar coin tumble across his knuckles, both hands, in either direction. Occasionally letting it disappear through a motionless finger to reappear somewhere else as if by magic. It helped him concentrate.

Everything should have been wonderful but Samuel had the feeling that someone, somewhere was torturing his spleen, in effigy, with pointy sticks and a lighted cigarette.

Spade Braithwaite

Samuel reassured himself by remembering that nothing happened quietly in Government. If someone was after his innards then the phone would have been ringing by now.

Samuel's phone rang.

"Hello?"

"Mr G., there's a man on the phone claiming to be Prime Minister Cartright. Should I get rid of him?"

"Yes. Wait, no. Put him on. Hello?"

"Sammy?"

Prime Minister Cartright oozed out of the earpiece.

The dollar coin spun across the room into a fish tank and Samuel laid his head in an empty out-tray.

"Hello! Mr Cartright! Lovely to hear from you. How can I help you?"

"Sammy, mate! How's things going with the call-up?"

"Good, Prime Minister. Almost exactly according to plan. There's been a few hitches but nothing that would attract attention."

"Good! Good. Do you ever read the National Clarion?"

"Shit-wipe! I wouldn't use it to house-break a puppy."

"Me either. But they seem to have their fangs in my arse. Something about Clausthowlersnauglerbogler. Have you heard anything?"

Samuel's bile rose. An unwritten rule of politics forbade gentlemen from asking other gentlemen questions that required a straight answer.

Herbert Brewer's Dirty Little Secret

"Mmm..., yes! I have heard some rumours from Claust-whatever-it's-called. Something about that Mayor of theirs trying to pull some scam to avoid the draught and win himself some votes. What've you heard?"

"The same. I had a look to see what we're doing about it and I managed to track down a copy of a note that went through this office last week. Your office made provision that, should things fuck-up-badly, a, "Federal Emergency Supervisor", was ready to step in and take control."

"You certainly run an impressive, political machine, Mr Prime Minister. One step ahead of the game, as always!"

"Yes..., your office recommended the appointment of, let me find it..., Laurence French, Senior Career Officer for the Northern Provinces."

"Did we? Remarkable! I'm sure he'll do a wonderful job. I'd like to take all the credit but I have to admit that much of what happens here is governed by procedural precedents that I inherited from my predecessor. I'll definitely look into it and keep you informed, minute by minute."

"Thank you. I also have to admit that I took the liberty of, "leaking", the note to a couple of muck-spreaders, just to show that we're on the case. I included a memo expressing my personal concern but, ultimately trusting the entire situation to you, personally. I think that this might turn out to be a watershed event in your career."

Spade Braithwaite

"I can't express my thanks, Mr Prime Minister. You gave them my name?"

"Yes. I wasn't sure how to pronounce it so I spelled it out."

"Mr Prime Minister, I can't even begin to...,"

"I know. The feeling's mutual. Take care now. Bye!"

Click.

Samuel Guarthje's eyes lost focus, roaming the walls before eventually picking out a knot in the grain of his desk on which to gather. From up close the knot became a Hindu Om.

"Fuck! Fuck, fuck,fuck,fuck,fuck!"

Samuel closed his right eye and the Om became an elephant saving a rat from a flood. His left eye made it an Om again.

"Fuck!"

Blue button, red button, one of the fucking buttons on the intercom had to do something!

"Mr G.?"

"Siva, my girl, in the middle of my rotodex, five red pages. The middle one, "Three Wise Men". Book the first one who answers his phone onto the next flight to Clausthowglerrugbytackler and tell him to phone me from the airport. Get 'im a hotel and a car, an' all that. Code red, as in, "red.""

"Is everything alright, sir?"

"Fucking A-one. Actually, everything's really shit, in a bad way. But that's just between you and me. Get right on it and we just might live to fight another day. When the going gets tough...,"

"...We're dead-meat, sir?"

"Probably. Get on that list. And see if you can track down Charlie Weber at the National Clarion. I think my last secretary put him under P, for, "prevarication", or B for, "it's-a-good-job-I've-got-my-Boots-on.""

"Charlie Weber. N, for Newspaper."

"Good girl! Tell him to meet me at the Duke of Woodstock, in Bisley at two o clock."

"Got it! Should I warn my husband that I might be late?"

"Up to you. Did we ever...ughm...?"

"No!"

"Wh-?"

"No!"

"Okay. Then I've no reason to imagine that you'll be late. Thank you anyway."

General Aemon Mussbiere ended his accelerated tour of Camp Good-News in the Largely-Duty-Free shop.

"...So, y' see, the modern soldier can expect his career to be individually tailored, within a huge network of opportunities and benefits. May I offer you each a case of Beaujolais Nouveau, not due in the shops for another month yet. I'm told that it's the genuine, crack-up gear."

"Thank you very much!"

Spade Braithwaite

Charles examined the display bottles dubiously and found that they were the real thing. Not available in Paris for three more weeks.

(Author's note: If you've just observed that the Beaujolais Nouveau wouldn't be available in Paris in the middle of June then the Author suggests that you go back to your Dick Francis novels. However, if you vaguely remember seeing something about Beaujolais Nouveau on Public Television and all you can remember was a lot of Frenchmen parachuting into Bexhill-on-Sea then the author suggests that you write to him, care of his publisher, and invite him to your home to discuss the French and the Bexhill-on-Sea Saab Owners Club in plain language.)

(Back to the story.)

Shirley Brown listened and made a good pretence of examining the perfumes as though she knew Eau de Toilette from French Dressing.

Colonel Cyril Neff stood attentively at-ease and admired Shirley Brown's arse as she bent over. Twenty four inches across the hips, give or take an inch.

It was standard procedure to put all visitors in the observation rooms at the Paradigm Hotel, just in case they might reveal idiosyncrasies that could be caught on video and later used in negotiations.

None of them had but Cyril had taken Shirley's shower video and watched it a few times on his own, just to be sure.

Herbert Brewer's Dirty Little Secret

Milky-white flesh from hair-line to toe-nails. Pink nipples and auburn triangle. Big, flat, sensible bum and frivolous, little breasts that jiggled. Pale blue floral pattern knickers, grey stockings and a garter belt. Crisp, white blouse and training bra.

There was something about mature women in suits, with crisp white blouses that reminded Cyril of his penis.

Not that any man needs much reminding.

Shirley examined a Gucci hand-bag on the bottom shelf and Cyril bent down to scratch some dirt from his shoe. It was quick, but Cyril had an idea that he might have seen almost a hint of stocking-top in the chasm.

Phwooaarr!

"Colonel Neff!"

"Gov'ner?"

"Would you mind having a wander into hospitality, see how close we are to lunch?"

"Gov'ner! I'll be right back."

"Good lad. In the meantime, we still have a little flexibility inside our, "Entertainment Budget", so if you see anything that you particularly like then I'm sure we can lose it in the stock-adjustment."

Charles particularly liked almost everything in the shop but contented himself with the case of Beaujolais.

Shirley admired a briefcase that would have been almost perfect except that it already had somebody else's initials, "Y.S.L.", branded down the spine.

Spade Braithwaite

Mamma Jen examined a, "Maori bridal pouch and wire tensioner kit", and for the first time in sixty years was completely mystified.

"Thank you very much Aemon but I think we're okay."

"In that case, ladies and gentleman, it's lunchtime."

Jon-Paul Clifton sipped his sherry and adjusted the binoculars on their tripod. From blurred to blurred, back to somewhere in between. Eventually finding focus inside his neighbour's back garden.

The foam mat was laid out. Her parents were away. She'd done it before. She might do it again.

Jon-Paul wondered if the Landscape Architects on the other side could see into her garden. Maybe, maybe not. They certainly wouldn't complain.

There she was! Jon-Paul's heart jumped into his mouth. The Speedo bikini!

She came out of the French-windows with a long drink in one hand, a magazine and a bottle of sun-cream in the other.

The binoculars swung wildly as Jon-Paul struggled to keep her in sight.

He lost her and found her sitting on the foam mat, pressing the magazine on the ground to keep it open at a page. Then she twisted the lid off the sun-cream and nestled it in the lawn to stand upright.

Herbert Brewer's Dirty Little Secret

Jon-Paul's heart nearly burst out of his chest when she reached behind to untie her top.

Knock, knock, knock, "Darling?"

Jon-Paul leapt into the air, kicking the binoculars into his hand and stashing them behind a roll of carpet in a single movement.

"Yes?!"

"Darling. Sorry to disturb you while you're writing, but there's a woman from the Government on the phone. She says it's really important."

"Bloody hell! I've told you about disturbing me while I'm writing!"

"I know, but she says that it's a matter of national security."

Shit!

"What, exactly?"

"She won't tell me. She wants you. Should I tell her you'll call back?"

"I'll be right there."

Bollocks!

Jon-Paul Clifton gulped down the rest of his sherry and stormed downstairs, past his wife to the phone.

"Yes?!"

"Mr Jon-Paul Clifton?"

"Yes?!"

"Mr Clifton. This is Mr Grr-arthur-jees secretary."

"Who?"

"Mr Gwa-wirth-jey, the Inland Attorney...,"

Spade Braithwaite

"Samuel Guarthje?"

"That's him! I'm his secretary. We have a situation developing and we need you in Clausthowler-babbler-babbler, as soon as possible."

"Clausthowlersnauglerbogler?"

"That's the place. I've booked you onto the next flight. In forty minutes."

"Okay. Can I talk to Sammy?"

"He said that you had to phone him from the airport."

"Is he there?"

"Yes. But he insisted that you phone him from the airport. You can be there in fifteen minutes."

"I know how long it takes to get to the airport! Can I possibly speak to Sammy, please?"

"I have lots of other names on my list. Should I call some of them?"

"No. I'll fly out to Claust' with no explanation. What do I care? It's only Friday afternoon and I'm supposed to be having a cook-out party!"

"Brilliant! I'll tell Mr G. to expect your call from the airport."

"Fine."

Jon-Paul Clifford put the phone back into its cradle and scratched his armpit.

"Anything serious, darling?"

"No. Just some secret, Government business. I have to be on a plane in half an hour."

Herbert Brewer's Dirty Little Secret

"That's nice, dear. I'll get your bag. Nicole 'n' Maurice 'll be sorry they missed you but we'll probably cook-out anyway. Formal?"

"No idea."

"That's nice, dear."

Alison Dawa kept her temper on the safe side of psychopathic by chanting her secret mantra, "W.W.J.K.D?"

What would Jacqueline Kennedy do? Firstly, and lastly, Jacqueline would have been decorously assertive and smoulderingly sexy.

A difficult combination to manage when you had to meet your new boss straight from an elevator rescue situation with a face full of fried chicken residue and a potty full of urine.

W.W.J.K.D.? What, the fuck, Would Jacqueline Kennedy Do?

The light behind the panel of buttons suddenly re-energised, illuminating the two options, "G", and, "2".

Alison pressed, "G", for Ground.

"Miss! Can you hear me?!"

"Of course I can hear you! I can see you! You're ten feet above me!"

"Miss! We think that we might be able to lower you back to ground floor an' get you out. Can you see the lift operation buttons?"

"I'm stuck in an elevator. I'm not retarded!"

Spade Braithwaite

"We've cobbled a manual-link from emergency power. I think we can get you out. Press the button marked, "G", as in, "G", for Ground Floor."

The lift descended four and a half feet to the ground floor.

"You're very efficient! Can I recommend you for an award?!"

"Thank you very much! My name's Edward...,"

"I was being ironic, okay! You've been fucking useless! As soon as I can afford it, I'll spend my own money to have you thrown in jail and raped by trans-sexuals."

"The door isn't open, yet!"

"Open the door, while you still have a dick!"

The elevator door opened.

Alison paused to refocus and emerge as Jacky at Arlington Cemetery.

Recently appointed Emergency Supervisor Laurence French was there to meet her.

"Oh my God, Miss Dawa! What a terrible introduction to the town! I'm Laurence French. Senior Career Officer for the Northern Provinces, recently appointed Emergency Supervisor of Claust'. Pleased to meet you. I can't begin to...,"

"Don't worry. We're only here because there's a problem. Let's do lunch. I look forward to hearing your prognosis."

"Well, ughm... It's a funny ol' town, Claust'. I don't know quite what to make of it. But let's do lunch. That's a good idea. I've got you a car, and a room at the Blandford. It's a lovely hotel. Do you fancy Chinese, Indian, Italian, French, or local?"

Herbert Brewer's Dirty Little Secret

Alison slipped out of Jacky Kennedy and lapsed, momentarily into Mae-West.

"I'll take it anyway I can get it!"

"I'm sorry?"

"So am I. It's been a long morning. Italian will be fine."

"Of course! I quite understand. Mae-West. You've had a strange morning. Let's get you to your room to clean up. Your bags came through hours ago. I had them sent on."

"Great. Lunch and a shower. In that order. I really hate this town, so far."

"I felt the same way. But you'll learn to love it. I promise you will."

"That would be nice. Lunch!"

"Okay! Italian it is. Welcome to Clausthowlersnauglerbogler!"

Inland Attorney Samuel Guarthje entered the Duke of Woodstock at five minutes to two. The smoke was almost impenetrable but the smell was worse. It smelled like a Bombay butcher's pyjamas and Samuel Guarthje's experience of what a Bombay butcher's pyjamas smelled like was nobody's business but his.

Charlie Weber, floating investigative journalist with the National Clarion was already at the bar, regaling the barman with tales of a large-breasted prostitutes that he'd personally caught in the act of having sex in return for money.

Spade Braithwaite

"So, anyway, you remember Monsignor Woomera? We got a call from some bird, an' when I met 'er, bloody hell, you wouldn't give it credence! Fuckin' Zepplins they were! All natural. So anyway, she reckoned she had a reg'lar gig, once a week with His Holiness, an' she wanted ten grand to set up a video camera to catch 'im. So we played along."

"Did y' get 'im?"

"Turned out to be some Anglican vicar who liked dressin' up. We gave 'er the money though. Amazin' video. I've still got a copy, somewhere."

Samuel Guarthje paused to control his stomach before saying hello.

"Charlie, mate!"

"Sammy-boy! Brilliant scoop! It's the first time we've had an exclusive since Rock Hudson turned out to be a poof. My Editor thinks I'm gold-dust. He's thinkin' of sendin' a reporter overseas somewhere, an' I'm on the shortlist!"

"Brilliant Charlie! Ughmm.., two pints and a pair of large cognacs. Can you put all these tickets on my bill, please?"

"Good lad, Sammy!"

"Charles. Look, I've got an even better story for you. You know I told you that this Clausthowlersnauglerbogler situation was about to bring down Dereck Cartright?"

"Sammy, I don't like your tone! That story had better be somehow, loosely based on fact, or we're both in it!"

Herbert Brewer's Dirty Little Secret

"Charlie, mate! It was a brilliant piece of investigative journalism! Completely true at the time. Can I offer you a chance to be so far ahead of the game that they'll probably name an award after you."

"Go on."

"News is just about to break that my Department anticipated the Claust' situation and we're completely on top of it. We had a trouble-shooter ready to step in take over, and the whole thing's probably going to be sorted out in no time. Another cognac?"

"Cheers boy! But no-can-do. Sorry mate."

"Wha' d'y' mean, sorry?!"

"Sorry! Our owners were practically wankin'-off at the possibility of two contested elections within eighteen months. Do you know how long it's been since we had a contested election?"

"But this is the scoop of your lifetime!"

"Sorry mate. News ain't shit compared to Paid Political Advertising. We're gonna make it a close race, jus' so that we can keep both sides spendin'. Christ, if I fucked this one up I wouldn't get a job writin' sell-by-dates on sides o' beef."

"But it's true, this time! I'm only offering you the chance to be first with it. The other newspapers 'll be onto it soon enough."

"Yeah! You just watch 'em!"

"You fuckin' bastard!"

"Sammy, mate! Of course I'm a fuckin' bastard! It's what I do. Maybe everythin' 'll work out. Here, let me get you a drink. Bar-keep! Two large tequilas. Look Sammy, don't be all pissed-

Spade Braithwaite

off. Y'r still inside the game. We'll both come out of this with new Porches. You'll see. Cheers!"

"Yeah. Cheers, mate."

Fuckin' bastard!

Chapter 20

The Correspondent & Sportsman was Amsarnie's oldest and most respected newspaper. Founded in nineteen fifty-eight and respected by hardly anyone, it was the best of a bad lot.

Canned vegetable magnate, Joseph Malakani took very little pleasure from owning it.

Its Head (and only) Office was in Tullamore Lane, just off Wheat Street. A converted nineteenth century cattle-market with Greco-Roman pillars added in the seventies.

Editor Maxwell Silverhammer loathed Joseph Malakani with religious devotion.

Joseph Malakanl suspected but said nothing. He didn't even read the Correspondent unless he had to but today, he'd read it and been very displeased.

Herbert Brewer's Dirty Little Secret

The Correspondent could honestly boast the best Board-Room off Wheat Street and Joseph phoned Maxwell from his car to arrange a meeting there in fifteen minutes.

Maxwell did some editorial stuff and then chewed his floor carpet for eight minutes, just to be three minutes late.

Joseph Malakani rolled in a quarter of an hour behind him.

"Maxwell."

"Joseph! To what do we owe this honour?"

"Fuck man, you talk clichés and you edit my newspaper?! What crap is that?"

"Joseph! Mate! What's eating you?"

"Have you seen the National Clarion?"

"The what?! The Clarion? I wouldn't use it to line my sock drawers! What are you on about?"

"The bloody Clarion! Running a front page story about this Conscription fuck-up!"

"What fuck-up?"

"Exactly! I look in our newspaper to get the real story and all I could find was a picture of young men, being called-up as instructed. Who's handling the damn story?"

"Pablo Harrison. Our finest young writer. He's as smart as a whip. I really think he's our next prize-winner."

"Damn your unnatural leanings! I want copy! This is the only real story we've had since World War Two, an' the pissin' Clarion scooped us! How did this happen? They get their news from prostitutes and drunks! We subscribe to the Reuters network, do we not? What do they have to say?"

"Ahh. Actually, we only get *foreign* news from Reuters. And, as we're the only subscriber in Amsarnie, they get all *our* national news from us. We've sold them two stories since I've been here. The atomic test, and Monsignor Woomera's speech about Anglicans. However...,"

"Get bloody Pablo Harrison in here, now!"

"Yes sir."

Maxwell picked up the board-room extension and was surprised to find himself connected to somebody, somewhere.

"...Hello?"

"Yes! Get Pablo Harrison in here immediately!"

"Yes sir. Where?"

"The bloody Board-Room! Thank you."

Pablo Harrison replaced the cafeteria extension phone into its cradle and scratched his chin, thoughtfully.

A bus-boy startled him from his thoughts.

"So, did it win?"

"No idea mate. I just picked up the phone and there was old man Silverhammer, shouting at me to come to the Board-Room. Very strange. Here, keep this warm. I'll be back."

The Board-Room was on the third floor. Pablo Harrison walked past it fifty times a day but he'd never heard of anyone being summoned to it.

Herbert Brewer's Dirty Little Secret

Damn, he wished he'd worn a tie. Too late to worry about that now.

Two knocks, with a pause between.

"Come!"

Pablo entered and swore when he saw Joseph Malakani. (Fuckin' hell!)

"Beg your pardon?"

"Uhmm.., looking well! I said you're looking well, Max. And you, Mr Malakani. What's up?"

"Please sit down. Pablo. Mr Malakani is quite, justifiably upset that the Clarion have scooped us."

"The Clarion? Christ, I wouldn't use it to stop my windows rattling. What 'ave they got that we missed? Don't tell me Mick Jagger's turned out to be gay?"

"Mr Harrison! Please, read this."

Joseph Malakani handed Pablo the newspaper and indicated a seat at the table.

Pablo sat and skimmed the article, incredulously.

"Bloody Nora! Well I'm damned. Charlie Weber?! I'd be willing to bet my salary that he couldn't name two Cabinet Ministers if he 'ad half an hour to think about it."

"Well the bloody story come from somewhere. And there must be something in it 'cause even the Clarion wouldn't tackle Dereck Cartright so harsh if they didn't know something."

"Damn sure they didn't count all the conscripts arrivin' at the airport."

Spade Braithwaite

"Neither did you!"

"Yeah..., I mean, no, of course not."

"Didn't we hear anything from any of our sources in Claust'?"

"What sources? I asked around and nobody knew anyone from Claust'. They've got one local newspaper that wouldn't run the Second Coming of Christ unless it happened in town. It's off the bloody map!"

"So what you thinkin'? Maybe ignore it?"

"Just..., give me a minute to think. Please."

Pablo stood up and stalked to the far end of the room, rubbing his temples pretentiously.

He paused and reflected that, when your owner asks you a question, it usually means that they think they know the answer. And what they really want is for someone to put the question back to them.

Pablo squinted at a flat patch in the artex above the fireplace and scratched his chin, even more pretentiously.

"Mr Malakani, how do *you* think we should handle this?"

"Good question, my boy! Firstly, you phone roun' your hack-buddies and give 'em an idea that we got somethin' big that we' just about to break with. Tell them Mr Dereck Cartright, my personal friend, is on very thin ice with accusations of corruption an' foreign bank accounts. Get 'em all running wild stories. Then we go in subtle, an' stick to what's true."

Pablo looked to his editor for support. Maxwell counted the hairs on his knuckles and wondered if there was a legal precedent for having a newspaper owner relieved of ownership on medical grounds.

"Mr Malakani! I have a few contacts in other papers, but they're all hard-bitten bull-shitters themselves! They're not likely to believe me if I just phone up for a casual chat and then let-slip the best story we ever had."

"One-time trick, boy! You phone 'em up, tell 'em you're not happy here and you want good money to come over with the biggest story ever. Fax 'em your résumé! Hint, and promise details as soon as you got a payroll number. It's a trick you can only do one time, but that's enough."

"Mr Malakani! Journalism is largely based on credibility! Why on earth would I do that, when I'm just beginning to make a name for myself?!"

"Because I'll give you a one-time bonus of four thousand dollars. And, quite honestly, we both know damn-well that your credibility wouldn't get you good seats at a dog show. Also, there's the pleasure of watching our competition make baboos of themselves."

"What if they offer me the job, and then want the real facts?"

Joseph Malakani made his, "what-are-the-chances?", face, and let it go.

Pablo Harrison scratched his groin because it itched, and mentally converted four thousand dollars into lifestyle.

"Eight thousand!"

Spade Braithwaite

"You know, boy, I could make you do it for nothing, but I like you. Eight thousand, and you can take me out whoring one night next week."

"Done. I do know a whore-house...,"

"Good boy! Now go and make some phone calls and send some faxes. Mention my personal friendship with Mr Dereck Cartright sometimes, to get them biting. Then find out what the truth is. Go!"

Pablo danced two paces before remembering to march, purposefully.

Joseph Malakani found the decanter on the window table and poured himself a memorable Scotch.

"Drink, Max?"

"Thanks. Small one."

Joseph half filled a tumbler and passed it over.

"I like that boy! He reminds me of what a little-shit I was, when I was his age."

"I can only imagine. Can I take the drink back to my office? I've got an awful lot of work to do."

"Sure thing, Max. Sorted! Can I get a direct, outside line anywhere? Without going through the switch-board?"

"Promise not to tell? Five five five, from that phone. Good luck, mate."

"Cheers, Max. Get back to your bullshit. I'll try not to bother you too often. Take it easy."

Maxwell trudged next door to his office, contemplating the practicalities of having Joseph Malakani professionally murdered.

Joseph Malakani moved the phone up to the head of the table and sat in the Chairman seat. The number was in Joseph's black book under D. Five five five for an outside line.

Prime Minister Dereck Cartright had resigned himself to a day on the phone. Every twat and their cousin had read the Clarion and decided that Dereck needed their opinion. There was no end to it.

..."Yeah? And you! You fat wanker! An' you can kiss your fuckin' bypass project goodbye aswell!"

Dereck replaced the phone and pressed the button that allowed him to speak to his secretary.

"Kev, mate, that's an end to it. No more calls. I've fuckin' had it!"

"One more that you might be interested in. Mr Malakani, the canned vegetable magnate who also owns the Correspondent & Sportsman."

"Good one! Put 'im on. Joe-Boy! A little ray of sunshine. How's it goin'?"

"Good, Dereck. Lovely. Tell your mum not to read the paper tomorrow 'cause they're prob'ly gonna carve you up badly."

"Goes with the territory, mate. Now, what were we discussin', last week? Something about import definitions?"

Spade Braithwaite

"Yeah! The fuckin' cans are made here. I think that should be good enough!"

"As soon as I've finished reading tomorrows papers, I'll definitely look into it. Cheers mate."

"And you, boy."

Chapter 21

In Bundawa, five hours behind and a world away from Amsarnie, all eight members of the Bantu Nation Redeemist Guerillas had separated and gone into deep hiding. Their locations known only to themselves.

Their leader, Abraham Unduwe had become Erazmus Gosh, a simple river-man, just arrived in Kinaida to escape a blood-feud. Flip-flops on his feet, god-almighty-trousers and a Limca bottle on a string. All his possessions, an international cell-phone, an advanced radio-control hand set, forty thousand US dollars, thirty thousand local francs and a clean pair of underpants, stashed inconspicuously in a filthy, Chicago Bulls gym' bag.

Abraham sat back and allowed himself a small sip of gin & tonic from the dirty, rag-stoppered bottle that was part of his disguise.

Herbert Brewer's Dirty Little Secret

He reckoned that it had been nearly forty eight hours since he'd closed his eyes for more than a blink. He was close to hallucinating from fatigue but he forced himself to focus on the moment, and specifically, the up-coming fight to get off the bus.

The bus guttered to a stop somewhere short of the Manuli River Terminal and hawkers climbed in windows faster than passengers could gush out the door.

"Banan'! Mango! Guava!"

"Cigarette! Holy Bible!"

"Hotel Côtedumore, cheapest an' cleanest, wi' free taxi!"

Every man for himself.

The tick-ulcer on his throat was real enough, as was the polyester allergy rash around his middle.

Erazmus Gosh, in the big city with a teaspoon-full of his life savings. Poor old Raz, even forgot his own family in the rush to save himself.

Everybody on the bus stank slightly different. Abraham stank only a little bit better than most of them because the cow shit he'd rubbed on his trousers had been fresh out the cow only the night before.

He pushed and shoved with the other passengers, down the aisle and onto the pavement. Into the sun, the unbelievable smells and the hellish noise. Jesus, it was going to be a hot one!

"Cheers, bwye!"

The driver nodded, without bothering to focus.

Spade Braithwaite

A fat woman, under full sail with a basket of audio tapes on her head knocked Abraham backwards into a barrow display of local rum and cigarettes.

Abraham apologised to the girl at the barrow and bought a pint bottle of Duq-de-Lait' and twenty five non-filters.

"Twenty franc."

A surprising advantage of the disguise was that vendors went straight to the final price, first time.

"T'anks."

The rum was settled into three layers. Cloudy, brown and black at the top, like refrigerated gravy. Abraham shook the bottle and put it in his bag for emergencies.

Cigarettes! The missing link in Abraham's disguise. Everyone in Bundawa smoked like New Jersey power stations. Abraham hadn't smoked a cigarette since he'd been caned at Eton.

He slapped the packet into his palm, pulled the film off and sparked one up from the burning rope on the girl's barrow.

It tasted of burnt rope but that might have been the tobacco.

First things first. Find a safe place and call-in the warnings.

Abraham looked around for the man that had been hawking the hotel.

In daylight, the man was a boy. Tall and thin in an orange, Chicago Bulls T-shirt, across the street, pestering a middle-aged white couple who'd obviously strayed from their tour group.

Abraham crossed the street to speak with him.

Herbert Brewer's Dirty Little Secret

"...An' it all modern, wi' swimmin' an' all type of electrical wonderment! Showers an' television, an' such!"

The white couple took a photograph of tiny, naked child, sucking a dirty carrot.

Abraham tapped the boy's shoulder and smiled.

"Y' tell me all about the electrical wonderment, an' such. M' want a good room, an' all."

The boy looked Abraham up and down, from head to toe.

"Wha'?"

"Me need a fine room. Cheapest an' cleanest. Free taxi, an' all. M' got the franc, look-see."

The boy hawked a big gob next to Abraham's foot and scowled, incredulously.

"Fuck off, nigger!"

Kevin Mackenzie loved Kinaida better than home. He'd been there for a week and, so far, it was more fun than Benidorm.

Bombardier, Second Class, Highland Blues and Fusiliers, (British Army), Kevin Callum Mackenzie was having the very best time.

"Shove over, betch!"

"Wha'?"

Kevin climbed over the girl and reached for his trousers on the floor. Left side pocket, cigarettes and lighter. He lit two and passed one to the girl next to him.

"T'ank y'."

Spade Braithwaite

Across the room, Bombardier, Third Class, Darren Frazer's skinny, little, white arse got up to speed between a big, luxurious set of brown knees. The steel cot making the only noise.

"G' on, laddy! Gi' it a good 'ne!"

"Fuck aff!"

Kevin sucked in a long pull of smoke and let it sit in his lungs for a moment, before exhaling.

Three hundred francs for the room. A hundred and fifty francs for two girls. Eighty francs for the bottle of rum. That worked out to twenty quid for the day!

When this shit was over, Kev was coming back to Bundawa.

He groped for the bottle, shook it and sucked down a gob-full.

The brown girl, next to him extended a hand so he gave it to her.

"T'ank y'."

Outside the window it was a beautiful day. It was always a beautiful day in Bundawa. When it rained it was hot rain. Not like fuckin' Glasgow.

Kevin swung out of bed and walked to the window.

A five minute taxi from the centre of the nation's capital and huge green trees grew, seemingly, just wherever they wanted. Vines with small, yellow gourds choked the fence and a bicycle stand. Mopeds, trucks and ancient cars fought, aggressively, for road space. An old lady hawked leaf-bowls of mutton and rice from a barrow with a propane burner. Anything that could float was loaded with cargo, taking its chances on the stinky river.

Herbert Brewer's Dirty Little Secret

In the courtyard, half a dozen boys, wearing a full set of old clothes between them played soccer with a bald tennis ball.

Kev rested his elbows on the sill and enjoyed the cigarette.

One of the goal-posts was a grey metal box, with yellow lettering, that reminded Kev of ordnance classes at basic-training.

Across the room, Darren got into the vinegar strokes and shuddered to a stand-still, with a grunt and a burp.

Kev rubbed himself, speculatively, and decided that it wasn't going to happen.

"Hey betch!"

"Wha'?"

The girl rolled over and opened her other eye.

"Breakfast, gal! Get across the road an' get us four portions o' grub."

"Wha'?"

Kevin hoisted the naked girl onto her feet and led her to the window.

"Yon costermonger! Four bayts o' scram!"

Kev pointed at the old lady with the barrow, then pointed to the four people in the room and held up four fingers.

"Plus rum, an' gaspers! Get y' gone, gal!"

He tucked a couple of hundred franc notes into her fist and allowed her to dress.

In the courtyard, one of the boys scored a superb goal from an inspired, overhead volley.

Spade Braithwaite

Kev smiled and clapped, quietly.

Across town, Silus Mantè, larger-than-life psychopath and full time Dictator to Bundawa sipped his coffee and made an effort to understand what his General was telling him.

"Wait, me say. What all for ..." Silus read the notes in front of him, "...*Amsarnie* getting' involved? Wha's *Amsarnie*, anyway?"

"Sir, Amsarnie's an island nation, somewhere in one of the oceans, somewhere. We supported them, indirectly, during some crisis, and so they're sending us a force of five thousand soldiers. We've reviewed their headquarters an' they seem quite professional."

"Why they *really* come?"

"Sir, with respect, politics is a capricious mistress, as you well know. Maybe their president needs votes, or something, I don't know. Anyway, as I said, they seem very organised. I'm meeting their Major tomorrow, where I shall propose combining our forces, under my leadership, for a systematic sweep through the up-country. I'm confident..."

Silus switched him off. There were always motives behind motives and it troubled Silus when he couldn't see what they were.

(Author's note: The author has just heard on the radio that Laurent Kabila, the psychopathic dictator of the Democratic Republic of the Congo has been killed in a failed coup attempt.

Herbert Brewer's Dirty Little Secret

Wow! That's really spooky! At least that means that he can't sue the author or his publisher. Not that the character of Silus Mantè was, in any way based on Laurent Kabila or anyone else, living or deceased.)

Silus stared out the window and wondered.

Raised voices in the outer office brought him back.

" ...in a classic, Sherman movement, co-ordinated by our intelligence..."

"'Scuse me, General. What all that fuckin' noise out there! W' bein' the President and a fuckin' General, in here! Not a fuckin' soccer match!"

A flustered Corporal hurried in, stood to attention, straight as a pig's leg, and saluted.

"M' exceedin'ly sorry, sir, but we 'ave ruckus downstairs! Two privates been caught tryin' to sell-off your personal Internet connection, so we' court-martialin' 'em with some rough tactics. It all done, now, sir. M' very sorry, sir."

"Sellin' off m' personal Internet connection?! M' don't have Internet connections, that I'm aware of! General?"

"Sir, as far as I know, the only Internet connection in the country is upstairs at the Plantation Club, in Albert Square. We looked into it but it wasn't cost effective. However..."

"See! What all y' talking about, Internet connections?!"

The Corporal straightened even more crooked and saluted again.

"M' uncommonly sorry sir. W' not disturb you again."

Spade Braithwaite

Back in the outer office, the Corporal wiped the sweat from his face. Twice, now, he'd spoken to Silus. Legend told that, the third time you spoke to Silus, he had your tongue cut out.

Fuckin' Internet connection! The Corporal stared at it hatefully.

A stupid, ugly, grey metal box with yellow lettering and a stupid wire dangling out the top.

The other Corporal patted his shoulder in congratulation.

"Silus goin' to promote us?"

"Fuck, is he! He practically tol' me to fuck off!"

"No!"

Both Corporals scowled at the stupid, Internet connection.

"Yeah!"

"Then y' can put d' fuckin' t'ing out o' my sight! In d' cupboard, adjacent to Silus' office. Nex' to dat box o' nails. Yeah, there! An' all d' trouble we made to discover wha' it was! Unbelievable!"

"Yeah!"

Mrs Matoo was late. Thank God that her aide was always early, to meet the children as their buses arrived.

She parked her moped in the staff section and hurried into school.

Friday. Fish for lunch and a lot of Christian nonsense from Father Breva, at assembly.

Herbert Brewer's Dirty Little Secret

At least it would be Saturday tomorrow. Sally Matoo enjoyed Saturdays. A day at her father-in-law's farm, probably weeding again. About the only time that she ever saw her husband, close-up, nowadays.

Principal O'Hara saw her scurry in and gave her the look that said, "Consider yourself caught!"

"What?! You must have heard about the accident on the South Arterial! Be thankful that I'm here at all!"

Principal O'Hara scowled and scurried back to his own office. Idiot!

Sally Matoo hurried upstairs to her class.

"Lyle, Mohamed?"

"Present."

"Mascale, Jeremiah?"

"Present."

Adrian the aide had started register without her.

"Sorry I'm late. You wouldn't believe the South Arterial. How we doin'?"

"Perfect. Munoz, Victor?"

"Present."

"O'Caplan, Francis?"

"Got bad tummy, sir."

"No Franky?"

"Not today, sir. Burstaspendix, his mother said. Better next week."

"Okay. O'Shaughnessy, Iqbar?"

Spade Braithwaite

Mrs Matoo put her bags under the desk and sat in her seat, trying to breathe deeply.

"Welk, Hans?"

"Present."

Adrian ticked the last name, counted them up and handed the register to Mrs Matoo for her drawer.

"Good morning, class!"

"Good-mor-ning-Miss-is-Ma-too!"

"Okay, we have assembly fifteen minutes. Has anybody brought anything for show and tell?"

Two hands popped up, excitedly.

"Iqbar?"

Iqbar stood up in the second row and held up a little, plastic medal that was too small for anyone to see.

"Lovely, Iqbar. And what is it?"

"It's a medal, "awarded to my uncle for donating money at the tomb of Saint Theresa of Calcutta." He came back two days ago, an' gave it to me!"

"Wonderful! And you, Sam?"

At the back of the room, Sam stood and held up a grey metal box with yellow lettering and a wire dangling out the top.

"Very interesting. What is it?"

"Please miss, it's a special type of computer."

"Very interesting. How does it work?"

"Don't know miss, I just got it. After assembly I'm going to take it to Mr Frost for him to tell me about it."

Herbert Brewer's Dirty Little Secret

"Very good. Okay. Paul, collect in the essays, five hundred words on Pollution. If any one needs the toilet before assembly..."

Shawaz Manerife poured himself a juice, turned on his T.V. and skipped up the channels to a hundred and fifty seven. The BBC World Service.

The picture took a few seconds to appear. Shawaz lit a cigar while he was waiting.

"...And again at seven thirty. At eight fifteen we have the weekly, omnibus edition of Eastenders, followed, at nine fifteen, by Come Dancing, with Terry Wogan..."

Britain, as a nation, had always been completely unfathomable to Shawaz. British culture was such an important influence in the world, and yet, the British seemed to take pride in having their heads stuck up their arses.

Perhaps that was their secret. Shawaz settled into his chair and turned it up.

"...Paul MacKay covering the Paris Summit..."

Shawaz hated the news. Everyday it depressed him but Shawaz had to know what was going on. By the time the Israeli Embassy told you to flee, it was too late.

"... with global weather. But first, the International News Headlines, with Peter Barker..."

Shawaz liked Peter Barker. At least he had the decency to look embarrassed when he told you bad news.

Spade Braithwaite

"Good morning. I'm Peter Barker and this is the World News. Our main story, today, in Hollywood, Sir Jasper Carrot spoke to journalists about his nomination for, "Best Actor", for his title role in the film, "Shakespeare's Lost, Really, Bad Play." We'll have a full report on that later. Meanwhile, British soldiers are reported to be, "settling in nicely", in the civil-war ravaged country of Bundawa. Over to John McHonagillycuddy in Kinaida. John, can you hear us?"

The scene cut to live footage from Leopold Street, outside the Presidential Palace. A hairy, young reporter in a loud shirt, holding his ear and a microphone.

"Thank you, Peter. Well, on the street, here in Kinaida, everything seems calm enough. We've tried to find some evidence of recent rebel activity, but apart from the hundreds of hoax bomb threats received by the government and newspapers everyday, there really doesn't seem to be much going on."

The camera zoomed out until the shot included an elderly man in uniform, standing next to John.

"I have with me, Colonel August Forsythe, of the Highland Blues and Fusiliers. Colonel...,"

"Haloo."

"Colonel. I understand that you've established a base, in the interior, ready for the arrival of the major part of our forces, tomorrow. Realistically, what efforts can you make to tackle an enemy that seems, to all appearances, to have disappeared back into their jungle hideaways?"

Herbert Brewer's Dirty Little Secret

The colonel folded his hands behind his back and smiled.

"Ahh weel, laddie. Yon fuzzie's a canny, wee skally, so 'e is! B' w' gradely maynded o' the weeves 'n' wee'ns cot up in t' bliddy miss, so's we'll nery gan'n wee gans blarzin, 'r oot. We canny, y' ken? Saftly, saftly, y' knar."

John McHonagillycuddy nodded his head, appreciatively.

"Of course. Do you see a quick end to this crisis?"

"Ahh weel. Tha's t' meeny withers t' coont. Wither th' weel, 'r wither th' want. Etcetera. 'M naa tay bathered a' the praspect o' a scrimmage 'n tee, o' such. Tha's wa' wur here fair."

'Wise words indeed, Colonel! One last question..."

Shawaz saw it a full second before John or the Colonel heard it behind them.

Two thirds of the front, upper and middle floor of the Presidential Palace suddenly erupted.

"...what would...?"

KABOOOOM!

The picture spun backwards and ended up on the ground, showing Peter and the Colonel flat on the road, arms over their heads.

Glass and lumps of concrete, torn from the Palace's steel reinforcement, raining down around them.

"Oh my...Oh my God! Keep rolling! Something's happened, we don't know what. Colonel, are you okay?"

A twisted window frame spun gracefully back down from a thousand feet and scythed into the road, twenty yards away.

Spade Braithwaite

"Weel, m' bladder still warks!"

Shawaz flicked half an inch of cigar ash into the ashtray.

"Okay! We'll keep rolling. London?"

"Hello, John! This is Peter, in London. Something dramatic obviously just happened. Are you okay?"

"I think so, Peter. The camera's still working…? You okay, Mike? Okay. We seem to be uninjured but, as I'm sure you must have realised, an enormous explosion has…"

Shawaz pressed the stand-by button on the remote control and rested his cigar in the ash tray.

With an inch of juice left in his glass, Shawaz stood up, crossed to the cabinet and added the same amount of tequila.

Then he sat back down and retrieved his cigar.

Shawaz noticed, for the first time, that, if he lost focus and crossed his eyes, he could make the porcelain horses at either end of the breakfast bar come together.

He gulped half the mix back in one go.

"Shug'!"

"Honey?!"

"Shug'. Phone the school. We're goin' home for a while."

"Today?!"

"Today."

"What if there's no flight?"

"Then we'll fly somewhere else an' have a vacation on the way home."

"You' sure?!"

"Yeah. Maybe we'll come back."

"Okay, Honey. If you're sure!"

"Yeah. It's time."

Chapter 22

Back at Camp Good-News...

(Remember Camp Good-News? General Aemon Mussbierre is giving Charles, Shirley and Mama Jen lunch, at which they discuss their options. I know it all seems a long time ago (the middle of chapter nineteen) but things are coming together alarmingly quickly so try to stay with it.)

...lunch concluded with cigars and cognac.

Charles had never heard of cigars and cognac after lunch, but the more he thought about it the more sense it made.

Mama Jen chose a ten-inch, Cuban, elephant leg and trimmed it with her nail-scissors.

"Cognac?"

"Thank you very much, just a small one."

Colonel Neff poured some tall measures and passed them round.

Mama Jen sniffed the brandy and lit the huge cigar from a small wick on the humidor.

Spade Braithwaite

Aemon Mussbierre watched her with awed respect.

"So ladies, Charles, what do you think of our proposition?"

Mama Jen blew a tall, thin smoke-ring and sipped her brandy, thoughtfully.

"I have to admit, General, that your reputation seems to be more than justified. I'd want Charles to sit in with you, while you edit the small-print, concessions and liabilities and such. But, overall, I think that it's the best idea that I've heard in years. Charles?"

"Well, Mama Jen, it certainly sounds like a wonderful plan. I'm a little concerned about the safeguards to our position. I'm not being suspicious when I point out that circumstances can change very quickly. Alliances can wane, just as they can wax. I'd be happy to see some guarantees worked into the package."

Aemon poured some brandy into himself and refilled his glass from the decanter.

"Quite honestly, Charles, I've seen enough of Mama Jen's operation to know that Claust' is *her* town. I don't doubt that if, at any time, you feel that you're being fucked-over, you could bring the whole thing to a stand-still, with significant losses all round. We're business men. We like to make a profit. I'm assuming that the three of you would accept honorary, senior military rank, with stock options?"

Mama Jen took a draught of spirit and blew a perfect smoke-ring in the shape of Texas.

Herbert Brewer's Dirty Little Secret

"All negotiable, I'm sure. I endorse Charles' concerns, but I think that we can give you tentative approval. Subject to the small print..."

"Perfect! One other thing, we got three recruits, and a corpse, from Claust'. Do you want us to do anythin' with them?"

Shirley drank some brandy to get the smoke out of her throat.

"Burghhh! 'Scuse me! The twins we don't want back. Do whatever you like with 'em."

"Okay. But, we got the impression that the other feller might be somethin' of a tough-guy. We appreciate a bit o' mettle, in the army."

"Josh Matenach! I mean, Herbert Brewer. Lovely lad. We're all very sorry that he had to leave town, for personal reasons."

"Quite, I'm sure."

"Can we put something in the contract, guaranteeing him the very best career?"

"We certainly can. But the twins, you don't care?"

"So long as they don't come back to Claust'."

"Lovely. Okay! All agreed. Can I just ask that we keep everything quiet for a few more days. Tell y'r people, back home, that we're sorted, but keep the town tied up until you read about it in the papers."

Aemon rose to shake everybody's hands.

"Sorted!"

Spade Braithwaite

Jon-Paul Clifton finally got through to Samuel Guarthje on a pay phone from Clausthowlersnauglerbogler International Airport.

"Samuel!"

"Jon-Paul! Where the hell have you been?"

"Your secretary wouldn't put me through until I called from the airport. Don't ask *me*, mate. Anyway, what's the crack?"

"You're in Claust'?"

"Yeah. At the airport."

"Good. You've read about the conscription situation in Claust', I presume?"

"Yeah, in the Clarion. Although I wouldn't use the Clarion to make papier mâchè."

"You've got your lap-top with you?"

"Yeah."

"Good, 'cause I've e-mailed you a full report. What I need you to do, is…"

Victoria Charring-Cross was the Mayoress of Braithwaite and she took the job seriously. The benefits included Luncheon Vouchers that Victoria could redeem at the Cattleman's Club.

"Cattle's", was two hundred yards from City Hall, along Younghusband Place and, on Fridays, they did a very passable Tex/Mex buffet.

Herbert Brewer's Dirty Little Secret

Sally Israel, Managing Director of Amsarnie-Microtech had an idea that Victoria would be at the Cattleman's and took the chance to catch her.

Victoria had a problem with fajitas. She felt that, if she' wanted to make her own lunch then she'd have brought a sandwich.

"Vicky! Allow me. Tomato?"

"Thank you Sally, everything."

"Two, or three?"

"Three, thank you. How are you?"

"Lovely. Have you seen the Clarion, today?"

"The Clarion?! I wouldn't use it to light my boiler. What have they got? Don't tell me they've found another Dead-Sea-Scroll with God's phone number."

"You haven't read about Clausthowler-thing-u-ma-jig evading the draught?"

"What are you talking about?!"

"It's a rash across their front page! Clausthowlerfowlerdoppler, in the western desert, isn't sending any soldiers to answer the draught, so there!"

"They can't get away with it. If you're called, then you have to go. I'm only sorry that we weren't chosen. We'd have done 'em proud, with our brave boys."

"I know, but, barbecue, or duck sauce?"

"Barbecue."

"I know, but it makes me wonder about that Federal Factory

Spade Braithwaite

Tax that they imposed last year. If Claustholwer-wherever-it-is can buck Federal Government over the draught, then maybe we could fight them over the Factory tax?!"

"I can't imagine. We submitted two hundred and fifteen million dollars in federal taxes last year, and received nearly twice as much in Federal Subsidies. I put a lot of time and effort into my relations with the Departments."

"But it doesn't seem right. Clausthowler-whatever, just defying the Prime Minister when they feel like it. It's unconstitutional."

"If they break any Federal laws then they'll get well screwed."

"Actually, I'm thinking of having a few of the chaps over to my place tonight. See if anyone's got any ideas about *us* challenging a couple of things."

"You can't be serious! Some bloody camel-stop town, that no one's ever heard of, pulls a stunt, and you want anarchy!"

"Don't be ridiculous, Vicky! It just seems, from what I've read, that old Cartright might be *on the outs*, and if we're going to have a change, well, then I'd like to go into it with a firm handshake. If you know what I mean."

"Bloody-hell, Sally! I'll read the article and phone my contacts at the Fed'. I think I might even have Cartright's number somewhere. DON'T, do anything stupid 'til I've found out what's going on! Okay?!"

"Vicky! We're not children. Drink?"

"Half a lager."

Herbert Brewer's Dirty Little Secret

"Fine. Isn't that Heston Mckane at your usual table?"

"Bloody-hell! Mr, "Octopus-hands". Don't ever dance with him. Or sit too near him."

"I think he's quite dishy."

"He's all yours. I'll be in the conservatory."

Valerie Benfield hadn't been into her office for six months. She did enough work from home to stop anyone bothering to look for her.

Valerie was almost the very best in her field. Information Technology, and the manipulation thereof.

Every morning her terminal clocked her in at eight and clocked her out after five. Her telephone extension diverted all calls, digitally, to her home. Not that anyone talked to anyone else, anymore.

The best thing about working from home was the Programme. Valerie had a Programme that logged every keyboard entry she made, twenty seconds behind the previous one. That meant that if Valerie put in two good hours in the morning she could take the rest of the day off and leave her PC entering data, with a short lunch, well into overtime.

The Friday afternoon classic movie was Rock Hudson and Doris Day in, "Secretarial Shenanigans!", on channel ninety three. Rock Hudson couldn't have been gay. Not with that chin.

"Blurrp!"

The extension phone!

Spade Braithwaite

"Shit. Hello, Valerie Benfield, Database Management. How can help you?"

Rock Hudson pulled up to the front door of his self-made, corporate empire in a Porsche convertible. A venerable, old doorman opened Rock's car door and tipped his hat, respectfully.

"Young sir!"

"Good morning, Gittles. How's the...,"

Valerie hit the sound button on the remote.

"Hello, is that Valerie Benfield?"

"Yes."

"Ughm, Valerie. Samuel Guarthje, Inland Attorney here. I've got a little job for you that might well prove to be your making, if it's handled discreetly."

"Mr Grrarth-chi, we all signed the National Security Act when we started. How can I help you?"

Rock Hudson burst, silently into his office, threw his hat onto the stand and paged his secretary to book a lunch table at Chez Groovy. Valerie had seen it fifteen times. She flicked two inches of cigarette ash onto the heap covering her ash tray.

"I'm sure that you've heard about our situation in Clausthowler-bogler-snaugler?"

Samuel tried to picture Valerie. She sounded like a dirty bitch. Career girl with a garter belt and silk underwear. Samuel liked a bit of that.

"Clausthowlersnauglerbogler?"

Herbert Brewer's Dirty Little Secret

Valerie scratched her belly-button, as deep as her pinkie could reach and opened her buttocks to pass gas silently.

"That's the place. I'm going to send you a small list of some solvent citizens currently on their Defence Register. I want you to tap into their banking details and freeze their transactions. As if it was a Domestic Revenue audit."

Samuel Guarthje sounded exotically husky. Like Johnny Weissmuller.

"I'll need the specific codes, for that."

"They should be in your system, already. When you've done it, I'll need you to forward the results to my man in Claust'. I'll send his address. I don't need to tell you, Valerie, that if you sort this little thing out, for me, I'll be extremely grateful"

"How grateful?"

Rock Hudson changed into plus-fours to play golf with Tony Randolph.

"Dinner, at Chez Grande-Femme?"

"Sounds perfect. Consider it done."

"Wonderful!"

Valerie hung up, hit the power button on the remote and resigned herself to doing some more work.

"Bloody Clausthowlersmellybuggers!"

Sure enough, there was one unread file in her secure folder.

Valerie typed in a password and opened it.

```
            20:5     13:37hrs
s_guarthje@inland.fed.com.ae
```

Spade Braithwaite

```
      TOP SECRET! ANY UNAUTHORISED
REPRODUCTION OR TRANMISSION OF ANY
      PARTS OF THIS FILE, BEYOND THIS
BUILDING, WILL BE PROSECUTED AND
      PUNISHED TO THE FULL EXTENT OF FEDERAL
LAW. WE'RE WATCHING YOU!


            Dear Valerie,
                 The following are all account
holders with the Randolph First National Bank
in Claust'. To access the bank computer and
ascertain their account numbers you will need
the code:
                 BYZ_3037574AUGBH_73747CLAU
            Banski, John Elmore, born:21:12:81
            Butterworth, George Town,
born:20:5:83
            Gordon, Brian Micheal, born:28:2:80
```
And so on.

Valerie copied the code and pasted it into her remote access programme.

It took three minutes to get through, with a tiny Elvis shaking his hips to show her that the computer was working.

The screen turned plain grey and black letters started to appear.

```
      Randolph First National Bank
```

Herbert Brewer's Dirty Little Secret

Surname:

Banski, enter.

First names:

John Elmore, enter.

Date of birth:

21-12-1981, enter.

Two seconds.

Herbert Brewer, nee: John Elmore Banski

37, Coronation Road

D.O.B.:21st December, 1981.

Employment history: June 1997, Draughting Apprentice, Brewer and Son, Coronation Road.

December 2000, Qualified: Junior Draughtsman

November 2001, Promoted: Draughtsman

Valeria expanded the, "action", menu and clicked on, "change paramaters".

The screen went blank before turning pink, with little hearts and flowers.

"What the fuck?!"

Bold red letters.

Expand Your Penis!

Naturally, herbally! She'll love you for it!

Spade Braithwaite

Gifts   -   Magazines   -   Contacts   -
Live Video Links

"What the fuckin' hell?!"

Valerie clicked *back* and Randolph First National Bank reappeared. With Herbert Brewer, nee: John Elmore Banski.

"Tools." Bottom of the list, "Manual options", "enter circumvention code:"

Valerie entered the code.

The screen immediately became pink, with little hearts and flowers. Bold red letters.

Expand Your Penis!

Naturally, herbally! She'll love you for it!

Gifts   -   Magazines   -   Contacts   -
Live Video Links

"Cock-suckin' crap!"

Back to Randolph First National. "Networking", "Direct Dial", "Verify secure link".

Valerie typed, skipped, linked and entered codes furiously for five minutes.

Enter.

A pink screen, with little hearts and flowers. Bold red letters.

Expand Your Penis!

Naturally, herbally! She'll love you for it!

Gifts - Magazines - Contacts - Live Video Links

"You! You fuckin' little shit-house! What the hell 'ave they done?!"

Valerie pushed the eraser-end of a pencil into her nostril and turned it, vacantly.

What, the hell, had they done? How, the hell, had they done it?

Valerie pulled the pencil out and bit the eraser clean off.

Samuel Guarthje sounded just like Tarzan, over the phone.

What the hell had they done?

Charles phoned Gary Crozier's office number straight after lunch.

Gary took the call at his desk.

"Hello?... Charles, mate! How's it goin'? ...No shit?! You've got to be shittin' me! That's brilliant news. Who's idea was that? ...Get-the-hell-out! Brilliant news, mate...For how long? No problem. I'll phone Laurence. Good job, Charles! Take care."

Janet listened to Gary's side of the conversation with interest.

"Good news?"

"...Nah, not really. Get Laurence on the phone, will y'. He's either at Don Ricci's or the Blandford. Close the door on your way out."

"Yessir, mas'er!"

Spade Braithwaite

    Janet closed the door behind her.

    Gary leaned back in his seat drummed a little tattoo on his belly.

    "Goo-ood day, su-un shine! Do d' do, Goo-ood day, su-un shine!"

    Laurence was lying on his bed, luxuriating in Blandford opulence when the phone rang. He rolled over two full times to get to the other side of the bed and pick up.

    "Hello?…Sure…Gary?… Get-the-fuck-out! Honestly?…Whose idea was that?…Fuckin' unbelievable! That's the best news I've ever heard! Fantastic!…Ahh, she's okay. Don Ricci made a fuss of her, which was nice… Havin' a shower, I think. We were' goin' to go to the Post Office, see if we could pretend to do something there… How long for?…I think we can manage that. Fuckin' brilliant news! I'll speak to you later. B'bye!"

    Laurence dropped the handset back into its cradle and sang a happy song.

    "Dere's an' ol' man called de Mississippi! Dat's de ol' man I would like to be! What does he care…"

    Assistant Emergency Supervisor Alison Dawa was drying her hair when Laurence knocked.

    "Hold on!"

    She switched the hair dryer off and quickly pulled a grey dress up, over her underwear.

    "Come in!"

Herbert Brewer's Dirty Little Secret

Laurence entered.

"Good news, Miss Dawa..."

"Alison, please."

Laurence paused for a moment to appreciate the sunlight on Alison's nearly dry hair. Pale, washed skin and bare legs, under a sensible, grey dress. Big brown eyes that looked almost vulnerable.

"I have good news, Alison. I've just received a call from my man in Gunswale and it seems that I've solved the problem."

"Solved the problem...? How?"

"I can't tell you any of the details, just yet, but we can relax."

"...And fly home?"

"Ahh..., not yet. I can't announce anything for a few more days, so we're going to have to sit tight and pretend that we're still working on it. We've got the afternoon off, though."

W.W.J.K.D.? What would Jaquelline Kennedy do. At this point, Alison had no idea.

"Thank goodness."

Alison fluttered her eyelashes and pouted, nervously.

"Would you.., would you like to stay with me..., for the afternoon?"

Alison noticed dirty underwear on the floor. She sat upright and flicked it under the bed with her left foot.

Laurence gulped.

"That..., that would be very nice. Should I get some wine sent up?"

"I'd like that. Can I ask..., one thing?"

"Go right ahead!"

"Can you..., can we, have a female-oriented sex scene?'

Laurence shrugged. What the hell was a female oriented sex scene? Eight chapters of nonsense before he'd even get to see her nipples, probably.

"I'll do my best, but our author, well..., he isn't exactly a Nobel Prize winner, or anything."

"I'd noticed!"

"How's this?"

Laurence assumed a pose that he considered masterful, and yet sensitive.

Alison took an ice cube from something nearby that had ice cubes in it, and rubbed her neck, seductively. Men really *did not* have a bloody clue!

Laurence enjoyed an uncharacteristic blood-rush to his loin.

Alison licked the ice cube and dropped it on the carpet.

"Are you married?"

Laurence couldn't help but notice a slight reversal of blood pressure.

"Ughhm..., yes."

"Thank you for being honest."

Alison stood up and let the dress fall to her ankles. Comfy, plain white Marks & Sparks knickers and big, white bra.

Laurence gulped again. Blood resumed its flow.

"Is this how a female-oriented sex scene goes?"

"No. I've given up. Let's just have a shag."

"Okay."

Alison reached behind and unclasped the bra.

"Our author isn't going to win any prizes for this, you know?"

"He doesn't care. Wow! They're beautiful! Can I put my nose in between 'em?"

"I suppose."

Chapter 23

Gunswale. 2 a.m., Sunday, the twenty second of May.

Stepanos Giraldo hated the Saturday night into Sunday shift. Everybody was drunk, tired and emotional, except Stepanos, who wasn't drunk.

He counted down the mailboxes and pulled up to the curb outside number 12A.

In the back seat, his passengers didn't even notice that he'd stopped. Stepanos saw a flash of nipple, in his mirror as the lout put his hand up the girl's blouse. Somebody's daughter. Stepanos shook his head.

"We're there! 12A, Kitchener Close. Safe an' sound."

"Thanks, mate! Lovely job!"

The lout dragged himself off and let the girl straighten herself.

Spade Braithwaite

Stepanos hated being called, "Mate". He wanted to say, "Do I look like one of your mates? Am I a spotty, fashion-victim? Do I parade myself like a Turkish catamite? Do *not* call me, "mate"!"

Instead, he said, "Nine dollars and thirty five, please."

"Here mate, keep the change!"

Stepanos pocketed fifteen dollars with a sigh.

"Thanks, buddy. You have a good night."

"Yeah!"

Stepanos got out the cab and lit a cigarette. Bloody, teenage bastards! Scum of the earth. But then, every job had a shitty side, or else people wouldn't pay you to do it.

"Car fifty four, where are you?"

Stepanos flicked the cigarette towards a storm-grate and reached into his cab for the radio mike.

"Stepanos here. I'm in Kitchener Close, by the Bisley Bowl-A-Rama. What's up?"

"You're gunna like this one!"

"My penis shrivels!"

"No, seriously. You're gunna like this one. Two calls on the same errand. Both wanting first editions of the Sunday papers. Double fare, almost. Get over to Wheat Street and do a round of the newspapers, picking up two copies of every Sunday edition. One lot to one address, and one lot to the other."

"Where?"

"You ready?"

"Yeah."

Herbert Brewer's Dirty Little Secret

"First, Prime Minister Dereck Cartright at Duncarin..."

"Fuck off!"

"Seriously! Duncarin, opposite the Parliament Assembly Building on Three Wheel Lane. The red door, next to the basketball hoop. Knock loudly. And then, a Mr Samuel Grarr-ith-chai."

"Spell that?"

"Can't! Mr Grarr-ith-chai, number two, Aerhardt Crescent, off Buxmont Road."

"I know where it is. Is this for real?"

"Sure is. Gentlemen, start your meters!"

"Fine! Good job."

By nine o clock, Samuel Guarthje had read every word of every Sunday paper published in Gunswale, including *City-Beat* and *Swing-Scene*.

Not one mention of his name. Not even an obscure reference.

Dereck Cartright, on the other hand, was getting carved up like a pepperoni. Every single newspaper headlined with news of an escalation in the Bundawa conflict and a different version of Dereck's incompetent handling of the situation.

Even the Dilbert was a joke about, "Anarchy in Amsarnie!"

The *Times* and the *Clarion* both hinted that they expected Dereck to be charged with corruption at any moment.

But no mention of Samuel Guarthje.

Spade Braithwaite

Samuel stared vacantly at the back page of the *Correspondent* and drifted away.

This is a paid advertisement: Amazing Developments in Follicle Resurgence!...

"Samuel! People are here!"

"Send them down!"

Samuel arranged the newspapers into a spread across the centre of the table.

Samuel's wife charmed the guests almost all the way to the family room.

"You know the way. Tea? Or coffee, anyone?"

Heavy feet tested the stairs.

"No thank you. Samuel!"

"Bernard, Charles!"

Bernard Kent, Foreign Advocate and Charles Mintion, the Cabinet Secretary, both sprightly after eight hours of innocent sleep.

"Is Stephen likely to be here?"

Bernard seated himself and picked through the papers.

"Not really. He phoned to say that he was still sodomizing some boy he met last night and he prob'ly wouldn't make it. How about the newspapers! Good stuff, eh?"

Charles picked up the *Clarion* to read, "**Claust-Gate! – Cartright's Final Waterloo?!**"

Samuel fetched three light-beers from the mini-fridge.

"Not really. Something's wrong. Something's very badly wrong!"

"Samuel! It's better than we expected. Cartright's got his dick properly in the snare this time."

"But something's not right. Cartright knows we're selling him out, and yet…,"

"He's last week's cheese, an' he knows it."

"No! Not Dereck. He hasn't denied anything, or made any counter claims, or done anything to save himself at all. He's up to something."

"You're paranoid, Samuel. He hasn't done anything to save himself because there's nothing he can do. I've already leaked a basket full of Internal Memorandums, washing my hands of the whole affair. I think I even initialled one of 'em!"

Samuel had to smile, in spite of himself.

"You leaked a memorandum with your initials on it, Bernard?! That was rather brave, wasn't it?!"

"Not really. There's a bloke in the outer office with the same initials, so I can always say it was him. Anyway, Cartright's down the u-bend and it's sink or swim for the rest of us."

Samuel took a pull at his light-beer and felt a little bit happier than he had for a couple of days.

"Yeah. Maybe Cartright knows he's screwed and he's just going gracefully."

The word, "gracefully", caught in Samuel's throat. Dereck Cartright had never done anything graceful in his life.

Spade Braithwaite

"It's the only explanation, Samuel."

Samuel nodded, thoughtfully.

Dereck Cartright wasn't a good loser. In fact, Dereck wasn't a loser, if he could sacrifice someone else in his place.

Samuel was sure that Dereck had seen into his soul. Dereck knew where the leaks had come from, and for Dereck to try to shift responsibility made perfect sense. But Dereck hadn't.

Dereck hadn't done diddley.

That meant one of two things. Either Dereck was laying a paper trail, even deeper than their Departmental Memorandums, covering his own arse and laying the blame somewhere else...,

Or else...,

By nine thirty Prime Minister Cartright was more than ready for bed. It had been a long night. John Sumwun was spread across on the carpet, snoring like a coal-shunt.

Twelve different newspapers, piled on the desk, all running different stories of bombs and bloodshed in Bundawa. The only common factor was their criticism of Dereck and his handling of the call-up. According to all sources, Dereck was yesterday's man.

It was time for something, shit-or-bust.

General Aemon Mussbiere had promised to phone at nine thirty. Dereck hated people that didn't phone when they said they would.

He turned the radio on.

Herbert Brewer's Dirty Little Secret

"...with the time coming up to nine thirty...,"

The phone rang. Dereck turned the radio off and picked up.

"Hello? Thank you, put him on."

John Sumwun woke himself up with a great, big fart.

"Is it...,"

"Shu' up! Hello, Aemon? Did they...,? Really?! But, did the...? Wow! And the...? Unbe-fuckin'-lievable! So you're sure? Brilliant! ... An' that's carved in stone, 'cause I need somethin' concrete, soon! Fuckin' brilliant, mate! What about these bombs goin' off in Bundawa? You reckon...? I'm not 'appy about that, but if you reckon... I'm tired an' emotional. Gi' me six hours sleep, an' then I wanna provoke 'em, just a little bit more. Can I announce it on... Tuesday 'll be fine! Cheers buddy, an' you! Take i' easy, mate...! And you! Good bye!"

"Did he...?"

"Yes, he bloody-well-did!"

"Brilliant! Hooray for our side!"

"Hoo-bloody-ray! Man, I'm tired! I'm going to sleep for a while. Don't let anyone disturb me."

"I'd take the bullet for you, man!"

"Don't be a cunt, an' don't let anything disturb me. Good-night. I'm fuckin' tired...,"

"Bye-bye. Sweet dreams."

Back in Claust', Samuel Guarthje's man, John-Paul Clifton parked his car in the cul-de-sac adjacent to Bloxam Terrace and cut through the trees towards the third house. An old wheelbarrow was propped against the fence, creating the perfect vantage point.

Jon-Paul took his binoculars and squatted on the wheelbarrow to reconnoitre.

Bloody-nora!

In the upstairs window, behind a three-foot gap in the curtains, a petite, Asian woman in a white bra was pacing up and down, apparently talking to someone else in the room.

After a couple of minutes the woman paused to face the hidden person. Hands on hips and an attitude that was visible from the fence. Suddenly she launched herself onto what Jon-Paul guessed was a bed. The top of her head still visible, bobbing up and down, and somebody's big, ugly, flat feet, waving around like antenna.

Jon-Paul felt his blood quicken.

"Mornin'!"

Jon-Paul keeled over backwards at the feet of an old man, walking his dog.

"Uh..., good morning! Western Desert Hoot-Owls! I think I saw an owl, on that roof!"

"I don't doubt it. Every Sunday mornin', and a couple o' times durin' the week. It's better when it's dark an' they got the lights on. Lucky bastards! There's pictures on the internet, if you're int'rested."

"Thank you, no. If I can confirm a Western Hoot-Owl then it'll be worth my trip."

"Good luck, boy!"

"Thank you."

Thirty-two minutes later, the owner of the flat feet appeared, dressed in a cardigan and sweat pants and disappeared out the front door. Jon-Paul guessed that he was going for a newspaper.

Ten minutes later, flat-foot was back, with a newspaper and a bag of Sunday breakfast groceries.

Jon-Paul contemplated his own Sunday morning ritual and hawked a big greenie onto a pile of brussel-stalks and broken glass.

Forty-seven minutes and flat-foot was on the move again, wearing khaki casuals and a pale-blue, short-sleeved shirt. Flat-foot was going to meet someone.

Through the kitchen window, the Asian woman tucked him in and pulled his chin down for a kiss on the lips.

"So long, flat-foot!"

Jon-Paul ran back to his car and drove around the block to their driveway.

Bloxam crescent contained fifty houses, numbered consecutively on the right side to the end and then returning back down the left side. Number twenty-four was in the turn-around at the very end.

Spade Braithwaite

Jon-Paul considered it for a moment before getting out the car.

The whole concept of the place was appallingly mid-middle-class, with a kidney-shaped, mulched shrubbery at the centre of two hundred square feet of front lawn. Jon-Paul could almost picture the Fonze living above their garage.

The doorbell would almost certainly be one of those Binge-Bong affairs, that people always associate with Avon cosmetics.

Jon-Paul got out of his rented car and walked up the drive to the front door. A stereotypical, polyurethane, replacement door with a guaranteed life of five hundred years.

Jon-Paul pressed the door bell.

Bluuurp...blup...bluruurp...blip.

The door opened almost immediately, giving Jon-Paul his first close look at the beautiful, Asian face that he'd seen through the window.

"Hello?!"

"Mrs Crozier? Mrs Bo-Bae Crozier?"

"Hello."

"Mother of one..., James Isaac Crozier?"

Bo-Bae turned her shoulders forty-five degrees to the visitor and kicked him, very quickly in testicles and then the stomach.

Jon-Paul felt himself losing the element of surprise. He let his body sag onto the crazy paving and hurled his breakfast across the herbaceous border.

"Please...!"

A fist like an axe-blow caught Jon-Paul between the eyes and he slumped into a neat heap, dreaming of his little, Scottish Grandmother.

Bo-Bae considered the unconscious turd on her doorstep and punched him once more, behind the ear.

"Pickle-head!"

Bo-Bae dragged the visitor by his ears, into the garage and covered him with an old carpet.

Then she swilled a couple of buckets across her hostas and phoned her husband on his mobile number.

"Hallo?"

"Honey! He came, like you said he might!"

"Who.., what?"

"The government man! He came and tried to find out where our-Jim was!"

"Wait.., someone came to the house?"

"Yeah! He came an' he interrogated me about Jim!"

"Shit! Where is he now?"

"He's in the garage, under a carpet."

"I'll be right there!"

"I love you!"

"I love you, too. I'll be right there!"

General Aemon Mussbiere took daily court at Camp Good-News, like the seasoned campaigner that he was. With two gentlemen of the press and a lot of reporters in audience.

Spade Braithwaite

"Next question?"

"General Mus'be-a', early reports indicate that six British soldiers were among the casualties in yesterday's terrorist attacks. Can you confirm that no Amsarnie soldiers were lost in the operation?"

"I can confirm that our army has incurred no casualties, so far. The six British soldiers that were killed were, in fact, in a hotel, doin' the local talent. Our boys 'ave been discouraged from this sort of activity due to the high incidence of S.T.D.s, namely, bum-rot. We are supplyin' prophylactic sheaths, an' educatin' our troops in the safe use thereof, but y' can't be too careful. Nex' question."

"General, how is the treason in Clausthowlersnauglerbogler affecting your plans? I understand that Mr Cartright's inability to execute the draught competently has left you dangerously short of soldiers. Would it..."

"Mr...?"

"Yarull Levinson, the *Cognoscenti*. Would it...,"

"Mr Levinson. For obvious reasons, the numbers of military personnel, and the specific nature of their deployment within our strategy of national security have always been an official secret. May I also remind you that treason is still a capital crime, so I'd be very careful about making accusations, if I were you. Nex' question."

Herbert Brewer's Dirty Little Secret

"General. Pablo Harrison, the *Correspondent*. General, given the recent escalation of violence, how can you guarantee the safety of our troops in Bundawa?"

"Mr Harrison, I can't completely guarantee my own safety in the shower. Of course I can't guarantee the safety of soldiers in a fuckin' war zone! But that's why we send soldiers, and not school-lunch ladies. I am able to guarantee that every possible precaution is being taken to minimise the likelihood of injury. Any real questions? No? Good! Thank you very much, ladies and gentlemen. We'll be available for questions tomorrow at the earlier time of nine thirty. Good morning."

Aemon and his two staffers rose from their seats and marched out of the auditorium through the back way.

"Wankers! The sooner we get back to obscurity, the better I'll like it!"

"Did you see that bird from the *TV Times*. Unbelievable tits!"

"The *TV Times* don't even publish any news! What were they even doin' here?"

"Maybe it affects scheduling, or something. She did 'ave some Bristols, though. I wouldn' o' minded."

Back in the command room, Aemon pulled his chair out from his desk and subsided into it.

"Arnie! Get me a plate-full of somethin'. Are they still doin' breakfast?"

"Prob'ly. Fo' you. I 'eard they were doin' a roast beef set-up for lunch."

Spade Braithwaite

"Perfect. Get me a roast beef sandwich, on that crusty bread, with horseradish and pickled onions. And a couple o' roasties with gravy. Good lad. What time is i', in Bundawa?"

"Uhh, half eleven, minus five hours. Half past six."

"Is Schooly's report in the system yet?"

"Prob'ly not. He should be up an' about, if you want to call 'im."

"Good lad. Get 'im on the line, will y'? The secure line. Wha's the date, today?"

"Sunday the twenty second."

Aemon let his attention completely focus on a quarterly requisition report from the Port Precaria Import/Export Office for thirty seconds until his phone rang.

"Mark! Find out why the fuck Barnacle-Bill thinks he needs eight new Cadillacs. Send some crew over, if you 'ave to. Yes, hello? Thank you, put 'im on. Schooly?"

Half past six in Bundawa but Major J Schooly had been up all night. A long night.

"Gov'ner! How is it in civilisation?"

"Don't know mate, never been there. What's goin' on?"

"It's been a long night. Let me tell you..."

Chapter 24

Six thirty a.m.in Bundawa.

Major J Schooly, Commander of Amsarnie's forces in Bundawa sipped his coffee and calculated the time difference. Six thirty, plus five hours, made it…, half past eleven in Amsarnie. The pubs would be open.

Schooly took another sip of coffee and scowled.

"Richard!"

"Boss-man?"

"Richey-boy. Give us a ciggy. Who's back yet?"

"Everybody, except for twenty crew at the barracks an' five medical-crew due back any minute. 'Ere y' go. Non-filter, I'm afraid."

Schooly took the cigarette thankfully. It was funny how smoking and alcoholism always got a bad press because they were both very positive aspects of Schooly's daily routine.

"That'll do. Good lad. Down-grade the alert to, "Caution". Keep twenty men on the fence an' the gate an' order everyone else to sleep until further notice. Let me know when we hear from anyone."

"'Scuse me, boss, the Gov'ners on the phone!"

"Put him through. Hello?"

General Mussbiere's voice crackled through the elaborate scrambler system.

Spade Braithwaite

"Schooly?"

"Gov'ner! How is it in civilisation?"

"Don't know mate, never been there. What's goin' on?"

"It's been a long night. Let me tell you…

It had been a very long twenty four hours. The previous morning, Major J Schooly had been on the phone, speaking to a General at the Presidential Palace when the line had suddenly gone dead. It had taken ten minutes on the radio to find out that a number of very powerful bombs had exploded in and around Kinaida.

Leaving a minimum crew guarding the fence, Schooly had taken every other man and arrived on Leopold Avenue twenty-eight minutes after the first explosion. Only just in time to control a major breakdown of discipline among Bundawa's armed forces.

The National Barracks were right behind the Presidential Palace and a lot of Bundawanese soldiers weren't as old or as experienced as their government claimed.

On arrival at the scene, Schooly's crew had shot three local soldiers trying to rape a secretary they'd pulled from the rubble of the Presidential Palace. Unfortunately, the secretary had also been shot, but Schooly's crew had learned an important lesson about fire-burst groupings from their new Kashmirnikov rifles.

Herbert Brewer's Dirty Little Secret

Half a dozen Bundawanese soldiers had witnessed the execution and within five minutes the entire Bundawan National Army were discussing it.

Schooly rode the momentum.

Both of Bundawa's tank crews were quickly identified and pressed into service, shunting wrecked cars to create control-points on all the Leopold Avenue approaches.

Two foraging crews had produced a crane-truck, back-hoes and fifty construction workers to help search the rubble for survivors.

A British television crew had been filming the Palace as the explosion happened. Schooly's crew had found them, terrified and tearful but apparently, still broadcasting, barricaded inside an abandoned ice-cream van.

With the telephone system down, Schooly had taken advantage of their live-link to London to find out what the hell was happening in Kinaida. Producers at the BBC had interrupted regular programming on both channels to carry live footage of the most exciting television that anyone had ever seen.

Also, an incredible piece of luck, the film crew had a Colonel of the British Army with them.

With Leopold Avenue in hand, Schooly had felt comfortable leaving it under the supposed command of a senior British officer and directed his attention to the other main situations.

Spade Braithwaite

The television office in London had passed on reports of five different explosions around Kinaida. The most serious of which was the bombing of the Hotel Côtedumore, with eighteen unconfirmed deaths including four British soldiers.

By the time Schooly arrived, the British had executed the controlled detonation of three further, suspicious devices and managed to drop a hundred foot chimney across their temporary command vehicle, killing two more British soldiers.

Schooly had reconnoitred and decided to keep his crew well out of it.

The second crew, he'd sent to a Catholic School off the north-arterial road, where a bomb had exploded in an outside lavatory. Two children had been killed and a lot of students and staff badly injured. Schooly's crew had secured the situation and organised a relief operation. No big deal.

The third crew had gone to an explosion at the Imperial Kitchener Tennis Club and encountered heavy flack from a horde of hysterical, middle-aged ladies with shooting-sticks and tea-trays. Beyond that, the crew reckoned about seven dead grounds-men and servants in a smoking crater where the maintenance buildings had once been.

What a fuckin' mess.

By four o clock all the crews were back on Leopold Avenue.

At half past four Silus Mantè's niece and protégé, Isabella had arrived to confirm her uncle's death and make trouble.

Herbert Brewer's Dirty Little Secret

Thirty-four year old Isabella Mantè, Director of Social Reform and the most obvious heir to her uncle's tyranny.

Schooly had flirted with the idea of killing her, just to change history. Like the hypothetical man in the debate, who committed the one immoral act to prevent an epoch of untold horror.

He'd flirted but he hadn't consummated.

Despots were a whole lot easier to deal with than interim coalitions.

He had, however, shot one of her body-guards for threatening his crew with a pistol, before introducing himself.

Thankfully, Isabella had accepted Schooly's advice and buggered-off to hold-up at her uncle's Beach Palace for a few days.

Schooly sent a truck-full of her own soldiers to look after her.

The Gov'nor would like Isabella. Six foot tall and frighteningly beautiful. Blacker than a tax-man's heart and more deadly than a Volvo full of frat'-boys.

At seventeen hundred hours Schooly had sent half of the operative crew back to camp, under order of intensive sleep.

Shortly before eighteen hundred hours, a report came in of another, serious incident. Murder and unbecoming conduct at the Brighton Beach Spa Resort, ten miles outside town.

Schooly had taken thirty men and gone to investigate. By the time they arrived everything was over.

Schooly counted seven heads amongst the scattered body parts, spread through four rooms. All of them, well fed, negro males. Hacked to pieces in a spontaneous outburst of mob-retribution. Looted, mutilated and then abandoned in an even more spontaneous occurrence of fleeing-the-scene when Schooly and his crew arrived.

The Resort Manager was beyond hysterical when they finally found him, hiding in a water tank.

Three horse-tranquillisers and half an hour of field-therapy had established the approximate identities of the dead men. Apparently, they were the entire Bantu Nation Redeemist Guerrilla Rebel Force, registered under false names but fooling no one.

When the BBC World Service had reported the explosion at the Catholic school, things had gone bad. A possè of tired, emotional house keeping staff had taken matters into their own hands, with swords and an oyster-knife.

Schooly rescued a bottle and a couple of cases of 'Tella beer to salute the end of a rebellion.

Schooly, five barmen, two ice-wallahs and thirty crew raised their cans in a toast. The Resort Manager had saluted by bitting through a vacuum cleaner lead, knocking himself out and shorting the entire ring-main.

Back on Leopold Avenue, Schooly was tired.

After the sun went down gangs of opportunists had tried everything imaginable, and a few things that even Schooly wouldn't have imagined.

Herbert Brewer's Dirty Little Secret

Under the supposed direction of British Colonel August Forsythe, Schooly had divided the Bundawanese army up into small missions and sent them to patrol the outlying suburbs. Schooly's own crews had covered the down-town district.

Fifty-eight reported murders. Somewhere between twenty-seven and thirty-two summary, military executions, depending on whose account you believed.

Shortly after eight o clock a British Captain and two Sergeants had turned up on Leopold Avenue, asking for their Colonel back.

Schooly had learned enough about the British to suggest a wee-dram and some good cigars before they left. By the time they had left, the two Sergeants were saluting the, "Honourable Dereck Cartright", and the Captain had given Schooly a photograph of his airdale setter.

The British were a bloody-funny crew to deal with. While Schooly himself was quietly relieved that his crew hadn't experienced a single casualty, the British seemed to be quite proud of their six deaths. And so, Schooly had toasted them, avoiding any reference to the circumstances or their negligent incompetence.

At midnight Schooly had ordered the sleepers, back at camp, to relieve operative crews and the operative crews back to camp to sleep.

Three armoured carriers, each with five crew, patrolling the streets. Twenty, big, ugly, security-crew, armed to the teeth, keeping an eye on the National Barracks and five medical personnel still out at the Memorial Hospital.

At four a.m., Schooly and his four die-hards had phoned for a taxi to take them back to camp, with a stop at the Gaslight Club on the way.

At five forty eight, Schooly was back in camp for a cold shower, a bacon sandwich and shot of orange-juice.

Six o clock. Opening time in Amsarnie. Major J Schooly just needed a cup of coffee and a cigarette.

"Non-filter, I'm afraid."

"That'll do. Good lad. Down-grade the alert to, "Caution". Keep twenty men on the fence an' the gate an' order everyone else to sleep until further notice. Let me know when we hear from anyone."

"'Scuse me, boss, the Gov'ners on the phone!"

"Put him through. Hello?"

General Mussbiere, as fresh as the dawn.

"Schooly?"

"Gov'ner! How is it in civilisation?"

"Don't know mate, never been there. What's goin' on?"

"It's been a long night. Let me tell you! The good news is that I reckon this civil war bollocks is all over."

"That *is* good news, but how so?"

"I told you that we figured there only was about ten rebels, altogether. Well, I reckon I saw at least eight of 'em dead, today. The report 'll be in your system in twenty minutes."

Herbert Brewer's Dirty Little Secret

"I can't wait. That is strange, good news. What's the lie of the land?"

"The *lay* of the land! Silus Mantè's niece is goin' to take over. That's safe-money."

"What's she like?"

"Isabella Mantè. Tall, dark and handsome. She's screwed 'alf the army, and they love her like a God, but she'd kill you 'erself for stealin' the flies off her garbage."

"Someone we can work with?"

"Perfect. I think she even likes me."

"Good boy! Any progress with the British?"

"It'll all be in the report. They're some bloody-funny crew, they really are! We had a small session with a couple of 'em last night and they seemed to think that loosin' six crew was somethin' heroic! We got ourselves invited to some *do* at their, "mess"!"

"Sounds lovely!"

"Exactly! It sounds like shite, but we'll try to make it work. It's a strange idea, an' I know how you feel about fightin', but 'ave you got anybody back there that's due for casualty status?"

"Nobody springs to mind. We haven't 'ad a confrontation in over eighteen months. Barnacle Bill's pushin' his luck, but I can't imagine."

"Oh well, just a thought. It wouldn't do us any harm, if you thought of somebody who needed toppin'. Ship 'em out an' we'll have 'em find a booby-trap or somethin'. We could make a

Spade Braithwaite

"mess", an' invite the British back over. An' it might look good, in the papers back 'ome. God knows their ain't gunna be any fightin', not now."

"Give me a couple o' hours to think about it. I'll 'ave your orders in the system by noon, your time. That's five o clock here, isn't it?"

"I think so."

"Okay, noon your time. Anythin' else exciting?"

"Nah! War, in a foreign land. Same ol' crap."

"Good boy. Get some sleep, an' then keep us informed. Stay out o' mischief, please!"

"Gov'ner! If you employ the best, you can sit back and let 'em do the job! Nothin' to worry your pretty head about, I guarantee it. Speak to y' later."

"Good boy. Sweet dreams."

"Bye. Over and out."

Chapter 25

Sunday evening. A lifetime away from everything else that had ever happened to Jon-Paul Clifton.

Jon-Paul opened one eye and tried to remember where he was.

Herbert Brewer's Dirty Little Secret

Slowly, it all came back. Firstly, there had been the phone call from Samuel Guarthje's office. Then, there was the little Asian woman with the fists of fury.

Jon-Paul conducted an internal damage report. Head, bruised and comfortably hung-over. Innards like a James Joyce story. Arsehole, sore until he moved but then really, really sore! Ow, Ow!

Jon-Paul resigned himself to farting very cautiously, for the next few days.

Then there was...

"Oh, my God!"

Jon-Paul remembered where he'd spent the afternoon. Waking up with a needle in his arm and then the very strange, not altogether unpleasant hour at a place that they'd called, "Shoop-Shoop".

It could have been a lot worse.

Jon-Paul picked up the photographs from the nightstand and gave them his one, good eye.

Jesus Christ! Where did they find these people?

The top one was a perfect 7"x4" of Jon-Paul, laughing like an idiot, being sodomized by an enormous black man. The next one was Jon-Paul felating a man with breasts, being felated by the black man.

Then one of Jon-Paul..., holy crap! Where did they find these people?

Spade Braithwaite

Jon-Paul dropped the photographs and rolled over enough to press the button for room service.

"Hello?"

"Yes, hello. Can I order a couple of lightly poached eggs and a pint of stout. Ughm..., I don't know what room I'm in."

"Eight eleven."

"Yeah, eight eleven. And some aspirin and a few tampons, if you can find them."

"No problem, sir. Ten minutes, thank you."

Jon-Paul rolled back onto his better side.

Every conflict had a winner and it was a wise man that recognised defeat.

Fuck Samuel Guarthje and his stupid career.

And fuck Clausthowlersnaugler-bloody-bogler.

Jon-Paul was going home.

Back home, in Gunswale, Inland Attorney Samuel Guarthje had finally admitted the awful truth to himself; that he, also, had been bum-shagged, figuratively speaking. Somehow, Prime Minister Dereck Cartright had out-flanked them all.

And Samuel couldn't even see how he'd done it. According to every indicator, Dereck's neck was mutton on a butcher's block. But something inside of Samuel told him that it was time to squeal like a pig.

Samuel ducked down behind his steering wheel as Dereck Cartright and John Sumwun came sneaking out the side door.

Herbert Brewer's Dirty Little Secret

He watched them creep furtively across the Hermitage lawn with their heads down, heading towards the Republic Archives Museum.

Samuel started the engine and slowly pulled around to see where they were going.

John Sumwun unlocked the doors of the only car in the car park, a brown Ford Malta hatchback.

Dereck and John climbed in and ploughed straight across six lanes of traffic, onto Three Wheel Lane. Eastbound, heading into town!

Samuel closed his eyes to cut through six lanes and then opened them to find himself three cars behind Dereck, perfectly positioned to follow without being too obvious.

Dereck drove, the same as he did everything else, like a bastard.

After only a mile, the brown Ford Malta turned off Three Wheel Lane onto Stanley Unwin Street and immediately pulled into the carpark of the Victoria Tavern.

Samuel drove past to park outside a donut shop and walk back.

The Victoria was a dilapidated, upper-lower-class boozer with delusions of country club. The signboard proclaimed, "Square-Dancing on Fridays! Old Time Rock'n'Roll, with Sid Ketchup this Saturday only! Every Sunday is Ladies Night! First Cocktail Free! Two-Dollar Draughts! Free Dart Board!".

Spade Braithwaite

Exactly the type of place that Samuel would have imagined Dereck enjoying his quality-time. Soon to lose its licence, if Samuel's, "Urban Clean-Up Bill", ever saw daylight.

The Victoria's car park was packed solid. A brown, Ford Malta hatchback was splayed, one half in the disabled parking space and the other across the fire lane.

Samuel shuddered and entered the, "Lounge Bar", through a big, purple gate.

Plastic palm trees and Billy Joel on the jukebox and yet, the Victoria somehow attracted quite a lot of fanny, on, "Ladies Night!". Samuel occasionally wished that he weren't so cultured, or discerning.

Dereck and John Sumwun were at the far end of the bar, doing very well with four women who, by their appearance, might easily have been a delegation from the up-coming Miners Union class action suit.

Samuel looked around for a likely alibi.

There were three, unaccompanied women at the bar. Two were absolutely out of the question but the third, Samuel might even be prepared to shag, under the right circumstances.

Samuel prided himself on his ability to judge people at first glance. She was fifty years old, give or take, with dyed blond hair, smiling at everyone and betraying a charming insecurity.

Samuel slipped into the roll.

"Hello! Aren't you...?"

"Of course! Weren't you...?"

Herbert Brewer's Dirty Little Secret

"I think I was. Look, you're going to think that I'm absolutely terrible, but I'm afraid that I've forgotten your first name...,"

"Rhian...,"

"Of course! I feel such a fool. By the way, out this way they just call me Sammy. No formality. Can I get you a...?"

"Singapore-Sling. Ice 'n' a slice. Cheers, Sammy."

Samuel leaned across the bar and waved a twenty-dollar bill.

"One for the lady! An' I'll have a Pimms, without."

"Without what?"

"Without the mint and the fruit, and all that nonsense."

"We haven't got any mint. Or fruit."

"What've you got?"

"We've got some cherries. An' umbrellas."

"Fine! I'll have another one for the lady, and a Pimms, without cherries or umbrellas, you pillak! Look Rhian, I've just seen one of my colleagues, over there. Do you think that you could play along with a little charade, and pretend that we're having an affair, just for a laugh?"

The barman plonked drinks at their elbows.

"Five-dollars-forty-five, please!"

Samuel dismissed him with the twenty-dollar bill.

"Cheers!"

"Cheers. So, Rhian, can you play along, for the joke?"

"No problem. In case it comes up, in conversation, I've got a cyst on my uterus and my ex- hubby, Carlos, gets out in three months."

Spade Braithwaite

Samuel smiled charmingly, "Thanks for the tip. Stick with me, and try to follow my lead. Here we go. Good-lord! Dereck! What are you doing here?"

"Samuel! Same as you, except better. Rhian! How's the cyst?"

"Enlarged, but benign. Carlos gets out in three months!"

"So I heard. What the hell are you doing here, Samuel?"

"Ughhm, me and Rhian meet here sometimes, away from the crowd."

"Yeah, and my arse is a vegetarian-buffet. I've been expecting you, since you followed us out of the Archives. Wha' d' you want?"

Samuel felt the floodgates of prevarication creak beneath a surge of emotion.

"Dereck! I just want to be on your side! I know that you've whipped me. I'm your bitch. Just let me be on the winning team."

"Hold it. Wait a fuckin' minute! Who've you been talkin' to?"

"No one. I just know that you've got some plan, and I don't know what it is but I'm frightened!"

"I'll credit you with remarkable perspicacity! Wha' d' you want?!"

"I want to be on the winning team! I'll do anything!"

John Sumwun made himself and the four women invisible while Dereck interrogated Samuel.

Herbert Brewer's Dirty Little Secret

"What could you possibly do, that anyone might be interested in?"

"I can be your man in the Cabinet. I can *sneak* on all of them, and tell you all the dirty little plans they're hatching."

Dereck Cartright sipped his ouzo, thoughtfully. He already knew his Cabinet and their black, little hearts better than their own wives did. A momentary inspiration manifested itself in a small twitch across Dereck's brow.

"Tell you what, Sammy…,"

"Yes, Dereck!"

"Tell you what, and this is the strictest secret that you'll ever get close to in the rest of your entire career, I'm goin' to announce the creation of a new Ministry, on Tuesday. I've been considering the candidates and, quite honestly, you're a bag o' shit, the lot of you!"

"I know exactly what you mean, sir. New Ministry? How exciting! I have Cabinet seniority, of course, if it were something that needed an experienced power-man. Or, I'll be happy to help you create an outsider, for the job."

"No Sammy, I think you're just the man. It'll mean spending a lot of time out of town, and pretending to do a lot of work…"

"Pretending…?"

"Exactly! Loads of media attention while you stay out of everybody's way for a few years, but then we'll have you back in the thick of government in no time! Dream job, mate!"

"Stay out of everybody's way…?"

Spade Braithwaite

"For a few years, Sammy. I think you've grasped it, like the professional that you are. Call in at my office tomorrow and I'll give you the Portfolio. Congratulations, Sammy! You're a real survivor!"

"Thank you..., cheers."

Beyond five p.m., weekdays, and noon on Sundays Amsarnie's army was managed by a skeleton crew.

General Aemon Mussbiere downloaded the quarterly figures for small-business protection revenue to help him think.

Pie charts, flow charts and graphs. Labour costs, income, incidentals. Logistical considerations of the recent recruitment.

A little voice in Aemon's subconscious suddenly came through with a really, good idea.

Aemon scanned the office for a face that he recognised.

"Arnie, m' boy."

"Gov'ner?"

"We got three recruits from Claust', didn't we?"

"Four, including the corpse with the boner."

"But it was three guys, right?"

"Yeah."

"The one guy that faced-off against Corporal Mohan..."

Everybody in the office paused to imagine themselves tackling Corporal Mohan, and shuddered.

"Yeah...! I've got it here, somewhere. Private Herbert Brewer, nee Joshua Matenach."

Herbert Brewer's Dirty Little Secret

"Put 'im in the Fast-Track Officer Course with a red-pen asterisk. But there was another pair wasn't there? The fat, pervy brothers that Claust' doesn't want back."

"The Herbert Brewer brothers, nee…, let me find it…, Alphonse and Hubert Pheobe. No, Claust' doesn't want them back, and an initial report from Induction gives me the impression that we don't particularly want 'em either."

"When's the next plane to Bundawa?"

"Nine thirty, tonight."

"Get 'em on it. Tell Schooly they're comin', an' they just might be the lambs that he asked for. Tell Schooly that it would be extremely media-positive if we could tout 'em as heroes, back here. The more dramatic the better, by tomorrow night at the latest."

"Gotcha, Gov'ner!"

"You all know how I feel about war, but if we've gotta get rid of 'em anyway…!"

Back in Clausthowlersnauglerbogler, the whole plot was coming together like custard in a school cafeteria, leaving a just few threads to tie into, "Strange, Monkey Sex.", the second novel in the series where Dereck Cartright tries desperately to sabotage his own career, only to have…, but that's another story.

Spade Braithwaite

Upstairs at Shoop-Shoop, in an unexplained, oriental dining room, Bo-Bae Crozier raised a glass of saki and toasted, "Tashi Delek!"

"Prost!"

"Saloo!"

"Bottoms up!"

Somebody else raised their glass...

(The author scanned down his notes and noticed Stella Davenport, a schoolteacher who shagged Charles in Chapter 12.)

It was Stella Davenport who raised her glass, "Cheers! So what, exactly, do they need, on Tuesday?"

Gary Crozier, the Chief of Police sipped saki and tried to look thoughtful as he leaned forwards to spread his buttocks enough to massage an embarrassing itch.

"Ooooh... Well, Prime Minister Cartright, himself, will be coming..."

Humner Speilding, the ex-Mayor could contain himself no longer, "So we're going to need snipers on the roofs, and barricades, and men with sunglasses talking into their lapels! And S.W.A.T. teams!"

"Ughhm, not as I understood it. Prime Minister Cartright will be bringing about a dozen government-wallahs, as well as General..., I've got it written down somewhere..., General Aemon Mussbiere,"

"Mus' be a what?!"

Herbert Brewer's Dirty Little Secret

"Quite honestly, I choose not to speculate. General Mussbiere and four senior officers. They'll all need overnight accommodation. Plus, about forty, "Friends of Government". Old-family names and pundits. Charles told me to splash fifty thousand dollars around and book it as, "Research and Development". I've reserved the top, two floors of the Blandford and everything at Shoop-Shoop."

"What about journalists? I thought that this was supposed to be the big, media snow-job?"

"It is, but Charles reckons that there's only twenty to thirty journalists, at most, that cover politics in the whole country. The Blandford is telling anyone who calls that they're completely booked, Tuesday night, but, Amsarnie-Air just happen to be laying on a charter-flight back to Gunswale at seven p.m., with first class seats and a lobster dinner for eighty bucks a pop. We're goin' to try an' time it so that journalists from every rag in the country attend the announcement an' then have to fight for taxis back to the airport. Job done."

Laurence French, recently appointed Executive Supervisor to the Office of Domestic Security smiled at Alison Dawa, recently appointed Assistant to the Executive Supervisor and tried to drag his thoughts away from the afternoon of sex that he'd just enjoyed.

"Bosoms…"

"Beg your pardon, Laurence?!"

Spade Braithwaite

"Ughmm, I was just wondering if I ought to be there or not. I'm still not sure whose side I'm officially on."

"The official line, from the Prime Minister himself, is that there only ever was one side, and you were on it. So the answer is yes. We'll all be expected to attend."

Stavros Nicolaus, the Greek Bank-Manager, gulped back the last of his saki with a vinegar-grin and refilled his glass with scotch from the bottle in his jacket pocket.

"You've got the marquee and the podium and everything booked?"

"All sorted."

"Bar?"

"The Shakey Man."

"How many people will there be, altogether?"

"We're setting up a hundred and fifty seats. If we count the numbers as they arrive at the airport, then we can fill the empty seats with a bus from the Legion."

"Which Legion?"

"Hale Avenue. Strictly vetted."

Detective Ian Metcalfe emptied the last of the saki into his glass and waved the empty bottle at a waitress, hopefully.

"Where, exactly, are we staging this do?"

"Out in the desert, just past the tyre depository."

"But that's not the real site, is it?"

"Fuck no! The real site is fifty miles out into the desert, but this place looks good. It's bleak enough that no one 'll give us

Herbert Brewer's Dirty Little Secret

any environmental crap, but it's not too shitty either. And it's twenty minutes by taxi.

Rahood Mahal, a mysterious, oriental businessman...

(Rahood Mahal?! The author checked his notes and realised that he wasn't supposed to introduce Rahood Mahal until the sequel!)

Rahood Mahal, a mysterious, oriental businessman, fingered the buckskin pouch containing his mother's covenant and the last of his father's ashes and signalled the waitress for a top-up.

"Cheers love! Lovely drop o' saki! So anyway, we're all organised for Tuesday, are we?"

(He might not sound mysterious, or oriental, but just wait for the sequel!)

"Yep! I'll expect us all to be there, halfway sober and dressed like citizens."

Judge Jacob Tethers poured the saki down his throat rather than poison the yucca plant in the pot, seated invitingly behind him.

"I think we can manage that. Can we get a couple of bottles of proper wine?! This stuff tastes like bat-piss. Excuse me, miss, have you got a Merlot, or something? Anything. Beer 'll do. So, any questions about Tuesday? No? Good. Shit or bust! Cheers!"

Chapter 26

Covering politics for the Correspondent & Sportsman, Pablo Harrison had never flown anywhere before.

He knew all about the check-in procedure from watching airport movies, but in the films the plane always crashed so the *check-out* procedure was still something of a mystery.

The seat-belt sign *bing-bonged* off and people started to retrieve bags from the overhead lockers.

The stewardess smiled, brilliantly.

"If you would please keep your seats while the plane is in motion, we will shortly be disembarking at Clausthowlersnauglerbogler International Airport."

Eventually, after the plane had been on the ground for what must have been five minutes, the passengers were allowed to exit.

"Excuse me, miss, where do I pick up my bag?"

"Just follow signposts to the, "Carousel". Have a nice day!"

"Thank you."

Pablo Harrison filed, slowly off the plane to the shuttle-bus, wondering how he might include, "business travel", in his résumé.

Clausthowlersnauglerbogler International Airport looked really nice. Pablo had expected it to be three sides of a shed, with rattlesnakes and tumbleweed, and old prospectors, half-mad from the sun, but it wasn't.

The shuttle-bus stopped outside a big, double door called, "Gate 1" and Pablo followed the other fifty passengers into the terminal.

Right in front of you, as you walked in, the biggest sign of them all stated, "Carousel", and an arrow pointing straight ahead. "Toilets", had an arrow to the right.

Pablo went into the toilet and tried to force a pee. He'd drunk enough beer on the plane that it ought to be through by now. He knew that as soon as he sat down at the press conference and Dereck Cartright started to speak, his bladder would suddenly bloat with a gallon of urine and strain the capacity of his boxers.

Pablo shook his penis and put it away dry.

Three hundred yards of gleaming corridors and four more signs led Pablo into a long hall dominated by a winding conveyor full of luggage. Pablo noticed his own bag amongst a hundred others and grabbed it, without bothering to ask.

"Provincial bloody airports!"

"'scuse me mate?"

"Ahhh, nothing."

Beyond this point the carousel seemed forgotten and all the signs were for, "Arrivals \ Meeting place", and the, "exit".

Pablo would have to get a look at the carousel on the way back, if he had time.

Spade Braithwaite

The corridor to the exit opened suddenly, into a wide, airy foyer with barriers to restrain two Welcome Committees.

One of the Welcome Committees could best be described as shit-awful. Maybe Iraqi dissidents, facing certain death if they ever returned home might have found it welcoming.

Pablo wondered how he would describe it in his memoirs and decided that, "…shit-awful!" summed it up nicely.

It was two men, an obvious bum in a bus driver's uniform and a younger man holding a piece of cardboard with, "Press", written in black marker.

Pablo was astonished to watch his newspaper colleagues jostle to introduce themselves.

The second, infinitely more welcoming committee was two, very attractive young women with courtesy glasses of champagne and a placard that read, "F.O.D."

"Friends Of Dereck", if Pablo wasn't much mistaken.

Pablo had a tenuous link and it was, after all, a good angle that made a good story. He strode boldly up to the more attractive of the women and proffered a firm handshake.

"Hi! I'm Joseph Malakani, Canned-Vegetable Magnate and owner of the Correspondent & Sportsman. I think my secretary told you that I probably wouldn't make it, but here I am!"

The woman pressed a glass of champagne into Pablo's hand and smiled, just as boldly.

"Good afternoon, Mr Malakani. I would have sworn that you were already here and that you'd asked me to keep an eye out for one of your reporters, "a cocky, little bastard called Pablo Harrison," but obviously I'm mistaken. Please enjoy your stay in Clausthowlersnauglerbogler!"

Pablo smiled, took the glass and allowed himself to be ushered to the F.O.D. shuttle.

Outside of the airport building, Clausthowlersnauglerbogler looked like dog-crap!

You'd think, with all of the money they'd spent, building a world-class, International Airport, that they'd at least put it in a good neighbourhood. Or maybe this was the nice part of town, God help us!

Pablo gulped back the champagne and boarded the shuttle.

The town actually wasn't as bad as it looked from the airport. Friends Of Dereck were taken, first to the Blandford Hotel to drop their luggage and then on to a reception at a big pub called Shoop-Shoop.

For all his urban sophistication, Pablo would have admitted that he liked the Shoop-Shoop. Joseph Malakani was there. Pablo told Joseph and couple of his billionaire-buddies the story of his attempt to use Joseph's name in vain and had them rolling in the aisles.

Good ol' boys, billionaires, when you got to know 'em.

Any one of them would have sacrificed Pablo's life for a fraction of a per cent on the dollar, but that was just them, being billionaires.

Spade Braithwaite

Pablo had long ago learned that you should walk a mile in somebody's shoes before you criticised them, so that when you criticised them, you were a mile away and you had their shoes.

Pablo couldn't get over the dozens of women that came into Shoop-Shoop, on a Tuesday lunchtime. Good-looking women that were quite happy to stop and have a drink with a lot of old men. And disappear with them for a while, and then come back to drink with other old men. What a bar!

A good-looking boy like Pablo could go through this town like a dose of funny-tummy.

All too soon, a steward notified everybody that the shuttles would shortly begin ferrying groups out to the site.

Just time for one more large one and a quick story before they left.

And all the while, Pablo forgot to pee.

Pablo remembered as the shuttle engaged gear. In fact, Pablo thought of little else during the twenty-minute ride to the site.

Mr Joseph Malakani, exuberant in his cups, poured them both a brandy from a flask cunningly disguised as racing glasses and told Pablo the most disgusting story that he'd ever heard about Turkish soldiers.

Funny as the story was, much of the humour was wasted as Pablo concentrated his attention anywhere away from his bladder.

Herbert Brewer's Dirty Little Secret

A few miles outside town they passed huge, ugly stacks of worn tyres but Pablo hardly noticed.

Eventually the shuttle stopped at a big marquee in the desert and Pablo was the first off.

"Excuse me! I gotta go!"

Pablo hobbled thirty yards behind the generator trailer, opened his fly and peed.

"Thank the lord. And they can't tax it!"

Pablo peed, and peed.

After a few minutes, Mr Joseph Malakani appeared next to him for a pee.

Pablo breathed deeply and peed.

Mr Malakani peed for a few seconds, shook his penis and then put it away.

Pablo peed.

"Jesus Christ, boy, that's some bladder you got on on you!"

Pablo smiled and peed.

Mr Malakani shook his head in wonder.

"I mean, I got horses and I know some of 'em would be happy to pee like that, once a week. Jesus Christ!"

Pablo felt the pressure subside and relaxed to enjoy the final minutes of his urination.

"Hell boy! I never seen anyone pee like that before. You must be part fish! Jesus Christ!"

Pablo massaged the last few drops from his jap's-eye and became a professional journalist again.

Spade Braithwaite

"Mr Malakani, shall we find our seats?"

"I guess. Jesus wept! I ain't seen no one pee like that before! You must be a freak o' nature! Holy Hell! Let's get a drink first. You got to learn, boy, that ninety-per cent of the world's news happens in the bar, or on the golf course. Come on, I'll introduce you."

The bar was an awning on the side of the marquee. Everybody seemed to be in it.

"Joseph, old friend! Come and have a snort!"

"Eddie! Lovely to see you, mate! Here, meet my boy, Pablo Harrison, bladder like the Nile! Pablo, this is Eddie Haffenschaft, Schlagel Holdings. Pablo's my ace-reporter, you know, at that newspaper I bought. Reminds me of when I was his age, delivering vegetables to the restaurant, you remember?"

"Good times, Joe. Pleased to meet you Pab'."

Pablo shook Eddie Haffenschaft's hand. Eddie Haffenschaft made more money while he was holding Pablo's hand than Pablo would ever earn in his life. It was a whole, different world.

The business end of the bar was a trestle table with two taps and a candelabra of inverted spirit bottles.

A man stood by the bar, entertaining a small crowd with a loud story about somebody's prostate. Pablo did a double-take because the man could have been Prime Minister Dereck Cartright's twin brother. Pablo hadn't ever met Dereck but he'd written the captions to enough photographs of him.

Joseph Malakani introduced him.

Herbert Brewer's Dirty Little Secret

"Dereck! Dereck I want you to meet Pablo Harrison. Ace-reporter at that rag I bought. Pablo, this is Dereck Cartright, our wonderful Prime Minister. John Sumwun, Samuel Go-with-joy, an' I don't know the rest of 'em but they're prob'ly just as bad."

Pablo shook a few hands. Dereck didn't look half upset, considering that, by all accounts, his career was past the u-bend and heading downstream.

"Pablo. Pleased to meet you, mate. I do love you Gentlemen of the Press..."

Snorts and howls from the crowd.

"...No, I really do! Honestly, and any friend of old Joe is in the loop, as far as I'm concerned. Catch me before I leave an' I'll give you my special phone number. Excuse me. Ladies! And gentlemen! Can I ask you to please refill your glasses and make your way to the seats. I'm afraid that I have some unhappy news."

A hundred and fifty people crowded over the bar for a top-up.

"Mr Malakani! What'll you have!"

"Better make it a pint of lager! Good boy!"

Pablo ordered two pints of lager and a couple of large whiskies.

Ten minutes later everybody was seated. Pablo counted his row and multiplied it by the number of rows..., giving him slightly over a hundred and fifty people, plus the twelve seats at the head of the meeting.

Spade Braithwaite

Prime Minister Dereck Cartright became a lot more impressive, commanding the ceremonies. Pablo suddenly understood Dereck's power. Dereck had an aura.

"Ladies! Excuse me, Ladies and gentlemen! First of all, I'd like to thank you all for attending this conference at such short notice. Before we go any further, I'm told that the relatives have been informed, so it's my sad duty to inform you that Amasarnie has incurred her first casualties from the Bundawa conflict! Two young soldiers, twin brothers as it happens, were killed this morning during a heroic operation to dislodge communist, guerrilla forces from a bunker in the mountains of northern Bundawa. This news is all the more poignant because the men were sons of this town, Clausthowlersnauglerbogler! I'm not supposed to reveal identities, as part of, "Operation Herbert Brewer", but General Mussbiere has allowed me specific dispensation to name our heroes. They were, Hubert and Alphonse Pheobe, aged thirty two. As I said, the relatives have been notified and there's a deductible fund being set-up at the Randolph First National to pay for a monument."

"Mr Cartright...!"

"Mr Cartright...!

"Dereck! Charlie Weber, *National Clarion*. Who were their relatives?"

"Excuse me Charlie, obviously I'm not at liberty to tell you, but, as journalists, I would expect any of you that track-down their mother, Lillian, to remember that she's a poor widow, and flex your cheque-books! Fair-do's?!"

"Mr Cartright! How do you justify military casualties, in a conflict that, obviously, has no relevance to Amsarnie's security?!"

Right there, in a moment, Dereck Cartright looked older. In fact, Dereck became suddenly, "Elder".

"Mr Levison, is it?"

"Yarull Levison, *The Cognoscenti*."

"Mr Levison. While I'm pleased to acknowledge that Amasarnie has almost no, strategic, military importance on the world stage, we have to remember that this is the twenty first century, and the only thing that world-terrorism needs, to prosper, is for good men to stand idle."

"Mr Cartright! Robin Mosaremba, *T.V. Guide*."

"Ms. Mosaremeba?"

"Mr Cartright. Can you give us any idea what, "Operation Herbert Brewer", might have involved?"

Dereck Cartright raised his hands in deference.

"Ms. Mosaremba, I may be the Prime Minister, but thankfully, I'm still only a Minister. When you employ the people, you have to let them do their jobs. Can I give the floor to General Aemon Mussbiere. Ladies and Gentlemen…,"

General Aemon Mussbiere slowly stood up as Dereck sat down.

Spade Braithwaite

Pablo knew General Mussbiere from the briefings and didn't rate him much above school gym'-showers in a list of life's experiences. Specifically, Pablo felt that the General was a grumpy old bastard.

"Hello. Most of you know me from the briefings. I'm pleased to see so many, distinguished members of the news industry here, with so little warning. Ms Mosaremba, Mr Harrison, ladies and gentlemen…"

Pablo suddenly liked him a whole lot more.

"…, For obvious reasons, while "Operation Herbert Brewer", is on-going, we can only be very vague with details, but I can tell you that the operation has been an unqualified success. The early reports that I'm getting from the, "field", lead me to believe that the violence in Bundawa has been dealt with…!"

"General Mussbiere…!"

"General…!"

"Excuse me, General Mussbiere!"

"Mr Harrison?"

"Pablo Harrison. *The Correspondent*. What do you mean, the violence in Bundawa has been dealt with?"

"You mean, what was I about to say, if you hadn't interrupted?!", Aemon thought to himself.

Aemon paused to look grave, and study notes on a clipboard in front of him.

"The reports that we've received, from Bundawa, over the last forty eight hours, are all entirely positive. Our operations, in collusion with the British Forces, have been entirely successful in pin-pointing the insurrectionist factions and negating the possibility of their continued antagonism. I can announce that the trouble in Bundawa appears to be completely contained, to the point where even the French are considering sending in a peace-keeping force!"

Dereck took over and stood-up to lead a standing ovation.

"Yeah! But, Ladies an' Gentlemen, we've learned a lot of lessons and we've realised that we really need our own Air Force. The second phase of, "Operation Herbert Brewer", is going to be the building of our first National Defence Airbase, right here, in Claust'."

"Prime Minister Cartright! John Chu, *The Morning Bombast*, don't we already have an Air Force?"

Dereck's turn to look grave, "Well, there's the rub. If you refer to the Municipal Mandate Act of 1947, then no, we never did. But eighteen months ago, before any of us even knew where Bundawa was, the Henderson Quasi-Autonomous Think-Tank published their Restricted White-Paper, high-lighting the importance of secure, international mobility for our forces and, I hope the records will show that my cabinet have done everything possible to facilitate the creation of this new branch of defence, without compromising national security. The world is changing and we have to be on top of it, or risk being buried under it. Our country owes the town of Clausthowlersnauglerbogler a huge debt of thanks for their discretion. I've wanted to tell you all about it, but I was advised that I would be putting the lives of our brave security personnel at risk."

Change to big smile, "Now, we've got four hours 'til the, "Press", plane leaves at seven. I suggest that we get the shuttles goin', and head back to town for a reception at the Shoop-Shoop Saloon. I think I might be able to re-open the bar, here, in the mean-time. Any questions?"

"Mr Cartright! Bart Adison. *Lawn & Garden*. Can we get lunch-receipts, from the bar?"

Dereck paused, to give full effect to his masterstroke.

"I'll tell you what, free-bar, while your waiting, and free-bar back in town!"

"Hurrah!"

"Hooray for World-Peace"

"Three Cheers for the French! Or whatever he was talkin' about, just a minute ago!"

The shuttles took the press back to town first.

Mr Malakani promised Pablo a room at the Blandford so they held out for a later shuttle.

"Can you do that thing again, where you pee for ever? I want to bet Eddie Hafenschaft that you can pee two gallons, all in one go?"

"Tomorrow morning, prob'ly. Although I wouldn't put my own money on it."

"You're a good lad! I like you."

Herbert Brewer's Dirty Little Secret

"I'm gasping. You got any more brandy in those racing glasses?"

"Sorry boy, have to move on to my emergency stash..."

Joseph Malakani flourished a bottle of Josè Cuervo from his day-bag.

"...the tequila! We can drink from the bottle. Our shuttle's here."

"You're a stand-up guy, Joe! You really are!"

Back at the Shoop-Shoop, Pablo peed an ordinary amount and started to feel quite queasy.

Without warning, Pablo Harrison felt drunkenness wash over him.

"Fuck!"

Cold water on the hands. Cold water on the face. Something with caffeine. Pepsi, or coffee or something.

Pablo checked his watch.

Five thirty. Just one more hour and then he could sleep for a while. Until then, caffeine!

Pablo trudged back to the bar and laid out a twenty-note.

"Burble, durble bleeber, an' a poke."

"I'm sorry?"

"Bloody, double brandy, and a coke! Extra cokiness in the coke."

Somebody, Pablo felt that it was probably a woman, said, "Urble-durble-burble. Eat this, mate. Harbble-bibble-dibble."

Spade Braithwaite

Somebody's fingers, maybe it was his own put a chalky, little pill between his teeth. Pablo washed it down with a mouthful of cola.

"Free bar!", somebody said. "Free bar, mate!"

Pablo stuffed the twenty back down the front of his shirt and took a another, longer draught of soda.

Reality slowed down, and, at the same time, accelerated beyond Pablo's capacity to understand.

"Plurple-barple-blample-Tottenham-Hotspurs away to Liverpool! With Charlton on the bench!"

Pablo's mind accelerated to speeds only imagined by Stephen Hawking, and calculated Tottenham's odds, in an away game.

"No fuckin' chance! Don't even bother watchin' it. An' a pint of lager, darlin'!"

Pablo fished a tip out of his shirt and took the drinks back to Joseph.

"...An' she said, have you got anything smaller?!"

Pablo didn't have a fuckin' clue what the joke was about but he laughed! And he laughed some more, until he was ready to stop laughing.

"So, Dereck! I noticed that you announced that we're going to have an Air Force, hey?!"

"You noticed that, Pablo? Joseph, keep your eyes on this boy. He's a card!"

Herbert Brewer's Dirty Little Secret

Pablo felt great! Never met the Prime Minister before, and they were on first name terms!

"Yeah! Air Force! What's the deal?!"

"Pablo, ol'-buddy, you know how, "Reporters", just report, but how, "Journalists", read between the lines! You got me, mate! We're creating an Air Force. With an Airbase in the desert outside Clausthowlersnauglerbogler. Conscription, within Clausthowlersnauglerbogler, has been tied into construction and related industry. Apprenticeships and training. We're creating a new Ministry of Defence, to co-ordinate our armed forces. Sammy Guarthje's gonna be the Minister. They're gonna have offices in Precaria, and give regular Press Conferences. I've fired most of the rest of the Cabinet. Laurence French, formerly the Senior Career Officer for the Northern Provinces is going to be my new Inland Attorney, and his assistant, Alison Dawa will almost certainly become rich and powerful in a subsequent novel."

"It wasn't much of an announcement, back at the site."

Dereck put his arm around Pablo's shoulder and gestured, generally towards the other reporters taking anxious advantage of the free bar.

"Pablo. Everybody's got a press-pack, with all the details, waiting for them on the plane home. Do you need me to tell you what tomorrow's headlines are gonna be?"

Pablo choked on his lager.

"Fuck! Tomorrow's headlines!"

Spade Braithwaite

"Don't worry about it, Pablo. Your boss, Joe Malakani got the press-pack a couple of days ago. It's all sorted."

Pablo tried to breathe deeply, to slow his heart down and catch his own, racing attention.

"What about a Navy?! We'd be really, "World Class", if we had a Navy."

"Pablo. You know, I really wanted to end the novel with the words, "It's all sorted." Yes, we've discussed the possibility of creating a Navy. Maybe, a few novels down the line. Judge Jacob Tethers and Shirley Brown got together and had magic sex last night. That's something else that the author forgot to work out in the final chapters."

Pablo shrugged, sadly.

"I feel…, you know…, it's only been a few chapters, but I feel so close to all of you!"

"Don' worry, mate. There'll be a sequel in the shops by Christmas."

Pablo sighed.

"But…?"

"Just…, shut-up! It's all sorted."

Herbert Brewer's Dirty Little Secret

Other novels in the Amsarnie series:

Strange Monkey Sex (Banned in China!)

In **Strange Monkey Sex,** the second Amsarnie installment the United Nations have offered Amsarnie's Prime Minister, Dereck Cartright, a sinecure-post in Bangkok that's just too good to pass. So Dereck decides to retire from elected politics.

Dereck has a comfortable relationship with Amsarnie's Army, who organise most of the nation's crime, and who want their own man to succeed him into office. The problem is that the Opposition Party are in such disarray, if Dereck announces his resignation, one of his Cabinet will take over and win any election.

So Dereck can't resign. He has to lead the Government to ignominious defeat to enable the Army's candidate, Janey Clickert, to take power as leader of the Opposition Party.

The Army take over and reinvent the Opposition.

Dereck calls a press conference and admits to beating his wife, smoking crack-reefers and being on a bowling team. The media carve him up. A few voices point out that bowling isn't illegal, Dereck was never married and also beg the question, is it even possible to roll crack-cocaine in a reefer?

The public, jaded after so many years of spin are suddenly excited about the issues. Dereck, unexpectedly, gets the highest ratings in history.

Spade Braithwaite

Dereck's Cabinet distance themselves and make wild claims of their own, with everybody over-playing their own sordid past. Private detectives are hired to disprove competing claims of depravity. College roommates are contacted and offered money to exaggerate old stories.

Meanwhile, tough, sexy, ample-bottomed lawyer, Janey Clickert establishes herself as the Opposition Candidate who can't be corrupted.

Amsarnie heads into election...

Coming soon:

Naked Vegetarians from the Planet Hot Dog

In his Summer ashram, in central India, after twenty one years of silence the great guru Wooli Baba uses his first utterance to inform his disciples that they are going on a mission to spread the wisdom beyond their own country. Very soon, he informs them, they will all be setting sail for Amsarnie. Jai Ganga, the guru's most faithful servant is horrified, believing Amsarnie to be somewhere in Wales. He is only slightly relieved to find that Amsarnie is, in fact, a mythical country, the location for a series of hilarious novels.

Herbert Brewer's Dirty Little Secret

The Guru and his entourage tour Amsarnie, fêted by unprecedented crowds of adoring fans at the biggest venues wherever they go.

After the tour has returned to India, Corporal Endicote of Amsarnie's army devises a cunning plan to perpetrate an ingenious land swindle by creating their own cult, oriental religion, occupying some forgotten real estate on the West coast. But the new religion captures the national imagination beyond anyone's expectations.

Very soon the army are forced to requisition every available holiday camp to create extra ashram space. The public are excited on every side of the issue. The established religions resort to dirty tricks to recover their errant faithful. Satanists arrive from America, sensing the coming apocalypse.

Recently recruited, twenty one year old Mathew DeSouza, of Indian ancestry, takes on his new role as Guru, the, "Infinitely Enlightened Babudev", in what must be the strangest military deployment ever assigned to a professional soldier.

Learn more at:

www.amsarnie.com

And please contact the author for a full synopsis, sample chapters and information about future Amsarnie adventures.

www.ingramcontent.com/pod-product-compliance
Lightning Source LLC
Chambersburg PA
CBHW020415010526
44118CB00010B/263